REVISITING GLOBALIZATION THROUGH THE GENDER LENS

REVISITING GLOBALIZATION THROUGH THE GENDER LENS

GEETA S. NAIR

SERIALS PUBLICATIONS
NEW DELHI (INDIA)

First Published - 2008

ISBN : 978-81-8387-136-5

Published by

SERIALS PUBLICATIONS
4830/24, Prahlad Street, Ansari Road
Darya Ganj, New Delhi-110002 (India)
Phone : 23245225. Fax : 91-11-23272135
E-mail: serials@satyam.net.in

Dedicated to all women of the world...

CONTENTS

FOREWORD

It gives me great pride and pleasure in sharing my thoughts on the book of Geeta Nair. First and foremost, the title, *'Revisiting Globalization through the Gender Lens'* is apt as it brings out the essence of the author's work and involvement with gender issues that are topical and will shape the world of tomorrow. Globalization has become omnipotent and omnipresent, and so have gender issues. Geeta has rightly brought out the increasing economic role of women that has enhanced our material progress, but also increased the gender divide. This is specially found in the burgeoning urban informal sector in India, where there is feminization of livelihoods, poverty, debt, and illiteracy. Thus, the focus is on the lack of gender-just development and increasing asymmetries in the neo-liberal growth pattern indoctrinated by the Fund-Bank agenda being followed since the nineties.

The new world order needs to take cognizance of women's participation in the world of work, along with their unpaid work at home and outside that requires correct estimation and market determined payment. The book uses detailed time use surveys to painstakingly point towards the rising contribution of women due to loss of income and employment of the male head as a result of globalization and informalization. Women's multi-tasking and rising burden of production, as well as reproduction has been woven intricately into the field work analysis. The book also throws light on the increasing divide between Mumbai's original settlers, the fisher folks and the migrants. Geeta has complemented the micro analysis of the impact of globalization on gender with a systematic secondary data analysis enriched by a comprehensive review of literature. The theme of the book concerns all of us, as the phenomena of globalization and gender have come here to stay!

I wish all the success to this book and my best wishes and compliments to Geeta.

Professor Parvathi Venkatesh
Dean, Arts Faculty
University of Mumbai-India.

ACKNOWLEDGEMENT

This book is based on my DOCTORAL Thesis entitled, "FROM COMMAND TO DEMAND-PROBLEMS OF TRANSITION" *completed successfully under the able guidance of Dr. Ritu Dewan, Professor and Chair, Centre for Women's Studies and Centre of Human Development submitted to the University of Mumbai on November 14, 2006.*

I would like to thank all my mentors and well-wishers starting with my wonderful guide, Professor Ritu Dewan, Professors Ajit Karnik, Avdhoot Nadkarni, Abhay Pethe, Romar Correa, Dolly Sunny, Hermione Salazar, and Bhagyashri Dabke for their continuous encouragement and support.

I would like to acknowledge the special role that my supportive husband, Dr. Sudhir Nair, my lovely children Aalaap and Abhiri, my brother Gaurav, and my parents-in-law have played throughout the long journey of my doctorate reinforcing the fact that women can chase their dreams and aspirations despite time constraints and multi-tasking that seem to be universal.

Last, but not the least, I admire the working women, especially the fisher folks I studied in Charkop Village for their 'never-die spirit' that provides inspiration for humankind.

1

INTRODUCTION

AN OVERVIEW

The introductory part gives a brief overview of the thesis that deals with the problems and impact of restructuring caused by the implementation of the 'New Economic Policy' in India. This chapter is divided into various sub-sections, beginning with globalization along with its bearing on gender, and then highlighting women's livelihoods in the urban informal sector in the Section 1.2. The subsequent section covers methodology and data sources in order to bring out different avenues of information at both the secondary and primary levels for analysis, comparison, and contrast. Section 1.4 chalks out the chapter scheme of the thesis.

This book is based on the doctoral thesis entitled, 'From Command to Demand-Problems of Transition' submitted to the University of Mumbai in November 2006 under the able guidance of Professor Ritu Dewan, University of Mumbai. A review and revisit of globalization needs to be undertaken through the gender lens as most of the literature and discussions on our borderless world misses out on the essential component of increased labour force participation and economic contribution of women, especially in the urban informal sector in developing nations like India. This revisit would help to focus on the socio-economic struggles and survival strategies of families adversely affected by globalization and industrial restructuring mirrored in the Neo-liberal 'New Economic Policy' since the nineties. It would throw light on the policy dimensions of 'inclusive growth' aiming at gender equality and human development.

GLOBALIZATION AND ITS IMPACT ON GENDER

Structural Adjustment Programmes initiated by most countries of the world have characterized the decades since seventies, and especially the eighties. As our study focuses on post 1990's, we state the basic relevant components, first in broad generic terms, then with respect to India.

"Structural Adjustment refers to the reshaping process undertaken by developing countries to introduce market forces. This is partially based on the failed experiment of the governments' endeavours in business and economic activity, as the traditional Smithian doctrine of least government intervention and larger decision-making by the free market forces had seen a comeback. These programmes have been generally introduced by the developing countries to correct perceived economic ills at the behest of world donors and international financial institutions" (Sparr, 1994, p. 2).

The post-nineties period is taken to be synonymous with globalization that mainly manifests itself in the internationalization of trade, investment, and finance. Increasing economic transactions on account of cross-border competition accelerates the mobility of capital and vulnerability of labour. Technological prowess and new flexible labour policies in turn speedily change the composition of workforce in order to continuously tackle surplus workers, majority of who are women (Jose, 2004, pp. 4447-4450).

The vulnerability of people and livelihoods are deteriorating, as pointed out by Nayyar (2002, pp. 6-9; 356-358), who states that globalization may have increased jobs and opportunities for some, but also accelerated the marginalization and exclusion of poor countries and peoples. This is mainly a result of unequal distribution, falling state participation, and equity-blind market policies. Thus, economic inequalities between the rich and poor within nations, as well as between nations have magnified.

Post-reform, a shift from the formal to informal segments of the labour market is seen to occur at a faster pace, especially in terms of female workers. The rise in informalization and feminization is brought out by Ramanujam et al (1998, pp.293-

295), thereby reinforcing that employment provides the link between poverty and economic growth. Also, livelihoods of majorities of workforce in developing countries depend crucially on the informal economy, as depicted by employment data, wherein the contribution of formal employment to total employment in 1999-2000 was barely 8 per cent and the remaining 92 per cent came from the informal sector. Interestingly, 92.5 per cent of women were found to work in the unorganized sector. Commenting upon the surge in informal activities and its rising feminization, the UNDP (1995, pp. 1-8; and 2003, pp. 2-9) observes that, "The sector accounts for 90 per cent of the total male workforce and 95 per cent of total female workforce in the country. The proportion of women is higher in especially the rural sector, where it is 98 per cent compared to 95 per cent of men. The urban area portrays a similar trend as 79 per cent of total jobs are of an informal nature, accounting for 82 per cent of women in comparison to 78 per cent of male workers. There is a mixed impact of globalization, particularly in case of women workers, as it has increased the opportunities and quantitative dimensions of some kinds of work; but the quality and nature of employment are quite questionable. However, women's increased participation in the labour market has not reduced their contribution to unpaid domestic work and the care economy. The value of unremunerated work estimated a decade ago was about 16 billion dollars, from which 11 billion dollars represented the invisible contribution of women". Thus, the divide between women's market and non-market activities is seen to worsen.

Apart from various functional changes, structural ones are also observed in labour markets. Directly, it entails longer working schedules with no guarantees or securities of employment. Indirectly, the Fund-Bank package has reduced food security and compromised on safety and health standards of workers. All this has caused labour market fragmentation, flexibilization, and more importantly feminization of work. Thus, precarious working conditions along with rising vulnerability have burdened women to a larger extent (Reddy, 2005, pp. 3-9; Veltweyer, 2004, p. 12).

The universality of globalization is mirrored in the policy impact of reforms in India. The New Economic Policy of 1991 has accelerated the process of liberalization, privatization, and globalization by shifting the focus from State planning to increased participation of market forces. Accordingly, the role of the government is seen to change, leading to an emphasis on private decision-making in contrast with the earlier trend of public domination.

The book based on the thesis deals with the impact of transition of India from a command or planned economy to a demand or market-led one, with a special focus on women. The term 'Command' is considered to be synonymous with planning directed by the government. Resource allocation, production, employment, and all other major decisions are taken by the planning authorities that are targeted to be attained in a time-bound manner. Economic plans of a nation are implemented by the ruling political party during their tenure, generally lasting for 5 years in case of India. In contrast, the concept of 'Demand' is usually associated with the market mechanism and its 'free' interplay without any public control. Shifts in policies and paradigms emerged in the process of change from a 'Command' to a 'Demand' economy since the advent of liberalization in the mid-eighties that was accelerated by the IMF loan and its attendant conditionalities from the early nineties. This era is associated with an increased play of market forces in decision-making, along with a reduction of 'un-necessary' rules, regulations, and procedural delays by the government. The trend of liberalization and privatization is seen to accentuate in the nineties due the imposition of the Fund-Bank strategy. The pace of reforms quickened along with a deepening of the Economic Policy of 1991 that has affected all major areas of the Indian economy. 'Integration' with the world economy on account of globalization has had far-reaching ramifications on the patterns of production, employment, and distribution.

Transition from a 'Command' to a 'Demand' economy has a multi-dimensional impact and has also created problems of adjustment. Also, the growth trajectory has been quite altered from a planned to a market-determined one that was largely governed by the IMF and its lending policies. Thus, the impact of these new structural adjustment policies following the Washington Consensus are bound to throw up new challenges and problems, especially in the absence of a Welfare State or social security mechanism in countries like India. Therefore, an attempt is being made to review these transitional problems.

This is not an easy task, and it is our endeavour to analyze the problems of change particularly with respect to female workers in the urban informal sector. The choice of the urban segment, and not the rural one is undertaken as there are few scientific studies on the former. The same logic applies to highlighting of women's contribution in the informal sector due to its general neglect, blurred by the intrinsic invisibility of the unorganized sector. The increasing presence of women laborers thus makes it imperative to re-look at gender blind macro policies. Any study on development to be complete or holistic in nature must incorporate the gender dimension, aptly brought out by Dr. Mahbub-ul-Haq's slogan, 'Development, if not engendered, is endangered' (http://www.undp.org.in, pp. 1-8).

OBJECTIVES OF THE STUDY (AS REQUIRED UNDER ORDINANCE 0.771)

The main purpose of this study is to examine the impact of transition and the 'New Economic Policy' on women in the urban informal sector. The specific objectives are:

- To review the gendered effects of Structural Adjustment Programmes and globalization on women workers,
- To revisit the importance and future prospects of the urban informal sector,
- To link up macro-economic policies with the micro-economic levels, along with coping and survival strategies adopted in the absence of an informal sector policy or in an environment of defective existing policy framework, and
- To highlight the debate between paid and unpaid work of women that is generally ignored, underestimated, and unaccounted.

HYPOTHESES

Keeping in mind the theoretical framework and objectives of the study, the following hypotheses are formulated:

Hypothesis 1: Structural Adjustment Programmes of the past and the on-going process of globalization have impacted the world of work and gender relations;

Hypothesis 2: The informal sector, especially in urban areas has been growing in importance in developing countries;

Hypothesis 3: Macro-economic processes have permeated to micro-economic levels affecting women more than men, thereby compelling them to devise coping strategies to combat unemployment, poverty, and inequality, especially in an environment of weak informal sector policy outcomes;

Hypothesis 4: To account for women's unpaid work by making it visible and countable via time use surveys at the micro levels.

METHODOLOGY AND DATA SOURCES

A time period analysis of over a decade to study the impact of globalization on women in the urban informal sector has been undertaken. The post-nineties period is chosen to enable a decade-long comparison of the pre-and-post globalization impacts.

The analysis is based on an integrated study approach, thereby referring to secondary data wherever available and applicable, along with primary sources generated by the field study. Methods used include structured questionnaires, personal interviews, and several life histories. The research is mainly based on field work, along with the use of non-primary avenues whenever available for drawing certain contrasts and comments, and utilizing both, quantitative and qualitative analysis.

Secondary sources help us to undertake data mining at different levels ranging from national to the ward. We have used various Population and Economic Censuses to get a macro picture. State-level data via Economic Censuses, along with various Economic Surveys of Maharashtra supplement the analysis. I have also interviewed several senior research officers at the Ward level, Directorate of Economics and Statistics, Annual Survey of Industries and other entities for gaining first hand information and field experiences.

The Directorate of Economics and Statistics generated special data for the thesis. Apart from that, the Annual Survey of Industries information on factory jobs in the country proved helpful in collating with National Sample Survey's data on Own Account Enterprises, enabling to draw rough comparisons of organized and unorganized sector employment.

The Directorate via its District and City Planning Surveys also provided the ward level information, supplemented by repeated visits and personal interviews with municipal officers. Macro and micro data sources have thus been tightly interwoven into the research.

The impact of macro economic reforms at the micro level has been brought out by field-level investigation. The choice of Charkop is influenced by the changing nature and extent of employment in the post-reform period that has bearings on women's livelihoods. Also, the field area represents a good mixture of the resident locals constituting two-thirds of the population, along with the migrant population accounting for one-third. Data collection and analysis was difficult due to the basic problem of defining women's work on account of various gray areas regarding their working status and multi-tasking, complicated by the lack of differentiation between economic and extra-economic activities. Thus, one had to use indirect methods of probing like expenditure patterns, standard of living status, and time use surveys to get a picture of the repercussions of the 'New Economic Policy'. The information has been gathered and studied for all households, with a special emphasis on female-headed ones. Women's occupations and changes in these units have been analyzed exhaustively. The tool of detailed questionnaires, mainly structured supplemented by unstructured methods have proved helpful. Also, the case study method for a detailed account of the past and present experiences of several respondents has been resorted to.

The total sample comprises 180 households, of which 120 are local residents. Economic and demographic data has been collected via structured questionnaires, personal interviews, case studies, and select life histories. A number of issues focused on include employment changes from formal to informal, different kinds of informal work of women, effect of declining male activities on females, and alterations in the expenditure patterns. Various parameters like employment, income, expenditure, assets, and standard of living are examined. Thus, we have attempted to locate field-based analysis in the macro perspective of reforms and its specific gendered micro-economic impact on the urban informal sector.

The following variables in the household survey to analyze the impact of reforms on women's employment have been analyzed:

- Demographic indicators like age, sex, literacy, and skill status;

- Economic variables like income, expenditure, and asset holding;
- Time use survey to measure both, economic and extra-economic work of women.

The above parameters have been applied to local residents as well as migrants, results of which are later compared and contrasted. Thus the qualitative aspect of fieldwork enriches quantitative analysis.

The analysis has tried to synchronize different aspects of reform to get a holistic and all-rounded picture of restructuring, and its implications for females in the urban informal sector. All the components covered by the study are important and relevant, as they deal with the inter-linked issues of globalization, the urban informal sector, and women workers.

CHAPTER SCHEME

The complicated issues dealt with in this research require that a strict logical analysis be followed. There is a logical presentation of the following sub-topics that are separately analyzed in various parts and synchronized towards the concluding section. The book is structured into the following chapters focusing on major issues.

Chapter 1: Introduction

Chapter 1 discusses the process of globalization and its universal nature. Later, the gendered impact has been examined, especially with respect to an increasing trend of female work participation, along with informalization of work. Reforms have led to restructuring of enterprises, thereby impacting employment of labour. Nayyar (2002, pp. 6-9; 356-358) brings out equity concerns and gender blindness of markets that result in exclusion of poor and underprivileged sections of society, especially women. Dewan (1999, p. 425) also states that, "The gender critique of institutional reforms has to go beyond the mere focus on individual and family levels. It is essential to investigate the implicit and/or explicit gender biases of economic reforms at the macro and micro levels. This implies an analysis of structures, institutions, and processes that are gender-ascriptive, and those that function as bearers of gender at all the levels". Leading researchers and economists suggest a gendered review of any new policy to get a holistic picture of grass root ramifications, especially in case of vulnerable groupings of society.

Chapter 2: Review of Literature

This chapter reviews major studies related to the impact of reforms on the employment of women working in the urban informal sector. Various gender studies of different researchers both at the national and international levels are covered. A review of literature helps to give a better and first hand picture of the effects of reform on females across different regions. It also enables us to observe the impact of restructuring on women from almost all strata of society and occupational backgrounds. Different researchers have used varying techniques and methodologies to collect and analyze data and focused on different aspects of women's work.

A majority of researchers through case studies have captured the emerging trend of informalization that could occur outside the formal sector as well as within the formal sector itself. All this has resulted in widening of the gender gap and reduction of female entrants into the organized sector in terms of availability of work and vertical mobility (Breman, 2005, pp. 2500-2506). Further, globalization appears to have increased the market and non-market burden of women, thus worsening the imbalance between paid and unpaid work. The last decade shows an acceleration in women's non-wage work burden, largely on account of new income-augmentation activities. Time use surveys across the globe document the fact that women carry a disproportionately higher burden of work than men and also bear a greater share of the care economy. Non-System of National Accounts Surveys of own-account services demonstrate that on an average, a female spends 34.6 hours per week as compared to barely 3.6 hours by a male in terms of household work (Economic Survey, 2001-02, pp.240-250). Labour market restructuring raises the dual burden of production and reproduction of women, thereby straining their already precarious balance on account of rigid gender stereotyping.

The U.N. Report of 1975 shows that two-thirds of the world's quantitative work is done by women for which they receive only 10 per cent of all incomes and own hardly 1 per cent of all means of production (Tripathy, S. and Soudamini Das, 1991, pp.1-9). Review of literature also focuses on a number of government policies and plan documents to analyze different national level initiatives with respect to the informal sector, thus enriching both, theoretical and policy issues, and providing a starting point for this study.

Chapter 3: Secondary Data Analysis

In this chapter, secondary data analysis is been undertaken to investigate results from various data sources in the area of study. Information from different government agencies at the national level like the Population Censuses of 1991 and 2001 are used. Regional information has been accessed from the Economic Censuses of the State of Maharashtra. National Sample Survey (NSS) findings of relevant rounds on Employment-Unemployment at the State level are incorporated. Also, the senior officers at the Directorate of Economics and Statistics and NSS, Mumbai have been extremely helpful by generating special data for this study. The Annual Survey of Industries data on the manufacturing sector has been incorporated. Besides, the Ward level information proved to be helpful in studying the field area.

Various NSS rounds on employment-unemployment show a decline in the annual growth of rural and urban employment for males and females in post-'New Economic Policy' period. In fact, the benefit of higher job growth due to restructuring has been negative in case of urban female labourers and nearly nil for their rural counterparts. Contrastingly, gains in employment in case of urban male workers are seen to work out lower than rural men. However, a dominance of women workers has been sometimes seen in the post-reform labour market, as depicted by an increase in regular employees. Nevertheless, this trend seems to be more prominent among urban female labourers. However, there is rising casualization, as self-employment is seen to drop marginally in case of rural women workers, and remain nearly unchanged for their urban counterparts (Talwar, 2004, pp.4-6). Thus, various segments of people have been affected differently, depending upon their worker status, labour category, gender, and also geographical area.

Rising home-based activities represent an essential part of globalization and informalization. Post-reforms, the world of work and workers have been restructured leading to a significant rise in the number of female workers, most of who are found in this segment. A recent survey shows that 36 per cent of women labourers in India are home-based workers (http://

hdrc.undp.org.in, pp.1-3). There has been a revolution in the spatial dimension of work due to greater worker flexibility and mobility that help transform people's homes into part-time offices. This trend is peculiar of women, who are increasingly being dubbed as 'mommy managers' seen to fine-tune their market and non-market work. These 'flexi-time' workers have been proliferating due to an emergence of the 'flexi-firm'.

We have also collated information in accordance with the National Industries Classification codes for 1987, 1998 and 2004 for major areas of livelihood of kitchen gardens, retail trade in fish, domestic service, and plastic products work areas relevant to the field study.

Chapter 4: Background of Area of Study

The rationale of studying the city of Mumbai is spelt out in this chapter. Post-reforms, various changes have occurred in the city, especially in terms of work becoming more informal due to a fall in organized sector jobs (Lever, 1991, pp.983-999). Consequently, a rise in employment ratios of the unorganized sector especially for women have been observed (Nagaraj, 2000, pp.3707-3715), thus depicting 'feminization of informal employment'.

Macro-economic policies have their bearings on all levels of the economy. Any analysis of the nation's reform and its gendered impact would be incomplete without the study of the metropolis, as it represents a microcosm of India's development. An in-depth micro level investigation helps to bring out these results more clearly. This justifies the choice of the field area of Charkop that enables to capture grass-root level impact. The investigation has been divided into two subsequent chapters that focus on the impact of labour reforms on different economic groupings comprising of resident local or Koli population, along with the migrants.

Chapter 5: Field Work Analysis of Local Population

In this chapter, the analysis of the local population or Kolis, who have been natives of Charkop for almost nine generations is dealt with. About 180 households, of which 120 comprising local residents have been surveyed. Various aspects like personal details of households with respect to the number of members, gender, and age composition are studied. Economic activities data is collected with respect to women's employment both at home and in the market via time use surveys. Also information on changes in occupational activities, along with income, expenditure, and assets via structured questionnaires has been analyzed. All these responses have been tabulated with an examination of survival strategies.

Chapter 6: Field Work Analysis of Migrants

The focus of this section has been on non-locals, majority of who hail from within the state of Maharashtra. Similar questionnaires and parameters have been analyzed for migrants and local residents as seen in the previous chapter, with additional aspects like data on migration and use of electricity.

Later, a comparison of findings for the two field samples for capturing similarities and differences between them is attempted. This has been of help in order to get a clear picture of the gendered impact of reforms at the micro level in two different economic groupings in Mumbai.

Chapter 7: Conclusions and Policy Recommendations

The last chapter tries to develop an interface between various aspects of the research via interconnections at different levels. The effort is towards viewing the impact of globalization with a gender lens to highlight the increasing contribution of women workers. Also, one tries to bring out field results by comparing and analyzing them with respect to macro economic trends. Thus, attempts at establishing various linkages and connections between emerging focal areas of globalization and its effects on the world of work have been attempted. The impact on participation of female workers has been observed in the post-reform period at macro, as well as micro levels. Subsequently, we come across the increasing trends of feminization and casualization of labour. The gender dimension also enables us to view informalization within the formal sector, along with the growth of the informal sector. Also, poor women seem to be affected the most by reforms, resulting in 'feminization of poverty'. This can be seen in the rising number of Female Headed Households. An attempt to distinguish between the headship of family on economic, rather than the traditional cultural basis is undertaken. This aspect will gain prominence in future, as income would become the major factor in decision-making.

Thus, females are affected as workers, as well as householders, compelling them to evolve new survival strategies. The duality and conflict between economic and extra-economic roles are seen to intensify that often escalate the visible and invisible burdens of women, thereby resulting in 'feminization of livelihoods and poverty'.

National and fieldwork experiences defy theoretical predictions of the transient and temporary nature of the urban informal sector, as it has shown to demonstrate an involutionary, as well as evolutionary growth. Thus, an interface between the two segments of labour market has been emerging. In fact, there is no watertight compartmentalization between the two, as the distinction is getting increasingly blurred in a borderless world. Informalization was seen to emerge on account of falling formal sector shares of employment that were unable to absorb all surplus labour thus making the 'push factors' more reliable than the 'pull factors'. Therefore, production should be viewed as a continuum of various forms, be it informal or formal. Labour market realities and contradictions could lead to differing impacts on men and women that become difficult to measure in the absence of gender-segregated data.

2

REVIEW OF LITERATURE

INTRODUCTION

The post-reform period is marked by the interconnected development of globalization, the urban informal sector, and women workers. This chapter is sub-divided into various sections highlighting the evolution, definitions, and characteristics of the urban informal sector, along with a review of literature and emerging trends in the post-nineties period.

Section 2.2 focuses on emergence of the informal sector, followed by coverage of its definitions and characteristic features. An exhaustive analysis of literature via international and national level studies to analyze the impact of structural adjustment programmes on women in the urban informal sector is carried out subsequently, the last section providing a broad conclusion of the gendered impact of globalization on the urban unorganized sector based on the review of literature.

EMERGENCE OF THE INFORMAL SECTOR

The origins of the informal sector can be traced back to the post-World War II period that focused on the 'accelerated growth' model. This involves a dualistic view of developing economies as comprising a 'traditional' and a 'modern' sector. The development process is thus based on the belief that the modern sector would lead to gradual absorption of surplus labour force from the traditional one (Lewis, 1954).

The theoretical presumptions led to the popularization of the 'trickle down' effect that would help transmit the benefits of economic growth via industrial growth and are perceived to solve problems of poverty, unemployment, and inequity. These are viewed as temporary issues arising out of migration and surplus labourpower. The reality, however, was quite contrary, due to the capital and import-intensive nature of growth, thus the focus of macro policies marked a shift to rural development, small-scale industries, and labour-intensive industrialization in the sixties.

The Institute of Social Studies Advisory Service (1985, p. 22) contends that, "The Social Marginalization Theory that emerged on the realization of the non-residual and non-transitory nature of the informal sector that was not absorbed into the mainstream, and led to the emergence of 'marginales' which represents a poor and powerless sub-proletariat. Neo-Marxists used a similar concept, but set it into a dependency framework wherein development of the modern sector depends upon the underdevelopment of the residual sector, constituting the 'industrial reserve army'. Unlike dualistic approaches, the radical marginality view gives importance to the economic role of marginality, as it is seen to sustain its formal counterpart. This represented the intellectual environment in which the concept of the 'informal sector' was launched in the early seventies and was characterized by a new concern with poverty and a growing awareness that urban social problems of developing countries cannot be resolved by industrialization and 'trickle down'. Research on the urban informal sector gained prominence almost universally with the focus subsequently shifting to Third World economies".

DEFINITIONS AND CHARACTERISTICS OF THE URBAN INFORMAL SECTOR

This section is sub-divided into two parts, wherein various definitions of the urban informal sector are reviewed in Section 2.3.1, and its characteristics in the Section 2.3.2.

Definitions of the Informal Sector

Keith Hart coined the word 'Informal Sector' in early seventies, "referring to a number of income and employment generating activities in the 'unenumerated' sector of urban settlements, thereby covering self-employed individuals and the urban proletariat" (Hart, 1973, p. 61). The concept of informal sector was formalized by the International Labour Organization (ILO) at its Employment Mission in Kenya, thereby giving an impetus to research, policies, and problems concerning this area. A reaffirmation to this commitment was sought at the 87th International Labour Conference on 'Decent Work' stating that, "The ILO is concerned with all workers. Because of its origins, the ILO has paid most attention to the needs of wage workers-the majority of them men-in formal enterprises. But this is only part of its mandate, and only part of the world of work. Almost everyone works, but not everyone is employed. Moreover, the world is full of overworked and unemployed people. The ILO must be concerned with workers beyond the formal labour market-with unregulated wage workers, the self-employed and home workers"(ILO Director General as quoted in Kundu, 1999, p.6).

In the nineties, the ILO revised its definition of the informal sector to include the emerging components of 'Own-Account Enterprises' (OAE's), and 'Enterprises of informal employers' that served as the first internationally approved guideline for the statistical measurement of the informal sector. According to the International Labour Organization's modern definition, "the informal sector refers to the working poor involved in the production of goods and services, where activities are not recognized, recorded, protected or regulated by public authorities" (ILO, 1999, p. 3). The basic reason for the introduction of the informal sector in the ILO's Kenya Mission was the time lag in development policies of 'trickling down of benefits' to the poorest sections of the population that represent the most vulnerable in the urban informal sector.

Researchers like Papola (1980, pp. 817-819) identify the following approaches to view the informal sector from different angles.

Structural Approach: It focuses on the nature of activities within a dualistic model. Modern economies emphasize the firm as the basis of production structures, while traditional ones focus on the old bazaar type economy. The former represents the formal sector and the latter the informal.

Distributional Approach: This classifies the informal sector on the basis of the mode of production or production systems used wherein a distinction is made between capitalist, socialist and peasant modes of production. Thus, different kinds of ownership of resources become the basis of differentiation, with the non-formal segment mainly associated with the peasant or traditional mode and the formal with corporate or institutional ownership.

Income Approach: This terms the informal sector as a family or household enterprise and distinguishes it from the formal sector which is characterized by a corporate production system using hired labour on a wage basis.

Economic Activities Approach: It covers different activities of the informal sector that deal with distribution, like trade, transport, and retail, along with provision of services relating to processing and furniture making, thereby typifying the jobs associated with this segment.

The criteria of size of workers and relation between the employer and employees to classify the informal sector are also utilized by others like Kundu (1999, pp.817-819) on the basis of the following two conditions:

(1) The first order condition basing its classification on the number of workers employed, generally ten or less;

(2) The second order condition goes further to use specific features to classify the informal sector like small-scale operation; direct participation of the owner; casual relationship between employees and customers; no security and certainty about employment and income, along with an absence of institutional factors in wage determination.

According to Bremen (1996, pp. 8; 260), "the most striking feature of the informal sector seems to be self-employment since the very introduction of this concept by Hart. The bifurcation of the economy into formal and informal sectors also leads to a dichotomy in society. This parallel duality is supposed to rest on two separate legal systems, each with its own logic and sanctions. The formal segment is associated with civil order and social justice, vis-à-vis the tacit anarchy characterizing its counterpart".

In the post-reform period, the dichotomy is manifested in terms of home-based work. Globalization leads to restructuring of production which results in an increase in home workers, majority of who are females. Despite their significant contribution to employment, they remain largely invisible in national data. This is evident from a recent survey estimating 36 per cent of women workers in India to be home workers. Informal workers are denied access to almost all kinds of organizational support like social and job security, wage protection, and the like (http://hdrc.undp.org.in). Thus, generally speaking, the non-formal sector refers to the unorganized, unaccounted, and unregistered activities involving easy entry and exit, requiring no formal training, skills, huge capital, and technology that is mainly labour-intensive, and lack formal working norms or rules.

In India, the informal sector covers the following economic activities:

- Household based activities as defined by the Population Census, National Sample Survey (NSS) or Own Account Enterprises (OAE's) given by the NSS;
- NSS and Central Statistical Organization's (CSO) definition of Non-Directory Enterprises' (NDE's) to constitute this sector that covers all units employing less than six workers, without power;
- A combination of Directory Enterprises (DE's) with OAE's and NDE's, as given by the NSS and CSO;
- Small-scale industries (SSI's) may be taken as constituting the informal manufacturing sector as covered by the Development Commission of SSI's (DCSSI's).

Consequently, in India, the term 'informal sector' is not used in official statistics or National Accounts Statistics (NAS). Instead, the terms 'organized' and 'unorganized' sectors are taken. The former comprises of enterprises for which statistics are available regularly from budget documents, annual reports in case of the public sector and through Annual Survey of Industries (ASI) in case of registered enterprises. Non-availability of regular information is the main criteria for treating the informal sector as unorganized. Activities of the private sector units not registered and governed by the Factories Act, 1948 get classified as the unorganized, including the ones that are not covered under the public sector. The National Sample Survey's 55th Round in 1999-2000 on the informal sector differs from the concept of unorganized sector used in the NAS, as it also covers the un-incorporated proprietary or partnership enterprises, enterprises run by co-operative societies, trusts, private and public limited companies (non-ASI). Thus, the informal sector could be taken as a part of the unorganized sector.

Characteristic Features of the Informal Sector

The above definitions of the informal sector by different researchers help to arrive at the salient features characterizing it. According to some economists, entry norms are easy in case of the non-formal segment as against the formal one, because there are no rules, regulations, or admission procedures in case of the former, while there are proper, systematic, and scheduled appointments, rules and regulations, selection procedures governing employees for the latter. Similarly, entry and exit are informal, verbal, generally without any contracts or appointment letters in case of the unorganized sector workers. The reverse is true for the organized sector employees. Also, the employees of the informal enterprises are mostly in temporary, flexible, irregular, casual working arrangements with no fixed working hours, wages, allowances, or facilities. This is contrasted by regular and permanent jobs involving fixed working hours, mutually determined pay and compensation packages for their counterparts.

Importantly, labour in the unorganized sector is not unionized, while trade unions and collective bargaining are generally an essential component of the organized workforce in formal enterprises with government regulation and protection. The non-formal segment is outside the purview of public policies as it is not recognized by official sources of data collection. Ownership of unorganized sector enterprises is usually vested in the family, while of their counterparts with governments or corporates.

Informal sector enterprises primarily use indigenous resources and labour intensive technology due to home based production. In contrast, the formal segment generally has access to imported technology and foreign capital due to its relatively large sized operations and product markets (Ramanujam *et al.*, 1998, p.56; Webster *et al.*, 1996, p. 6). Big firms that manufacture goods mainly for the upper income groups primarily control the non-formal sector. On the other hand, the informal sector is owned by a large number of small producers mainly selling to low-income groups (Papola, 1980, p. 819).

Informal sector establishments are not transitory and in most cases are found to have survived over a decade. Structurally, these units are largely linked to the informal sector only and have a large employment potential. This segment is found in rural and urban areas, and is generally of a subsistence nature in case of the former and market-oriented in case of the latter. Rural informal enterprises are usually male-dominated, while their urban counterparts are controlled by females. Home-based work is forming an increasingly important constituent of the informal sector, especially in terms of women's activities accounting for 60 to 70 per cent of its total employment (Awasthi *et al.*, 1994, p. 56).

Some researchers characterize the informal sector as heterogeneous, and claim that it is becoming an integral part of the mainstream economy, though traditionally it was predicted to be transient. It was believed that this segment would ultimately fade away or merge with the formal sector as the economy grew. On the contrary, the sector has been proliferating and gaining prominence. Also, an involutionary growth resulting in the spread of tiny enterprises, rather than growth of enterprises is on the rise (Ramanujam, 1998, pp. 4; 25). Currently, various debates and controversies about the unorganized sector are emerging to discuss its existence and role in development. In contrast with the predicted short-run appearance, experience proves that this segment is not a temporary phenomenon, but is at an early stage of its own transition (Sanyal, 1991, pp. 9; 42). Therefore, despite general predictions of the non-permanent status of the informal sector, it represents a part of the modern economy that is growing at a faster pace than the organized sector. The World Labour Report estimates of 1992 showed that while the formal segment grew at about 2 per cent a year through the eighties, the urban informal sector managed more than double of that, providing up to 60 per cent of urban employment. Thus, different perceptions and predictions about this segment have emerged. The twenty-first century is characterized by reforms, structural adjustments, and globalization that affect labour markets and their structures. It also leads to interconnections across the globe which has their bearings on both, the formal and non-formal markets. We should not dichotomize these two segments due to inherent linkages between them, and thus see them as a continuum of production forms (Brigitte, 1985, pp. 279-280; Panitch *et al.*, 2001, p. 295).

Various researchers have been studying the impact of structural adjustment programmes and globalization on different nations, which will be covered in the subsequent section of review of literature.

ANALYSIS OF LITERATURE

In the analysis of literature, a brief introduction discussing national and international trends in employment is given in Section 2.4.1. Subsequently, we focus on various intertwined issues that impact wages in Section 2.4.2, followed by working conditions. Other developments like feminization of work, poverty, indebtedness, illiteracy, and the rise in Female Headed Households is brought out in the last section.

Trends in Employment in last ten years (1991-2001)

In this section, an analysis of national and international trends in employment in the decade of 1991-2001 is analyzed. Despite a few individual studies by researchers, little work has been done on the impact of structural adjustment programmes on the urban informal sector, and hardly any on gender. We found gender studies on this aspect of economic reforms to be largely rural-based or socio-cultural in nature, thus making our area of research relevant, as well as significant. Also, a brief look at international experiences gives a broader perspective, as the new millennium has resulted in the universality of globalization with reforms becoming common to most nations.

A review of literature has enriched our own study and is discussed briefly in the subsequent sections. World over, reforms and structural adjustment programmes have resulted in changes in the production process. Privatization and denationalization leading to changes in ownership and policy framework have impacted employment and livelihoods. The continuous search for competitive methods of manufacturing low cost goods aided by internationalization of capital and technology that is hastened by globalization has its bearings on the human factor. Labour market reforms are seen to be speedily implemented by almost all countries since the nineties. Job changes could vary in the severity of their impact depending on the degree of restructuring and in accordance with country-specific measures. Generally, the type and nature of employment gains or losses are difficult to measure and estimate. Also, a few sectors may experience an increase in work, especially due to a rise in exports in the special economic zones or in the area of information technology. Thus, it becomes imperative to view labour market reforms on a larger canvass beyond temporary gains in employment that could be sporadic, ad hoc, and sector/industry specific.

Another emerging trend associated with globalization is trans-nationalization due to speedy integration across the globe facilitated by back-processing offices (BPO's) and sweat shops. Thus, multinationals find it cheaper to outsource production and assembling processes to third world countries. Reforms have drastically altered people's livelihoods as work is seen to become casual, contractual, temporary, and highly uncertain. This has led to the strengthening of the informal sector, as workers are being pushed out of formal employment, especially in case of males. Retrenchment of men compels women to take recourse to the unorganized sector for income augmentation. Thus, competition for these jobs increases due to the crowding out effect on employment that directly depresses wages. Also, the secondary status of females comes into focus, as they are generally 'target earners'. Apart from the gender divide, women as a group face dichotomy on account of employers' preferences for young and unmarried girls without any encumbrances due to their inherent docility and exploitability (See Mukherjee, 2004, pp.284-285; and Sparr, 1994, pp.16-29). Casualization and informalization of jobs and livelihoods have their bearings on wages, working and living conditions, headship of households, and other related issues. Globalization is generally associated with the information technology (IT) sector and its related services that help to transform multi-national operations into trans-national ones, as the scale of production becomes global. Another emerging issue of globalization and immigrant Indian women facilitated by the information technology revolution, in particular shows a spectacular rise in their numbers. Paradoxically, during the decade of eighties, it was at 2.62 lakhs and decreased to 1.92 lakhs post-globalization in the 1991-95 periods. This drastic fall was due to their preference of reproductive activities over productive ones. The irony is that qualified or unqualified, females' roles are socially constructed and could lead to a 'behavioural duality' among women at home and at work (S. Uma, 2002, pp. 4421-4427).

Some researchers observed a paradoxical development of men losing their jobs more to women than automation, as regular male employees fell from over 44 per cent to just above 39 per cent during 1990-91 to 1992, denoting a higher impact of casualisation in a shorter period (Ramaswamy, 1984, p. 221). The Indian case shows that the post-nineties have witnessed a 'jobless growth' due to stagnation in employment. Major industries like cotton textiles and food products accounting for about one-thirds of jobs experienced 20 to 25 per cent cut in employment on account of restructuring and reform. A decline of these traditional sectors has adversely impacted trade unionism, as voluntary retrenchments were negotiated between employers and unions without involving the government. Thus, many people lost their livelihoods without getting any compensation guaranteed by law which in turn further weakened collective bargaining and unionism. Globalization promoted by the Washington Consensus is largely responsible for labour market flexibility and deregulation. This in turn has resulted in temporary jobs without any guarantees or securities, along with an absence of regular earnings and benefits of jobs whatsoever. Thus, the 'low road to growth' of reduction of wages and labour standards has been used extensively by a majority of firms. Few employers have been resorting to the 'high road to growth' by accelerating productivity with the use of innovations in technology, product design, and organization or development of new segments. However, new sub-sectors like electrical machinery, chemicals, transport equipment, rubber, plastic and petroleum products all experienced a growth in output of over 7 per cent that was not matched by an expansion in work opportunities. Another emerging divide is noticed in case of 'insiders' and 'outsiders' entering the labour market. The interests of insiders or existing workforce are being protected at the cost of restricting entry for new entrants. These developments mirror the changing job maps for men and women. They also portray the basis of gender differentials in earnings inherent in the nature of employment and source of incomes. Overall, an acceleration in growth rates have been accompanied by a deceleration in employment as the former has recorded gains from 8 to 9 per cent, while the latter a dip from 2 per cent to barely 1 per cent along with continuously falling employment elasticities from 0.41 to 0.15 in the pre-and-post nineties, respectively (Sharma, 2006, pp. 2078-2080). The latest NSSO survey on 'Employment and Unemployment Situation in India' highlights the accentuation of 'jobless growth' as 58 per cent of employable population is found to be unemployed in 2004-05. The nation is also seen to portray a gender and rural-urban divide as more women than men are found to be unemployed. The urban locations demonstrated higher unemployment ratios at 45 per 1000 workers in contrast with 17 in case of rural areas. Interestingly, nearly one-third of urban males were seen to be employed in the 'trade, hotel, and restaurant' sector followed by 'manufacturing' and 'services' segments that provide livelihoods to 24 and 21 per cent, respectively. These results are contrasted by nearly 36 per cent of female employment in the 'services' sector followed by 28 and 18 per cent in 'manufacturing' and 'agriculture', respectively (NSSO, 2005).

Impact on Wages

The changing labour scenario impacts earnings and benefits of permanent employment like pension, gratuity, provident fund, leave, traveling expense, house rent provision, dearness allowance, and the like. This results in direct downward pressure on wages, as the nature of work changes to casual, ad hoc, and temporary. Payments are generally made on daily or hourly basis and are mostly arbitrary. Thus, money and real earnings of workers decline as they are based on verbal and informal agreements without any contracts and guarantees of regular jobs. Further, competition among different segments of workers like men and women in general, along with special cases of retrenched males in the formal sector and females in informal jobs, married women and young girls in the unorganized segment intensifies due to industrial reforms, thereby depressing wages. All this increases the vulnerability and exploitation of unprotected workers due to rising uncertainties of jobs and earnings.

United Nations International Children's Educational Fund's study (1988, pp. 66-67) on 'The Invisible Adjustment' shows that poor women work harder thus enabling the bottom one-third population in Latin America and the Caribbean to physically survive the economic crisis. These developments clearly show that reform brings in paradoxes of rising unemployment in the formal sector, and increasing employment in the informal sector, that have bearings on gender, thus involving major opportunity costs and adjustments for women (World Development Report, 1995, pp. 7-9). Therefore, labour market changes generally result in falling male employment due to the implementation of 'exit policies' and 'golden handshakes'. Employment is becoming more casual, temporary, and erratic in nature, adversely affecting male employment, thus having repercussions on female employment.

Women are taking to employment on a larger scale than earlier to augment family incomes (See Bullock, 2000, pp. 1-2; OECD, 1994, pp. 19-20; and 'UN Inter-regional Seminar for Women and the Economic Crisis', 1987, pp.95-98). Thus, females become target earners causing a further fall in wages due to their 'surplus' worker status. Strangely, labour market policies put a downward pressure on both money and real earnings that affect livelihoods and standards of living directly as well as indirectly. Falling and uncertain money wages coupled with no benefits of employment experienced by a majority of workforce particularly in the informal segment is worsened by inflation, cut backs in government spendings and subsidies. Paradoxically, surplus labourpower emerging from the formal sector's restructuriong, along with a natural growth of labour force leads to competition among labourers themselves that depress their earnings. These trends have been supported by micro studies of labour flexibility across 1,300 manufacturing firms in 9 industry groups in the post-nineties. Results show that while downsizing occurred in a few firms, employment gains in others largely accrued to non-regular 'flexi workers', majority being women (See Deshpande et al, 2004). Thus, the 'race to the bottom' seems to be reserved for female workers who can be easily exploited. Majority of labour was found to be non-unionized due to their lack of 'permanent worker' status, thereby accepting any wage for survival and income augmentation.

Impact on Working Conditions and Security

Globalization is rapidly altering the nature and conditions of work that jeopardize security of employment. Transnationalization and outsourcing of production processes on grounds of economic efficiency, along with informalization in domestic segments are on the rise. Thus, a third world is being created in the first, as globalization is seen to perpetrate the myth that sweatshops exist outside rich countries. In fact, developed countries are competing with developing countries in terms of lowest possible labour standards. This is demonstrated by numerous cases where especially women workers in the garment industry in America are found to work in unsafe, unhealthy conditions, and earn low wages for putting in long hours- ranging between 8 to 10 hours per day. The Silicon Valley provides a glaring case of exploitation and discrimination of immigrants working long hours in high tech industries with carcinogens, acids, and highly toxic gases. These fast growing segments are known to flout labour and environmental standards as people are employed on contract basis that results in international exploitation of workers (Chossudovsky, 1997, p. 84). There are no formal agreements of work, as labour laws or trade unionism is absent in these segments. Besides, there are no guarantees or benefits of regular employment like leave, medical allowance, pension, provident fund or gratuity.

Industrial restructuring in countries like India is partly responsible for employment stagnation during the 'jobless growth' period. This is largely attributed to major cuts in jobs in the two main sectors of cotton textiles and food products due to industrial sickness or rationalization. Cotton textiles used to account for a share of about 20 per cent in total employment, and they experienced a fall of 3.6 per cent per annum in employment. Food products were the second largest employer to the tune of 13 per cent of organized manufacturing sector employment and saw a similar downtrend as cotton textiles. The decline of these traditional industries adversely impacted trade unionism, as voluntary retrenchments were negotiated between the employers and unions without involving the government. Thus, many workers lost their jobs without getting any compensation guaranteed by law, which in turn further weakened the trade union movement. New sub-sectors like electrical machinery, chemicals, transport equipment, rubber, plastic and petroleum products, machine tools and wood products all experienced a growth in output of over 7 per cent. Despite positive employment growth, it accounted for just one-third of the total output growth that was worsened due to subcontracting to small units outside the formal sector.

The post-reform period of nineties show an impressive growth of over 10 per cent in output, but data gaps in the recession period of 1996-97 are left out. The two major changes in the labour market witnessed are the fall in share of wages, and change in the trade-off towards employment growth, rather than wage growth. All this results in a substantial increase in employment elasticity, though it may not reach the high value of the first period. The structural adjustment programmes of the government have been adversely affecting women's employment by wage reduction, and contractualisation of work by making it temporary. This casualisation is on the rise, especially for women from an already high figure of 38.5 per cent in 1987-88 to 43 per cent in 1993-94. Therefore, the adverse trends in labour market in terms of informalization, casualization, and feminization are clearly emphasized. Working conditions for females are worse than men in various ways like the quality of employment, extent of underemployment, and unemployment, especially for educated women that worsens on account of a gender gap in wages (See Bhalotra, 1998, p. 13; Ghose, 2004, pp. 5106-5111; Kundu, 1999, pp. 3-6; Majumdar *et al.*, 2004, pp. 3017-3021; and Papola, 1992, p. 13). The Fund-Bank package may lead to an increase in employment prospects for women, but may tend to place additional burdens in terms of greater pace, longer hours of work, compulsory overtime, no wage increase related to productivity increase, lack of safety standards, reduction in food security, declining health, denial of implementation of labour legislation, along with restrictions on trade union organization (Visvanathan *et al.*, 1997, pp. 191-203). Thus, mere increases in the quantum of work may be offset by its poor quality or lower remuneration. Globalization has also reduced male employment due to enterprise restructuring and closure, leading to under-employment, unemployment, and subsequent entry into the informal sector. Apart from this direct impact, many women have been forced to take to income-augmenting activities, thereby worsening the dual burden of women's production and reproduction activities.

Other Issues

Literature on women's work does not explicitly cover the impact of structural adjustment programmes and globalization, as most of them are sociological in nature. The ones that deal with economic issues are largely concerned with the rural areas, leaving us with only a few on the urban informal sector. We shall emphasize on the economic aspect by critically reviewing the findings of the major studies. Various other issues important for our analysis like feminization, emergence of female-headed households, and their impact on society are brought out in this section. Gender analysis of the emerging employment trends becomes important on account of a few basic aspects that need to be considered. Studies at the international level bring out varied experiences of different countries with respect to structural adjustments undertaken, thereby affecting the urban informal sector and women's work. It becomes difficult to generalize the Indian case due to its diversity in terms of various regional, religious, social, and economic groupings. Nevertheless, a synchronization of results for both the international and national levels is attempted in the subsequent part.

Historically, women's economic role has been marginalized the world over as seen from the debates on the issue of recognizing women as workers dating back to the first population Census of England in 1870-71. This official data considered six broad classes, wherein one of them categorized 'domestics' considered women as the ones either with occupations in the family or personal service. The Bombay Province dropped this classification as they found it difficult to differentiate between women's work as a wife and as an agricultural labourer. Thereby, females and children were taken as consumers and not producers. Women thus acted as a 'reserve army' due to industrialization and restructuring, which conceptually draws its parallel in Marxian work (Kalpagam, 1994, pp. 17; 125-126). Since the sixties, low employment elasticity in the manufacturing sector has plagued the third world countries, which are traditionally characterized by over-population and surplus labour, especially of females. Restructuring increasingly results in the employment of women's cheap, surplus, and docile labour that is substituted for male workers, thus further masking their invisibility (Brigitte, 1985, pp. 279-80).

Globalization leads to 'feminization of labour force' as almost universally the ratio of women to men in economic activity has risen from 37 to 100 in the seventies to 62 to 100 in the nineties. Women also carry a bulk of unpaid work to the extent of 70 per cent that is known to escalate with restructuring with restructuring and informalization. This in turn causes 'feminization of livelihoods, poverty, and the informal sector'. Consequently, labour market schisms, especially for females worsen and could have major socio-economic ramifications (See Date-Bah, 1997, pp. 2-5; and Mazumdar *et al.*, 2004, p. 3017). The non-market burden of women rises, as their market activities increase. Their contribution to the care economy is typified by gender stereotyping, and hence cannot be measured accurately, thus further escalating the dichotomy between paid and unpaid work.

According to Sen (1992, pp. 154-155), "The gender division of labour also extends to the household, wherein the dynamics of bargaining, decision-making, and gender relations impact production and consumption. The household emerges as a non-homogeneous unit, depicting 'cooperative conflict' based on the general assumption of male headship".

Post-reform periods depict a rise in women's unpaid work, thereby making them continuously devise new coping strategies. Government's adjustment and stabilization policies are often gender blind, and lead to cutbacks in subsidies, social services, and higher prices of necessities. For combating this, females are seen to either stretch their limited funds due to which their domestic responsibilities rise, or spend more time shopping for cheaper items, as food preparations take longer because they buy less of processed food, and also in smaller quantities on account of lower incomes. Post-liberalization and currency devaluation, women were observed to cultivate vegetable gardens to meet higher food prices, and even walk more or avoid public transport to save money (Cornia *et al.*, 1987, pp. 95-96). The gender gap in wages further increases with a drop in formal sector employment, and its resultant spillover into the informal sector. Thus, workers lose out on relatively high wages and benefits, along with labour rights and job security offered by the organized segment. This leads to the "feminization of work and poverty". Women, thereby become poorer absolutely and in relation to men, as the numbers of poor households headed by women increase, either due to death, loss of employment, migration of the male head, as seen particularly from the Brazilian and Carribean cases that portray about one-thirds of poor households headed by females. Consequently, women are compelled to mortgage or sell their jewelry that further raises their indebtedness. All this jeopardizes old-age security by making them more vulnerable and insecure, thereby resulting in 'feminization of debt' (Institute of Social Studies Advisory Service, 1985, pp. 22-28).

Other researchers reiterate these findings and also bring out several paradoxes in the labour market, as restructuring reduces formal employment, thereby pushing people into the informal sector. Male and female workers compete for these jobs, as the former experience retrenchments, thereby forcing them, and their counterparts to enter the labour market to augment family incomes. Thus, it reinforces the secondary status of women, as they are generally 'target earners'. Strangely, apart from the gender divide and competition from males, women workers as a group are divided, as employers prefer young and unmarried girls on account of maternity, and child care benefits associated with married women. This increases the vulnerability and exploitation of females that exert a downward pressure on wages, and benefits of employment. Increasing social costs of women's labour market participation cause delays, stress, and frustration in their marriages. They are found to go through more mental health problems, as they are unable to cope with insufficient incomes, and find lesser time to care for children. Female fertility and childbearing gets adversely affected due to the economic compulsion of work, stress, improper diet, and inadequate nutrition. The burden of new roles leads to further neglect of their health, especially in case of pregnant and lactating mothers. The well-being of children also suffers that leads to malnutrition, diseases, morbidities, and mortality. In a majority of cases, especially girls are found to bear the burden of their working mother's income-augmenting activities that lead to neglect of their health and education (Sparr, 1994, pp. 16-29). This is documented by the United Nations study that points to a slowdown in the rate of improvement in female: male enrolment ratios in general education, particularly in case of second-level schools in Africa and Asia since the eighties. Deteriorating female enrolment appears to be directly related with an increase in unemployment. A rise in absenteeism and school dropout rates is found to further decline female human capital. Women tend to remain under qualified, illiterate, and untrained leading to low employability in the future (World Survey, 1989, pp. 27-35). Another paradoxical situation on account of export-led globalization is seen to have mixed employment results for women. Exports of traditional items that employ a majority of women in tea, handlooms, and handicrafts are found to stagnate, thus not actually helping these workers. On the non-traditional export front, demand for garments, fish, and shrimp processing has grown, but females do not gain again as they are hired on a temporary or apprentice basis. Despite this, women still continue to work in such uncertain jobs, as these wages are relatively high compared to alternative opportunities (Mahmud *et al.*, 1989, p. 31). UNICEF's (1988, pp. 66-67) country studies show that worst hit categories among women are those who are least educated, unskilled, poorest, and household heads. This is documented in its cases of Egypt and Ghana, where public enterprises avoid hiring females to keep the gender workforce below the threshold set by law to run enterprises more 'efficiently'. Women are losing job protection, security, and benefits due to a cut in public sector work that affects the least skilled among them the hardest. The Mexican example shows that young rural women are forced to emigrate to work as domestic servants in other countries under 'extremely vulnerable conditions'. Young women and wives are pulled out from land to work as day labourers with no benefits or social security and made to live in sheds, thereby additionally making them easy targets of sexual abuse. Other rural females take to contract work through a 'putting out' system for income augmentation. The social position of women is adversely affected especially in cases of income-supplementation as their unpaid work at home increases. Women feel the extra burden of household chores to be now accomplished within the same time thus jeopardizing their physical and mental health. Also, family tensions and clash of priorities like child-care versus income earning, or productive versus unproductive activities emerge. Apart from an increase in the number of hours of women's work time, more importantly there is an observed shift on how time is being spent. They have to now allocate more time to income generation and community management at the expense of reproductive work. In extreme cases, role clashes lead to marital discord, break-up of families, and divorces. This could also occur due to women's demands for more money for running family expenditures in the event of falling family incomes.

Women try to fine tune this dichotomy by resorting to home or flexi-time working. This trend is on the rise almost universally, as females are reported to contribute 83 per cent of part-time workers, 70 per cent of family workers, and 50 per cent of casual workers even in countries of the European Union. Thus, it worsens the valuation and visibility of women's work, further increasing the risk of their exclusion (Ratna Kumari, 2001, pp. 3603-3605). Home-working, facilitated by information technology, along with new structures of governance and contracts is rapidly spreading to developing countries, especially among women who find it easy to intersperse with their household responsibilities. This could blur the distinction between the formal and informal sectors, and mask the visibility of the latter (Sudarshan R and Jeemol Unni, 2003, pp. 19-20). Other contrasting trends at the other end of the spectrum show that well qualified women who migrate to America for lucrative jobs, unfortunately choose to become 'homemakers' and thus, enter the care economy. All this leads to the emergence of a new trend of 'feminization of migration', as employers prefer women to men. The current occupational class structure produces two groups of women in relation to domestic work and child care: those who have got no time to do it and those who have no alternative but to do it. Thus, the growth of luxury goods production and consumption in a globalizing world results in a strange contradiction of producers not being able to consume goods produced by themselves (See Chaganti, 2004, pp. 2220-2224; Dubey, 1996, p. 56; and Panitch *et al.*, 2001, pp. 280- 295).

The International Labour Organization's (1989 and 2002) findings reiterate the increasing presence of women in the changing labour market, especially in the informal segment that lacks gender parity in work, wages, and benefits. Thus, their work becomes more insecure, flexible, and vulnerable than men. Globalization may have sometimes created more and new jobs for females, but family and social relationships have placed them in a subordinate sphere, thus reinforcing their 'secondary' status inside and outside the household. Women's involvement in the informal sector is marginal, temporary, and supplemental, that is worsened by interspersion of productive and reproductive roles, thereby making their 'work' increasingly difficult to define and segregate. A borderless world is characterized by increasing mobility of labour, capital, and new technologies, which result in 'feminization of migration'. Globally, there is a rise in Female Headed Households associated with 'feminization of poverty', worsened by migration, unsafe living, and working environments and policy apathy. The Report on Global Employment Trends for Women (2004, p.24) reiterates that, "Despite entering the job market in record numbers, women still face higher unemployment rates, lower wages, and represent bulk of the world's 550 million working poor. In the transition economies and East Asia, the number of women working per 100 men is 91 and 83, respectively, and as low as 40 in Middle East, North Africa, and South Asia. Worst still, of the 550 million 'working poor' in the world living on less than 1 American dollar a day, 60 per cent are women". Females continue to be asset less, as they own less than one per cent of property largely on account of patriarchal laws of inheritance. Worst still, working women do not have control over their own earnings as they are supposed to work for the family, and spend nothing on themselves. Contrastingly, their counterparts seem to be exempt from this obligation, as they can give a part of their incomes at home and spend a large proportion of it outside without being questioned (Dwyer *et al.*, 1988, p. 21). Thus, labour markets, institutions, and policies are gender blind, as they promote and perpetrate asymmetries that have larger ramifications on society and gender stereotyping.

Nevertheless, historical and socio-cultural forces circumscribe women's economic participation that could act as a constraint for parity with men. Gender stereotyping emphasizes the household headship of men, while reserving the care economy for women. Traditionally, females are not supposed to work outside their homes for wages, and thus, special cases like that of India demonstrate the irony of development adversely affecting the status of women. Generally, female work force participation is directly related to the family's poverty, and male unemployment. Subsequently, a rise in wage rates do not necessarily lead to an increase in women's work, as their labour market behaviour is primarily affected by the pattern of fertility and 'home responsibilities'. However, the economic power enjoyed by men could be diluted in a few exceptional cases, as the underlying socio-cultural conditions change (See Glover *et al.*, 1995, pp. 37-57; Morgan, 1984, p. 298; and Neft *et al.*, 1997, pp. 298-99).

Women in India, thereby confirm to the 'contingent' labour status that is universally true. The socio-cultural environment is in favour of male employment vis-à-vis their female counterparts and is reinforced by the marginal rise in labour force participation of women from 36 per cent to 40 per cent in the two-decade period from 1970-1990, matched by low increases in female adult literacy, as well as school enrollments. These developments point to gender biases and gaps in education that tend to worsen their employability and inequity with men. Globalization and associated technological developments have impacted women's work, as almost 94 per cent are employed in the informal sector. Most of them are contingent or surplus workers like landless agricultural labourers, cottage industry workers, and also migrants, generally employed as domestics, street vendors, daily workers, and the like. Thus, they mirror the trend of the post-reform labour market, which is temporary, non-formal, and irregular (See Bhalotra, 1998, pp. 5-32; Dube *et al.*, 1990, p. 131; Dunlop *et al.*, 1999, pp. 1-3; Gandhi *et al.*, 2002, pp. 170-71; Ghose, 1999, p. 2604; Kundu, 1999, pp. 3-6; Lebra *et al.*, 1984, pp. 20-23; Majumdar *et al.*, 2004, p. 3017-3021; and Papola, 1992, p. 13).

Women represent the most vulnerable segment of the labour market, as they are doubly disadvantaged due to their gender, and informal work status. Thus, the perception of females as a 'secondary' labour force gets reinforced on account of increasing competition at work that is gender biased. Paradoxically, despite a rise in their numbers as main workers which is faster than their male counterparts, they account for a small part of the formal sector labour. This is documented by a few studies which show that despite male main workers rising by 23 per cent and female by 40 per cent, the latter accounted for only 23 per cent of the total workforce. The situation was seen to deteriorate in terms of work participation rates that were low at 22 per cent. These further declined to 9 per cent in case of urban women workers. The share of organized sector employment in total employment was at around 8 per cent in the eighties, which dropped to 7 per cent in early nineties and fell still further to 5 per cent towards the end of nineties. This is largely attributed to industrial restructuring leading to a fall in public sector employment. In industry, deceleration in employment growth in the post-reform period has occurred due to capital deepening resulting in the adoption of labour-saving technologies. Employment in public sector factories grew at only 0.4 per cent per annum between 1990-91 and 1997-98. This segment was responsible for 70 per cent of the nation's employment that fell to a negative level of 0.03 per cent p.a. The graph gets more skewed when women's employment in the organized sector is considered, as it is low at only 17 per cent, with a majority doing menial jobs and barely a few at the managerial or decision-making levels. Declining jobs affects women both directly and indirectly. Directly, because women employed in low-paid and low-skilled jobs are adversely affected in comparison with men due to the import of capital-intensive technology, and indirectly, in competition with men for low-paid and low-skilled jobs that were primarily held by women (See Dewan, 1999, p. 427; Planning Commission, 2002, p. 225; and Srivastava, 1997, pp. 527-43).

The United Nations Report on Third World Women for 1970-90 thus points out that the informal sector is not a panacea for women and is far less secure than formal sector work as it generally pays lesser than even the minimum wage (Patel, 2002, pp. 22-23; 31). Globalization could accentuate the vulnerabilities and exploitation of female workers hastened in a borderless world, thus, the increasing the commodification of women (Mies *et al.*, 1986, p. 170). In fact, global trends confirm women to be 'last in, first out', especially in female-dominated industries of South-East Asia like textiles, garments, and shoes that employ 30-40 per cent of females. Paradoxically, they are seen to form a larger part of the unemployed like 43 per cent of Jakarta's 13 million unemployed (Tsikata, 2003, p. 1-2). This 'feminization of production and exports' is also confirmed by the United Nations study in Bangladesh that employed over 2400 people, 90 per cent of who were women (United Nations, 1999, pp. 9-10).

However, gains in labour markets for women could be transitory, as they lose them to men later as products and technologies become sophisticated and advanced. This is amply clear from Korea's electronic industry, as well as Singapore, Taiwan, Mexico, Malaysia, Philippines, and Sri Lanka's export processing zones, where female employment fell from 75 to 54 per cent between the decade of eighties and nineties. These paradoxical trends associated with high employment followed by higher proportions of unemployment in case of women are emphasized by other economists also (Bagchi, 1999, pp. 3219-3230). Thus, females have always been working and are observed to be highly mobile in terms of both entry and exit into the labour market (Moser, 1980, p. 28). Their earnings constitute a significant proportion of the household's income, particularly among low-income groups. The spread of their economic activities outside the household may be sequential or may co-exist, largely determined by the socio-economic conditions and their position within the household. Any reorientation of their involvement in the informal sector only implies the changing nature of priorities of market versus non-market work. Most of these workers are target earners, as they augment family incomes, with their mobility depending upon factors of age, marriage, and migration (Phongpaichit *et al.*, 1984, pp. 43-45).

The gender lens clearly shows us the disadvantaged position of women vis-à-vis men on three counts. Ray (2000, pp.3-4) observes that, "Firstly, globalization being technology driven, women are marginalized in economic activities as men continue to be offered new scopes of learning and training. This increases the casualisation of female labour. Secondly, globalization has led to an increase in unemployment of men, resulting in more frustration, tension, fear of job insecurity for which women are made to pay the social cost. Family violence, rape, and dowry deaths are escalating. Thirdly, strains are put on women's health and education resulting in mortality, morbidity, and ill health. In a few cases, it also leads to a rise in female-headed households". Globalization tends to be biased in favour of industry against agriculture, leading to informalisation and migration of the poorest workers, especially women (See Breman *et al.* 2000, p. 156; Eapen, 2001, p. 2392; Goldar, 2000, pp. 1191-1193).

Therefore, almost universally, women's contribution to the economy, society, and the household is undermined due to the non-market nature of their work. Also, most of women's work being interspersed with other household chores makes it difficult to measure their economic work and differentiate it from the extra-economic tasks, which is perpetuated by gender stereotyping. Few others feel that this non-recognition in economic activities is not only an outcome of their work being intertwined with household activities, and being unpaid, making it difficult for enumerators to identify women as workers but is largely due to definitional problems that are worsened in subsistence activities, especially of developing economies such as India (See Bardhan, 1985, pp. 2261-69; and Dewan, 1999, pp. 425-427). Emerging casualization and flexiblization of labour is worsened by the new trend of home-working and self-employment of women, as it does provide an entry into the world of work, but no benefits of regular employment, thereby increasing their over-representation in all types of irregular jobs (National Sample Survey, 2000, p. 21). In fact, this rising trend of home-based workers in the information technology enabled services employ majority of females, especially to the tune of 37 per cent in areas of call centers, medical transcription centers, and back office services like data entry that are expected to further generate a million jobs by 2008 (Mukherjee, 2004, p.282).

However, this positive entry of women into non-traditional areas may not be of a permanent nature, vis-à-vis its Asian competitors. Also, at the macro level, the picture gets smaller as the computer software industry accounts for only one per cent of national employment, thus creating jobs for only a small fragment of women, who are professionally qualified (See Chakrabarty, 2001, p. 3257; Kumar, 2001, p. 4284; and Roy et al, 1996, pp. 33-35). Paradoxically, there is also an increased trend towards feminization of the work process, as women are preferred in certain areas like export industries or export-processing zones due to increased profits from sub-contracting, which have increased from 10 per cent in 1970's, doubling to 20 per cent in the eighties, further rising to 35 per cent in 1990's. Thus, globalization enabled by new information technology leads to an expansion in informalization and feminization of formal employment, thereby raising the proportion of non-rural population that depends upon the informal sector at a faster pace. The urban informal sector provides livelihoods to a majority of women in urban India, four out of five, in 1993 that continues even a decade later. However, the new reform process creates a rift within females themselves, as employers prefer young, unmarried girls to their married counterparts. The former are easy to employ and exploit without any encumbrances, while the latter have a number of domestic problems, absenteeism, and have to be provided with benefits of maternity and childcare (See Noronha, 1996; and Roy, 1996, p. 33).

It appears that globalization is resulting in an increasing entry of multinationals and transnational into traditional local industries, thereby threatening livelihoods and the environment. A few examples that could be cited are especially in cases of fishing which have been taken over by giant corporations. Thus, traditional fishing is operated on a large scale using modern technology, sophisticated tools and equipment like mechanized boats, trawlers, nets, storage, packaging, and the like. All this entails a challenge to the local fisher folk, as they are unable to buy modern tools and adopt latest technology, and most of it being labour displacing, thus adversely affecting local employment. Another major area of livelihood for females, comprising the handloom sector, is also hit due to restructuring, reform, and trade unionism, especially in

Mumbai. All this jeopardizes the employment of unskilled, illiterate, and poor workers.

Studies reveal that the textile sector in the metropolis, which formerly employed about two-and-a-half lakh workers in 1985, experienced a drastic fall to less than one-fifth at 54,000 in 1996. The problem was more acute in terms of women's employment share in this sector, which dropped to a mere 0.01 per cent in late nineties from 40 per cent in 1950's. Other examples show that women accounted for 600 of the total 1500 workers in the multinational factory of Levers in Mumbai in the sixties, which fell to only 3 of the reduced workforce of 800 in the nineties. This clearly brings out the gender bias in employment and retrenchment. Other female-dominated home-based activities being threatened due to the entry of multinationals are hosiery, textile, and pickle making. Also, retrenchment drives in the organized sector first target women. Modernization and skill-development programmes benefit men, as they are preferred over women. This in turn, pushes them into assembly line and low paid jobs in the short run, and also handicaps them in the long run (See Dewan, 1997; and Menon, 1995-96, p. 1165). The study of four informal sector industries in the city of Mumbai, namely Bakeries and Savouries, Food Processing, and Fish Processing portray that globalization and restructuring increase the proportion of workers, as well as manufacturing activities in the informal sector. Data gaps, lack of a detailed break-up, along with the further bifurcation of the informal sector into Own-Account Manufacturing Enterprises and Non-Directory Manufacturing Enterprises undermine its importance. Most of these industries have a strong gender-based division of labour, where women dominate the 'delicate' tasks of packing and cake making in the bakery section, along with drying and salting of fish carried out exclusively by migrants. All this creates a rift and escalates inequalities among the 'white collared' workers and 'blue collared' ones (Dewan, 1999, pp. 14-54).

A new emerging trend is of 'feminization of migration' as most of the migrants are poor women from the villages. Researchers highlight the findings of their study to show that, migrants generally resort to domestic work due to an ease of entry and no special education or skills required. The survey of about 7000 domestic workers in eight states portrays the low wages, menial nature of jobs, and deplorable working conditions. Employers' preferred young girls and boys below 20 as they are generally docile. Also, three-fourths of these are females, being traditionally role-molded into this job (D'Cunha, 1987, pp. 1-3). Thus, a 'gender trap' emerges, as a combination of negative forces like low wages, low schooling, and training, appalling conditions of work lacking basic infrastructure and sanitation all lead to the degradation of the 'worker status' of women. Globalization has led to declining public expenditure in the eighties and nineties in critical areas of health, housing, rural development, education, and the like. Data clearly shows that the outlay on social services and rural development as a per centage of net state domestic product has fallen from roughly 7.3 per cent to 6.4 per cent, and from 1.3 to 0.9 per cent from 1990-91 to 1998-99, respectively (See Dev *et al.*, 2002, pp. 853-866; Kapadia, 2002, pp. 69-135; 329-32; Pillai, 1985, p. 33; and Savara *et al.*, 1986, pp. 6-8). There is an increase in the feminization of poverty, as women face relatively more burdens. Reforms have to a large extent created a surge in Female Headed Households of widows, single mothers, and deserted or divorced women. These are the poorest of the poor households, thereby showing a connection between Female-Headed Households and poverty (Parthasarthy, 1982 and Visaria, 1985).

A study by the National Commission on Self-Employed Women and Women in the Informal Sector (Shramshakti, 1988) depicted that women's work, even via Census data, is under-reported by 30-40 per cent due to poor data collection. An increasing proportion of over 90 per cent of females are involved in the unorganized informal sector doing menial, casual jobs of a time-consuming and unremunerative nature, with wide wage differentials vis-à-vis males. Thus, they are trapped in the vicious circle of subsistence, deprivation, and survival. They are asset-less or even if they own them, do not control them. Unfortunately, their labour is never perceived as 'work' in the productive sense due to the pre-conceived notion of their homemaker and non-primary status. Thus, her work is uncertain, vulnerable, and lacks recognition and protection.

CONCLUSION

The multi-dimensional review of literature points towards certain universal trends emerging in the labour market that could be summed up as under:

- There is an increasing feminization of work, as more women are entering the labour market, mostly in the informal sector. Thus, females are generally temporary, casual, or marginal workers and are not part of any organized labour force or trade union, thereby increasing the vulnerability of their employment and exploitation;
- The gender gap in earnings increases, as women workers are generally under-employed, underpaid, and overworked. This is worsened by increasing labour market segmentation, and inherent gender biases, thus making 'women last in and first out', as unemployed men seek jobs out of the organized sector competing with already employed women;
- In the post-reform period, females' income augmenting role is on the rise and generally gains prominence in times of loss of employment of the male head. Unfortunately, there emerges a divide amongst women workers themselves, as employers prefer young and unmarried girls to their married counterparts;
- Women's dual burden rises, as they have to multi-task between their 'productive' and 'reproductive' roles. This could worsen role conflicts, increasing the burden of girl children at home that results in absenteeism in school, neglect of health due to the drudgery of household chores, all causing deterioration of physical and mental health of girls and women. Thus, females get further trapped in the vicious circle of poverty, illiteracy, low skills, and deprivation;
- Globalization also raises the number of Female Headed Households, along with single parent families due to death and unemployment of the male head, or divorce and break-up of families.

Thus, the International Monetary Fund-World Bank package on reforms could lead to an increase in the growth of tradables and employment prospects for women. But industrial restructuring and liberalization could result in greater costs for women in terms of new technologies and skill learning, longer hours of work and additional burden on the home front. The scenario becomes worse in the absence of social security or labour law protection/implementation for women (Viswanathan et al, 1997, pp. 191-203).

Research has focused on the gendered nature of globalization and how global processes absorb and shape labour. Other concerns include women's exclusion from modern industry, their selective inclusion in global factories, the role of capital in gender relations, and the existence of patriarchal relations at the workplace. This analysis helps to give theoretical insights into the exploitation of women workers and focus on the gendered nature of labour markets. Unfortunately, this theorization has two inadequacies. First, it concentrates on export-oriented industries, bypassing women in domestic industries in the informal sector which do not necessarily employ unmarried and young women. Second, it is concerned with the 'demand' side or the needs and strategies of capital and not the 'supply' side of women workers. Some economists see the study of household responses and survival strategies to overcome adverse effects of globalization as handy tools to understand the dynamics of poverty due to methodological difficulties encountered (See Cornia *et al.*, 1987, p. 95; and Gandhi *et al.*, 2002, p. 192). Paradoxically, the 'New Home Economics' treat the household as an undifferentiated unit, solely governed by altruism, thus pushing women's issues to the background (Becker, 1981, p. 17). Therefore, divergent theories and opinions have resulted in lack of synchronization on women's market and non-market activities that greatly undermine their working status within and outside the household.

However, the nineties are known to show a number of hypotheses that provide insights for the analysis of women's work. The most prominent among these is the 'Flexibility theory of labour market' that focuses on streamlining of the work force, regulating wages and working hours, casualizing its permanent workforce and curtailment of collective bargaining for the 'flexi firm' and 'flexi workers'. 'Labour deregularisation' is linked with the 'feminization of work force' in that insecure, low wage jobs attract the employment of women. Feminization refers to a rise in female labour force participation that is accompanied by a fall in male participation rates and the feminization of certain jobs that are traditionally performed by men that is the substitution of men by women. Other researchers criticize this gender substitution by pointing out that though there is a rise in women's labour, it could be difficult to pinpoint the exact cause of substitution, as employment could have risen because of rise of low wage and flexible jobs (See Atkinson, 1986, p. 13; Chhachhi *et al.*, 1996, p. 12; and Standing, 1999, pp. 583-602).

In conclusion, there is a rethinking of the role of globalization, coupled with reforming domestic public policies. Harris-White (2002, pp. 173-184) feel that, "Despite the existence of global institutions of regulation, economic globalization does not replace 'defective' state regulation with a new international framework. The regulatory framework, on the contrary becomes more complex producing indeterminate outcomes. In fact, the forced adoption of 'national competitive advantage' policy effectively creates a new field of discrimination at the national and global levels".

The critical review of literature indicates that few economic studies have been conducted, especially with respect to women's work. Most of these lack statistical measurement of female employment due to definitional problems of work, lack of distinction between their productive and reproductive activities, absence of gender-disaggregated figures, and invisibility due to the nature of their activities. Also, most of the available data is rural and agricultural based, with little information on the urban informal sector and women workers. These shortcomings make it imperative for us to look at the micro level to study the impact of reforms on females in the urban informal sector.

3

SECONDARY DATA ANALYSIS

INTRODUCTION

In the earlier chapter, we looked at various definitions of the urban informal sector and also reviewed literature covering different studies for the purpose of data mining. Economic reforms world over and especially in India have led to an unprecedented rise of the unorganized segment. This is also caused due to the restructuring of the public sector, resulting in unemployment, underemployment, and 'voluntary retirement'. The 'New Economic Policy' has its ramifications on people's livelihoods, incomes, and living standards. Export-led growth has increased employment for few, but the nature, and quality of work is highly questionable. These labour market developments have resulted in the casualisation, informalization, and feminization of work leading to marginalization of workers. The surge in new industries and the services sector has led to a simultaneous increase in jobs accompanied by exploitation.

Researchers reiterate this trend that has largely emerged due to industrial and labour market restructuring, as it reduces formal sector employment for the new entrants, and also increases unemployment of the present organized sector workers. Thus, the informal segment is negatively associated with organized factories and positively with urban poverty (See Kundu, A. and Lalitha Kundu, 1998, pp. 4284-4287; and Mitra, 1998, pp. 3-6). Mukherjee (2004, pp. 293-304) also brings out the importance of these enterprises in post-reform times and states that, "Thus, the urban manufacturing informal sector is anticipated to be a distress phenomenon having close association with high incidence of poverty, slackening factory growth and the like by a few scholars. However, an overview of the growth pattern and dynamics suggests that the informal sector in India cannot be labeled either a distress driven sink, where people without any earning opportunities come in, or a dynamic alternative economic avenue in blanket terms. Parts of this sector do seem to have linkages with the organized sector in the urban areas and the agro sector in the rural areas, and are likely to act as an engine of future growth, especially in terms of its employment-providing role". This clearly highlights the inter connections between the formal and informal sectors, focusing on the employment potential of the latter that is generally taken recourse to by the unemployed and poor on account of the inability to create or sustain existing work.

IMPORTANCE OF SECONDARY DATA FOR THE INFORMAL SECTOR

It is necessary to incorporate secondary data with respect to the informal sector due to its growing prominence in recent times. A study of both, primary and secondary information is important for any analysis to be complete and balanced. The former helps devise micro connections, while the latter a macro perspective. Both these aspects provide a macro base that could formulate the theoretical and general picture which can be applied to the grass root level to make our study more methodical, empirical, and sound.

Any research to be complete needs to incorporate the available information already gathered by other researchers or bodies. This may seem an easy task due to it's apparently 'ready reckoner' nature. Unfortunately, experience proved otherwise, as it was tedious, more difficult and time-consuming, especially due to the lack of data availability with respect to the gendered informal sector. Most of the information is generated by government authorities who find it difficult to cater to the needs of individual researchers due to several reasons like pre-occupation with multiple political and administrative duties; lack of proper records; constant shifting of files and documents to different government offices; constant transfers of government officials leading to a problem of continuity; and funding problems of publishing data. Despite limitations, generality and difficult accessibility, secondary sources enrich research and present a holistic picture at different levels. It thereby links the macro-economic level with the micro-economic one of fieldwork analysis.

SECONDARY DATA SOURCES

After the detailed review of literature in the previous chapter, we now commence on the analysis of secondary data that is available on the central issue of our study. Secondary sources ranging from the national level to the State of Maharashtra and further to the urban segment, followed by Mumbai, R/S Ward, Kandivali, and field level of Charkop for the chosen areas of economic activity are studied. Section 3.3.1 brings out various non-primary information sources that present a general macro picture. The focal areas of activity of the thesis are highlighted in the subsequent part.

Different Levels of Data Availability

There are various bodies undertaking research and data mining at the macro levels. The most important secondary data sources are provided by the Population Census held every decade, the National Sample Survey (NSS) carried out by way of different rounds, and the Annual Survey of Industries (ASI) conducted every year.

Data collection for employment and unemployment has been carried since the 9th Round of the NSS in 1955 to assess the volume and structure of employment-unemployment. The Planning Commission has provided the conceptual framework since 1970 by setting up an 'Expert Committee on Unemployment Estimates' (popularly known as the Dantwala Committee) to review various surveys and the indicators generated.

Based on the concepts and definitions recommended by this Committee, the first quinquinnial surveys of employment and unemployment situation in India have been carried out by the NSSO. These six surveys were conducted during the 32nd (July 1977-June 1978), 38th (January 1983-December 1983), 43rd (July 1987-June 1988), 50th (July 1993-June 1994), 55th (July 1999-June 2000), and the 61st Rounds (July 2004-June 2005). Besides these, the NSS has also been regularly collecting information on certain key items on employment and unemployment from a limited sample of households since the early nineties (Sarvekshana, 2001-02, p. 1).

Microeconomic Activities to be Studied

As seen earlier, secondary data mining is undertaken at the levels of the All-India, Maharashtra State, the urban sector in Maharashtra, Mumbai City, and R/S Ward levels. We have used almost all the sources of information to develop a macro database, and focus on the following sub-sectors that are relevant to field work:

- Growing of vegetables and retail sale of fresh fruits and vegetables, or kitchen gardens;
- Retail sale of fish;
- Manufacture of plastic products;
- Domestic service.

The focus on the above is determined by the gendered economic reality prevailing in the selected region of research-viz. Charkop in the northern suburbs of Mumbai. Also, the choice of these activities is on account of their prominent share in employment, especially of women. A study of these shows the retention of traditional occupations like fishing and kitchen gardens, along with the adoption of new activities like plastic products assembling. Also, domestic service is mainly undertaken by migrants in order to augment family incomes, as it provides an easy option in the absence of resources, skills, and investments. People of this village were found to resort to other less important occupations like toddy tapping, casual factory employment, or illicit sale of hooch. These are not emphasized due to an involvement of smaller proportions of people in such activities.

CODE CLASSIFICATION AND CLARIFICATION

The introductory comments to code classification used by the NIC are discussed in this part. Sub-Sections 3.4.1 deal with NIC codes for 1987, followed by 1998, and 2004 subsequently. Later, a comparative analysis for all these years, along with the Concordance table is undertaken to draw clarifications and relevant observations.

At the outset, it becomes imperative to go through the exercise of code classification and clarification for the sectors chosen at the macro level due to changes in code numbers and components of categories over the years, along with re-groupings at different digit levels. We have considered all the three available codes of the National Industrial Classification for 1987, 1998, and 2004 at the one, two, and three digit levels of analysis.

Codes Applicable as per NIC-1987

NIC-87 clubs together economic activities that are similar in terms of process type, raw materials used, and finished goods produced. It incorporates a new titling system for various levels of economic classification in accordance with the recommendations of the United Nations Statistical Office. The codes are at different digit levels, like the one-digit constituting the Section, two-digit the Division, and three-digit the Group. There are no major changes at the one-digit level, the economy being divided into 10 Sections with special Section X for activities not adequately defined in Sections 0-9. The two-digit has 73 codes, while the three-digit uses 462 groups.

One-Digit Code Applicable as per NIC-1987:

0 : Agriculture, Hunting, Forestry, and Fishing;

2 & 3 : Manufacturing;

6 : Wholesale and Retail Trade, Restaurants and Hotels;

9 : Community, Social, and Personal Services.

Two-Digit Codes Applicable as per NIC-1987:

00 : Agricultural Production;

06 : Fishing (including collection of sea products);

31 : Manufacture of rubber, plastic, petroleum, and coal products; processing of nuclear fuels;

65 : Retail trade in food and food articles, beverages, tobacco, and intoxicants;

99 : Services not elsewhere classified.

Three-Digit Codes Applicable as per NIC-1987:

006 : Growing of roots and tubers, vegetables, singharas, chillies, and spices (Other than pepper and cardamom);

313 : Manufacture of plastic products not elsewhere classified;

652 : Retail trade in meat, fish, and poultry;

960 : Domestic services.

There are no four or five-digit codes available in accordance with NIC-87 (Census of India, 1991, pp. iii-v, 1-45).

Codes Applicable as per NIC-1998

NIC-1998 has broadened the definitional scope of activities to include certain specific categories, which were either not defined earlier or were a part of some broad category. From the viewpoint of our study, the following activity codes are important:

One-Digit Codes Applicable as per NIC-1998:

A : Agriculture, Hunting, and Forestry;

B : Fishing;

D : Manufacturing;

G : Wholesale and Retail Trade, Repair of Motor Vehicles, Motorcycles, and Personal and Household goods;

P : Private Households with Employed persons.

Two-Digit Codes Applicable as per NIC-1998:

01 : Agriculture, Hunting, and Related Service Activities;

05 : Fishing, Operation of Fish Hatcheriès, and Fish Farms; Service Activities incidental to Fishing;

25 : Manufacture of Rubber and Plastic Products;

95 : Private Households with employed persons.

Three, Four and Five-Digit Codes Applicable as per NIC-1998:

The tabular representation of NIC data at the three, four, and five digit levels for our chosen activities is seen below:

Table 3.1
Three, Four, and Five Digit NIC-1998 Codes for Selected Economic Activities: 1998

Type of Activity	*3 Digit*	*4 Digit*	*5 Digit*
Growing of Vegetables	011	0112	01121
Manufacture of other Plastic Products	252	2520	25209
Retail Sale of Fruits & Vegetables	522	5220	52202
Retail sale of Meat, Fish, & Poultry	522	5220	52203
Private Households with Housemaid/Servant	950	9500	95001

Source: NIC 1998.

We need to also look at the Concordance table for converting NIC-87 based data in terms of NIC-98, as the former is at the three-digit level, while the latter at the four and five-digit levels. Also some of the four-digit groups of NIC-87 have been sub-divided and distributed to two or more five-digit sub-classes of NIC-98, the classic case being presented by the bifurcation of vegetables (code 006 in NIC-87) into growing of vegetables and retail sale of the same, along with fruits as codes 0112 and 52202 respectively in NIC-98. Few activities at the three-digit level are covered under the same code, viz. 522 and 5220 in accordance with the three and four-digit classification, but have got separated at the five-digit level into different codes of 52202 and 52203 for retail sale of fresh fruits and vegetables; and retail sale of meat, fish, and poultry, respectively.

A one-to-one correspondence cannot be met in the 2 classifications of NIC-87 and NIC-98, as NIC-87 is a four-digit classification, whereas NIC-98 is a five-digit one; and because some of the four-digit groups of the former classification have been split into two or more five-digit sub-classes of the latter, as seen earlier. Thus, data collection, analysis, and collation at the secondary level become an extremely difficult and time-consuming task.

Codes Applicable as per NIC-2004

The NIC-2004 classification that was introduced in 2005 bifurcated Category 0112 of NIC-1998 into two separate codes of 0112: Growing of Vegetables, Horticultural Specialties, and Nursery Products; and 0113: Growing of Olives. Also, codes for the primary sector have been partially allotted to other NIC sections like agriculture, fishing, construction, etc.; thus making comparisons between the two NIC codes of 1998 and 2004 almost impossible (nic-2004-struc-detail; nic-2004-concor-tab).

OVERALL ANALYSIS OF VARIOUS DATA SOURCES

We have analyzed the following 4 data sources available in India in the subsequent sections to get a macro picture. Sub-section 3.5.1 covers the Annual Survey of Industries (ASI) data, while the Population Census of 1991 and 2001 are covered subsequently. The Economic Census of Maharashtra and the National Sample Survey (NSS) are dealt with in Sub-sections 3.5.2 and 3.5.3, respectively.

Annual Survey of Industries (ASI) Data

The ASI data relates to organized sector on the basis of yearly returns received from the factories registered under the Factories Act, 1948 in the prescribed format of Form number 27. At the outset, mention needs to be made about this information source specifically relating to the formal sector, and being available at the national and state level only. ASI's Volume VII (out of its 14 volumes) is important from our viewpoint, as it gives a broad and general view of the sub-sectors, and pertains to code 31 that deals with the 'manufacture of rubber, plastic, petroleum, and coal products'; which is relevant due to the field activity of assembling of plastic products. Thus, only one area is covered at the two-digit level, viz. manufacture of plastic products not elsewhere classified (n.e.c.). This too is clubbed with various other products, as seen above, thereby not giving an accurate picture.

Our focus relates primarily to employment status, and we have examined the total number of workers, and their sub-division into male and female, along with the total number of factories. According to the ASI (1993-94, p.xv), "Workers are defined to include all persons employed directly or through any agency whether for wages or not and engaged in any manufacturing process or in cleaning any part of the machinery or premises used for manufacturing process or in any other kind of work incidental to or connected with the manufacturing process or the subject of manufacturing process". Thereby, only formal sector workers are covered, leaving out majority of labourers in the informal segment. Thus, this definition is inadequate, and deficient. We were constrained to use data for a very ambiguous classification code of ASI, viz. 3029, as our category of work was not clearly defined in the ASI classification. Code 3029 has been accorded to the category 'plastic products not elsewhere classified' in accordance with NIC-87 classification, which was subsequently given a five-digit code of 24139 in NIC-1998.

Data for 1990-1998 for code 3029 dealing with the manufacture of other plastics in primary forms (n.e.c.) can be seen as follows:

Table 3.2
Employment Status of 'Plastic Products not Elsewhere Classified' at Maharashtra level: 1990-1998

Years	*No. of Factories*	*Male*	*Female*	*Total Workers*
1990	48	2352	56	2408
1991	50	2899	98	2997
1992	48	2295	85	2380
1993	77	2656	79	2735
1994	79	2608	116	2724
1995	86	3385	125	3510
1996	94	4195	139	4195
1997	90	3853	144	3853
1998	94	3845	150	3845

Source: Special data generated by ASI, 2000.

The above table depicts a doubling of workforce as seen from total and male employment in case of industry code 3029. Female employment was low at barely 2 per cent in the beginning of 1990's, which rose to 3 per cent towards the end of the decade. These workers also depicted a three-fold rise from merely 56 to 127 workers for the same period.

The year 2000 shows a totally different picture, as the total number of working factories increased from barely 88 in 1999 to 368 in 2000. There has been a 5 per cent rise in women's employment, despite a fall in overall figures, especially of males who ironically continue to constitute the majority.

Mixed trends characterize the nineties, showing a modest growth at the start, accompanied by a slight fall in 1992, followed by a rise of about 25 per cent in the subsequent year. A 5 per cent spurt observed in mid-nineties was offset by a similar drop towards the end of the decade. This has been the result of general economic slowdown, along with denationalization and closures in the private sector. The sluggish investment and restructuring has manifested itself in erratic patterns in employment accentuated by the 'New Economic Policy' and reforms undertaken in the dual areas of enterprises and labour. The later part of nineties has experienced falling employment shares, more so in case of males, thus portraying the impact of Structural Adjustment Programmes and labour market reforms in India.

Population Census Data

Our analysis has considered the 1991 Censuses, along with Paper-3 of 2001 Census. In sub-sections 3.5.2.1 and 3.5.2.2, an analysis of the per centage shares for the Census years of 1991 and 2001 respectively, for Greater Mumbai in Urban Maharashtra, R/S Ward in Mumbai, and Kandivali and Charkop in R/S Ward have been carried out. Subsequently, we have tried to locate various shares with respect to the national level at five different levels of the State, Urban State, Greater Mumbai/Mumbai, R/S Ward, and Kandivali and Charkop for the chosen areas of activity; wherever such comparisons exist. The following section looks at the comparative analysis between the two decades of 1991 and 2001.

Per centage Shares for 1991 Census

Here, we look at various per centage shares at different levels of geographic analysis of Greater Mumbai, R/S Ward, Kandivali, and Charkop as under:

(1) Per centage Share of Greater Mumbai in Urban Maharashtra

The metropolis represents over one-thirds of total main workers, with no male dominance. Cultivators form barely 1 per cent depicting gender equality. One-thirds of the secondary sector labourers are found in the metropolis with a male majority.

The 1991 data has clubbed a number of activities from the primary, secondary and tertiary sectors in activity (4) of 'other than household activity' showing 40 per cent representation at the Mumbai level with no major share of females.

(2) Per centage Share of R/S Ward in Greater Mumbai

The ward accounts for 4 per cent of main workers, with a similar proportion being found in case of males, while females represent half of this ratio. Cultivators constitute approximately same figures of 4 per cent of the metropolis' share with almost equal shares for men and women. Only a per cent of workers, with a male majority are involved in 'livestock, forestry, fishing, hunting and plantations, orchards and allied activities' at the ward level.

The ward represents 6 per cent of household industry, with a male majority, as females account for half of their male counterparts' ratio. In terms of 'other services', there is a smaller share of just a per cent in case of total, male, and female workers.

We cannot look at the respective shares of the ward in terms of the metropolis in areas of 'other than household industry', and trade and commerce, as these have been clubbed together at the Greater Mumbai level in the 1991 Census.

(3) Per centage Share of Kandivali and Charkop in R/S Ward

Kandivali and Charkop represent half of R/S ward's main workers, with a female share of 60 per cent. Cultivators account for a similar proportion of labourers that is contrasted by a male dominance of 70 per cent, with female figures at only 24 per cent. Two-thirds of the ward level workers were seen to be occupied in the category of 'livestock, forestry, fishing, hunting and plantations, orchards and allied activities' depicting a female bias of 80 per cent at the Kandivli and Charkop level. A similar domination is mirrored in the categories of household and non-household industry. Kandivli and Charkop constitute two-thirds of workers in the section on trade and commerce. Over half of the labour in the category 'other services' reiterates the predominance of women. Therefore, the area represents a mixed occupational structure that combines relative shares at the ward level.

Per centage Shares for 2001 Census

The per centage shares at different geographic levels in accordance with 2001 data are analyzed as under:

(1) Per centage Share of Greater Mumbai in Urban Maharashtra

Mumbai represents 25 per cent of Urban Maharashtra's main workers, 40 per cent constituted by men, and 20 per cent by women; thereby showing a male bias. The metropolis accounts for barely 1/10th of cultivators of the urban state level, depicting a natural decline of cultivation in urban areas due to urbanization and progress. The picture gets magnified at the worker level, as seen in the negligible proportions of 0.05 per cent of agricultural labourers in case of total, males, and females in Mumbai.

The household industry has shown male-dominance, accounting for 1/10th of employment of men in Urban Maharashtra, which is slightly higher than the total person rate and double of their counterparts. The category of 'other workers' employs 10 per cent of the city's labour force, when considered as a per centage of the urban state.

(2) Per centage Share of R/S Ward in Greater Mumbai & 3) Per centage Share of Kandivali and Charkop in R/S Ward

Both these per centages are not available in a disaggregated form, and thus no comparisons can be drawn, as the 1991 Census has clubbed together activities like livestock, forestry, fishing, other than household industry, trade, commerce, and other services. On the other hand, the 2001 Census has introduced 2 new categories of 'household workers', and 'other workers', which cannot be compared with the earlier decade due to lack of reference category.

Regional Shares of Main Workers by Industry in terms of National Level Data

In this section, we try to locate various regional shares at the Maharashtra, Urban Maharashtra, Greater Mumbai/ Bombay, R/ S Ward, and Kandivali and Charkop levels in terms of All-India

Table 3.3
Classification of Main Workers by Industry at the All-India level: 1991

(in millions)

Category	*Code*	*Male*	*Female*	*Total*
Total Main Workers		216.0 (77.4)	62.9 (22.6)	278.9 (100.0)
Cultivators	I	85.6 (80.0)	21.5 (20.0)	107.1 (100.0)
Livestock, Forestry, Fishing, Plantations, Orchards, and allied activities	III	4.3 (81.0)	1.0 (19.0)	5.3 (100.0)
Manufacturing, Processing, Servicing, and Repairs: (a) Household Industry	V (a)	4.5 (67.1)	2.2 (32.9)	6.7 (100.0)
(b) Other than Household Industry	V (b)	19.2 (88.4)	2.5 (11.6)	21.7 (100.0)
Trade & Commerce	VII	19.4 (93.2)	1.4 (6.8)	20.8 (100.0)
Other Services	IX	23.3 (81.8)	5.2 (18.2)	28.5 (100.0)

Source: Statistical Outline of India, 1991.

Census data for 1991 and 2001 in terms of total main workers and our chosen 5 categories of economic activities.

Relative Shares in Accordance with the 1991 Census

Turning to the classification of main workers by industrial classification in accordance with the Population Census of 1991 at the following 5 different levels, we observe the following:

The 1991 census shows a better picture in terms of female participation that has doubled in most categories, except, 'other than household industry' and 'trade and commerce', thereby retaining the male majority in technologically advanced and lucrative areas.

Table 3.4

Classification of Main Workers by Industry in Maharashtra: 1991

(in millions)

Category	*Code*	*Male*	*Female*	*Total (15-59 yrs)*
Total Main Workers		19054913 (67.4)	9195690 (32.6)	28250603 (100.0)
Cultivators	I	5338034 (59.7)	3601973 (40.3)	8940007 (100.0)
Manufacturing, Processing, Servicing, and Repairs: (a) Household Industry	V (a)	297103 (66.7)	148735 (33.3)	445838 (100.0)
Livestock, Forestry, Fishing, Hunting & Plantations, Orchards, and allied activities	III			
Mining & Quarrying	IV			
Manufacturing, Processing, Servicing and Repairs in other than Household Industry	V (b)			
Constructions	VI			
Trade & Commerce	VII			
Transport, Storage & Comunications	VIII			
Other Services	IX	9965810 (87.0)	1492328 (13.0)	11458138 (100.0)

Source: Census of India, 1991.

The State level data denotes an improvement over the national level, as women represent 1/3rds of the total workers, and also in the category of 'Cultivators and Household Workers'. Unfortunately, their participation continues to remain low in other sectors, which are all clubbed together in the 1991 census.

Table 3.5
Classification of Main Workers by Industry in Urban Maharashtra: 1991

(in millions)

Category	*Code*	*Male*	*Female*	*Total (15-59 yrs)*
Total Main Workers		7749895 (84.8)	1394597 (15.2)	9144492 (100.0)
Cultivators	I	182090 (76.0)	57892 (25.0)	239982 (100.0)
Manufacturing, Processing, Servicing, and Repairs: (a) Household Industry	V (a)	111303 (87.0)	55983 (13.0)	167286 (100.0)
Livestock, Forestry, Fishing, Hunting & Plantations, Orchards, and allied activities	III			
Mining & Quarrying	IV			
Manufacturing, Processing, Servicing and Repairs in other than Household Industry	V (b)			
Constructions	VI			
Trade & Commerce	VII			
Transport, Storage & Comunications	VIII			
Other Services	IX	7217161 (87.0)	1086072 (13.0)	8303233 (100.0)

Source: Census of India, 1991.

The Urban Maharashtra scene denotes a fall in total female main workers as a per centage of total main workers from over 20 per cent to 15 per cent in the decade of 1981-1991. The male occupational prominence continues and has increased in 1991in almost all the activities.

Table 3.6
Classification of Main Workers by Industry in Greater Bombay/ Mumbai: 1991

(in millions)

Category	*Code*	*Male*	*Female*	*Total (15-59 yrs.)*
Total Main Workers		2851702 (86.3)	450090 (13.7)	3301792 (100.0)
Cultivators	I	2602 (82.6)	550 (17.4)	3152 (100.0)
Manufacturing, Processing, Servicing and Repairs: (a) Household Industry	V (a)	36264 (76.0)	11353 (24.0)	4761 (100.0)
Livestock, Forestry, Fishing, Hunting & Plantations, Orchards, and allied activities	III			
Mining & Quarrying	IV			
Manufacturing, Processing, Servicing and Repairs in other than Household Industry	V (b)			
Constructions	VI			
Trade & Commerce	VII			
Transport, Storage & Comunications	VIII			
Other Services	IX	2811191 (87.0)	437501 (13.0)	3248692 (100.0)

Source: Census of India, 1991.

The Greater Bombay data shows an all-round improvement in female per centages in comparison to the earlier Census.

Table 3.7
Classification of Main Workers by Industry in R/S Ward: 1991

(in millions)

Category	*Code*	*Male*	*Female*	*Total*
Total Main Workers		118964 (90.7)	12325 (9.3)	131289 (100.0)
Cultivators	I	110 (81.4)	25 (18.6)	135 (100.0)
Livestock, Forestry, Fishing, Hunting & Plantations, Orchards, and allied activities	III	478 (92.2)	40 (7.8)	518 (100.0)
Manufacturing, Processing, Servicing and Repairs: (a) Household Industry	V (a)	2352 (84.8)	424 (15.2)	2776 (100.0)
Manufacturing, Processing, Servicing and Repairs: (b) Other than Household Industry	V (b)	48263 (94.8)	2664 (5.2)	50927 (100.0)
Trade & Commerce	VII	31136 (93.3)	2218 (6.7)	33354 (100.0)
Other Services	IX	15501 (73.0)	5701 (27.0)	21202 (100.0)

Source: District Primary Census Abstract, 1991.

Table 3.8
Classification of Main Workers by Industry in Kandivali and Charkop: 1991

(in millions)

Category	*Code*	*Male*	*Female*	*Total*
Total Main Workers		59890	7319	67209
		(89.1)	(10.9)	(100.0)
(As % of R/S)		(50.3)	(59.4)	(51.2)
Cultivators	I	76	6	82
		(92.7)	(7.3)	(100.0)
(As % of R/S)		(69.0)	(24.0)	(60.7)
Livestock, Forestry, Fishing, Hunting & Plantations, Orchards, and allied activities	III	320	32	352
		(91.0)	(9.0)	(100.0)
(As % of R/S)		(67.0)	(80.0)	(68.0)
Manufacturing, Processing, Servicing and Repairs: (a) Household Industry	V (a)	889	175	1064
		(83.6)	(16.4)	(100.0)
(As % of R/S)		(37.8)	(41.2)	(38.3)
Manufacturing, Processing, Servicing and Repairs: (b) Other than Household Industry	V (b)	22639	1530	24169
		(93.7)	(6.3)	(100.0)
(As % of R/S)		(47.0)	(57.4)	(47.4)
Trade & Commerce	VII	19629	1359	20988
		(93.6)	(6.4)	(100.0)
(As % of R/S)		(63.0)	(61.2)	(63.0)
Other Services	IX	7468	3610	11078
		(67.4)	(32.6)	(100.0)
(As % of R/S)		(48.1)	(63.3)	(52.2)

Source: District Primary Census Abstract, 1991.

The 1991 Census does not show any different results at this level, except a negligible fall in terms of per centages of the ward level. In terms of Total Main Workers, surprisingly, Maharashtra data shows that females account for a higher per centage at approximately 15 per cent, as against 10 per cent of male and total workers, thereby showing an improvement in women's participation over the last decade. However, a reverse trend was documented at the Urban State level, accounting for a male majority (4 per cent) seen to half in case of both, female and total workers. Greater Bombay figures confirm the same results, the only difference being a reduction of these per centages to one-thirds. The category of Cultivators at the All-India and Urban Maharashtra shows a similar result of 1/5th participation of women, that is found to almost double in case of the overall State level. A marginal drop in these figures are observed at Mumbai and Ward locations, that is still higher than the cases of Kandivali and Charkop, thereby denoting the falling importance of cultivation. The Maharashtra segment of 'Livestock, Forestry, Fishing, Hunting and Plantations, Orchards and Allied Activities' and 'Other Than Household Industry', 'Trade and Commerce', and 'Other Services' accounts for 1/10th of total workers, and also a male majority. The same trend continues at the Urban Maharashtra and Mumbai level, with slightly higher proportion of males. Household industry in the State accounts for less than 1/10th of All-India figures with male majority increasing in the metropolis. The Ward, as well as, Kandivli and Charkop figures portray similar results as Mumbai, and have not been considered on account of their negligible figures.

Relative Shares in accordance with 2001 Census

Let us analyze the distribution of work force at different levels, as the earlier two Censuses, in accordance with our chosen occupations.

Table 3.9

Classification of Main Workers by Industry at the All-India level: 2001

(in millions)

Category	*Code*	*Male*	*Female*	*Total*
Total Main Workers		240,520,672 (77.0)	72,652,722 (23.0)	313,173,394 (100.0)
Cultivators		86,328,447 (68.0)	41,299,840 (32.0)	127,628,287 (100.0)
Household Industry Workers		8,312,191 (51.0)	8,083,679 (49.0)	16,395,870 (100.0)
Other Workers		123,468,817 (82.0)	27,571,491 (18.0)	151,040,308 (100.0)

Source: Census of India, 2001.

The above table brings out the male majority in terms of main workers along with cultivators and other workers having a two-thirds representation. The only exception is seen in case of household industry labourers depicting gender equality due to the intrinsic nature of this activity that permits women to multi-task.

Table 3.10
Classification of Main Workers by Industry in Maharastra

(in millions)

Category	*Code*	*Male*	*Female*	*Total*
Total Main Workers		24,485,209	11,185,627	35,670,836
		(69.0)	(31.0)	(100.0)
Cultivators		6,765,759	5,244,144	12,009,903
		(76.0)	(24.0)	(100.0)
Household Industry Workers		540,611	505,538	1,046,149
		(52.0)	(48.0)	(100.0)
Other Workers		14,689,601	3,016,732	17,706,333
		(83.0)	(17.0)	(100.0)

Source: Census of India, 2001.

The male-bias is seen at the State level also, with similar results in case of household industry.

Table 3.11
Classification of Main Workers by Industry in Urban Maharastra: 2001

(in millions)

Category	*Code*	*Male*	*Female*	*Total*
Total Main Workers		10,895,473	2,023,275	12,918,748
		(84.0)	(16.0)	(100.0)
Cultivators		218,191	75,414	293,605
		(74.0)	(26.0)	(100.0)
Household Industry Workers		236,181	223,178	459,359
		(51.0)	(49.0)	(100.0)
Other Workers		10,800,135	1,893,432	12,693,567
		(85.0)	(15.0)	(100.0)

Source: Census of India, 2001.

The Urban State level also has identical results as the general State level.

Table 3.12
Classification of Main Workers by Industry in Mumbai District: 2001
(in millions)

Category	*Code*	*Male*	*Female*	*Total*
Total Main Workers		1,078,949 (86.0)	182,690 (14.0)	1,261,639 (100.0)
Cultivators		251 (78.0)	72 (22.0)	323 (100.0)
Household Industry Workers		26,180 (68.0)	12,534 (32.0)	38,714 (100.0)
Other Workers		1,096,425 (85.0)	189,806 (15.0)	1,286,231 (100.0)

Source: Census of India, 2001.

The Mumbai level data also shows us similar results as seen at other levels, thus reinforcing the male bias even in case of household industry, which was missing earlier. This brings out the gravity of the labour market situation, which makes males take to all kinds of jobs to eke a livelihood in this mega-city.

Decadal Analysis of 1991-2001

In this section, we look at the trends between 1991 and 2001. The national level figures depict an almost unchanged gendered pattern of main workers with a male domination at 75 per cent. A notable rise of over 10 per cent is visible in case of female cultivators due to a decline in male ratios. Unfortunately, a parallel cannot be drawn in case of other categories of workers, as the 2001 Census has clubbed them together. At the Mumbai level, a rough comparison for the ten year period shows that the total main workers have reduced, as only 40 per cent male, female, and total workers (as a per centage of 1991) were found in 2001.

A similar decline is observed in case of cultivators, as 2001 data shows roughly 1/10th representation of 1991 figures. The female figures are marginally higher than their male counterparts, thereby mirroring the direct impact of the 'New Economic Policy' on especially male employment, which is adverse, thereby forcing their counterparts to join the labour market.

No comparisons can be drawn in terms of other occupational codes, as the 1991 Census has clubbed together various activities like livestock, forestry, fishing, other than household industry, trade and commerce and other services. On the other hand, the

2001 Census has two new categories of household workers and other workers, which cannot be compared with the earlier decade due to lack of reference category.

Economic Census of Maharashtra Data

The Economic Censuses of the State of Maharashtra for 1990 and 1998 according to major industry groups are studied for an analysis of persons usually working:

Table 3.13
Persons Usually Working in Maharashtra: 1990-1998

(in thousands)

Major Industry Groups	*Persons Usually Working*			
	1990		*1998*	
	Urban	*Total*	*Urban*	*Total*
Agriculture	54 (100.0)	534 (100.0)	65 (7.0)	968 (100.0)
As % of Total	(0.9)	(6.0)	(0.9)	(9.0)
Manufacturing & Repair Services	1870 (71.0)	2652 (100.0)	1547 (64.0)	2408 (100.0)
As % of Total	(31.0)	(30.0)	(23.0)	(23.0)
Community, Social & Personal Services	1693 (67.0)	2509 (100.0)	2062 (71.0)	2914 (100.0)
As % of Total	(28.0)	(28.0)	(31.0)	(28.0)
Total	6113 (68.0)	8960 (100.0)	6756 (65.0)	10445 (100.0)

Source: Economic Survey of Maharashtra, 1998-99, and 2000-2001.

The above table shows us that persons usually working in the urban areas as a per centage of total persons employed has decreased in agriculture over the two censuses, and has marginally risen when taken as a per centage of total employment in case of these areas. It points to the continued importance of the primary sector in the rural areas.

The share of manufacturing and repairs in total employment in the State portays a decline in shares from a 1/3rd to 1/5th, along with a 5 per cent fall in the urban areas, despite their majority in terms of total employment. Retail trade continues to be important constituting 2/3rd of urban majority, inspite of a marginal per centage fall in the Fourth Economic Census of 1998. Community, Social, and Personal Services account for 1/3rd of total employment, with a 10 per cent rise in the urban areas in absolute and relative terms. The above trends clearly point out the importance of the tertiary and secondary sectors in Urban Maharashtra (Economic Survey of Maharashtra, 1998-99, pp. T-56; and 2000-2001, pp. T-58).

National Sample Survey (NSS) Data

The NSS conducts various Rounds on Employment-Unemployment at the National and State level. The 43rd, 50th, and 55th Rounds have analyzed different areas of economic activity. There is no two-digit level information for our chosen sectors, as either the results are not generated or are too small and negligible to be tabulated. Thus, only the 50th and 55th Rounds are considered. The old and new NIC codes for 1987 and 1998 have been observed for the chosen codes. The five-sector analysis is carried out in Section 3.5.4.1, subsequently followed by concluding remarks on NSS data.

Analysis of Chosen Sectors at the Maharashtra, Urban Maharashtra, and Mumbai levels

The following five sectors have been considered for analysis:

- Retail Sale of Meat, Fish and Poultry (NIC-1987 Code: 06, 652, 0500; and NIC-1998 Code: 52203);
- Manufacture of Rubber, Plastic, Petroleum, and Coal Products; Processing of Nuclear Fuels (NIC-1987 Code: 31, 313, 2520, and NIC-1998 Code: 25209);
- Domestic Service (NIC-1987 Code: 96, 960, 9500, and NIC-1998 Code: 95001);
- Growing of Vegetables (NIC-1987 Code: 01, 006, 0112, and NIC-1998 Code: 01121);
- Retail Trade of Fresh Fruits and Vegetables (NIC-1998 Code: 52202).

The figures in brackets deal with the activity codes at the two, three, four, and five digit levels in accordance with the NIC-87 and NIC-98 classification codes. We have considered data for the 43rd, 50th, 55th Rounds in terms of total and female employment. The two-digit code does not give any specific details for the chosen sectors, as the results could not be generated or were too small or negligible to be tabulated. Thus, we shall take only the 50th and 55th Rounds into account.

Let us look at each of our chosen sectors at the following three levels of Maharashtra State, Urban Maharashtra State, and Mumbai level.

(1) Retail Sale of Meat, Fish, and Poultry

Maharashtra Level

The 43rd Round at the three-digit level shows less than half a per cent of workers employed in this sub-sector in terms of both, principal status (pp), and principal and subsidiary status (pp + ss), with slightly higher figures of 0.4 per cent in case of females.

The 50th Round at the three-digit level portrays a reduction in employment in all categories with the most prominent one observed for females. Personal interviews with the NSS officials show that these figures are negligible and thus, we take them to be nil in a small sized sample.

Constancy in total employment with respect to the earlier figures was observed in the 55th Round at the four-digit level. A positive trend is documented by an increase in female employment to 2 per thousand vis-à-vis the falling figures in the earlier information.

The data trends should not be interpreted at its face value, as here one needs to take caution and avoid generalizations. The 50th Round gave negligible results due to the small sample size taken. Again, the actual retailing of fish may turn out to be still lower as the NSS has clubbed fish, along with meat and poultry.

Urban Maharashtra Level

The 43rd Round showed higher employment figures at 5 and 7 per thousand respectively, in case of total and female principal status, as well as principal and subsidiary status with respect to the State level. This could probably be explained by the rising importance of these items in the urban diet, thereby promoting demand and employment.

A further decline at the 50th Round was again due to a smaller sample size.

The 55th Round demonstrates higher growth in total employment, and constancy in female employment.

Mumbai Level

Tne 43rd Round shows overall higher figures, more so in case of female employment, which has risen more than 2-times with respect to the urban level and 4-times in comparison with the State. This is documented in the NSS data for all categories due to the increasing importance of this activity in Mumbai in recent years, along with its traditional prominance in the field area.

A similar downtrend is depicted at the 50th Round on account of the small size of sample, despite which female employment is observed to be almost double of total, thus, reinforcing their prominence.

The subsequent data shows an increase in total employment, with no major improvement in case of women workers.

(2) Manufacture of Rubber, Plastic, Petroleum, and Coal Products; Processing of Nuclear Fuels:

Maharashtra State Level

The 43rd Round at the three-digit level indicates only a single person to be engaged in this entire division, with surprisingly no females in almost all categories.

Subsequently, a higher proportion of total workers were observed at the three-digit level that depicts almost 3 per thousand in both, principal status, as well as principal and subsidiary status. Female figures account for only 1 per thousand in both these statuses, especially, in case of plastic workers.

The 55th Round at the four-digit level depicts a further improvement, as the figures were seen to rise to four per thousand with an equal gender distribution.

Urban Maharashtra Level

The 43rd Round at the three-digit demonstrates an improvement over the state level, as three-four times more employment generation is seen amongst females and total workers engaged in this industry.

Three-digit level analysis at the 50th Round shows an almost doubling of employment with respect to the earlier data on urban figures for total and female plastic workers.

The similar uptrend is observed to continue at the subsequent Round as the figures rose to 8 per thousand in case of total and remained at six per thousand for females. This clearly highlights the importance of the plastic industry in employment generation in urban areas.

Mumbai Level

At the 43rd Round at the three-digit level, an increase that is nearly double of the urban level in case of both total and female plastic workers is observed. The rise is higher in case of females, which is even more than that for total plastic workers.

A doubling of total employment of plastic workers with a three-fold rise in case of females over the earlier figures characterizes the 50th Round at the three-digit level. In fact, women are at an advantage as their gains are nearly double that of total job expansion. These trends are a result of the prominence of the sector in Mumbai's economy in terms of livelihoods due to persistently rising demand for plastic products and its propagation in order to save trees.

The 55th Round at the four-digit level depicts a negligible fall vis-à-vis the earlier figures in case of totals, but the decline is highly pronounced in case of females due to contraction in employment to less than half in comparison with the previous data. This falling employment in plastic industry is due to a variety of reasons like Structural Adjustment Programme (SAP) and globalization leading to a cut in jobs, decreasing male employment in other formal sector activities, thereby pushing them into plastics, and females out of it. The popularity of this industry cuts across the gender divide largely on account of its home-base nature.

(3) Domestic Service

Maharashtra State Level

The three-digit 43rd Round shows that 6 per thousand people are involved in domestic service, in both statuses. This figure is observed to more than double when data of female domestic workers in both principal status, and also principal and subsidiary status is considered.

The subsequent Round at the three-digit level depicts similar results for total domestic workers. In fact, the number of females rose in the principal status, while the combined principal and subsidiary status figure remained unchanged.

The 55th Round at the five-digit level shows nil figures for total, as well as, female domestic workers. This does not mean that people engaged in domestic service have decreased, as the NSS sub-divides different domestic services into various subsections like 95001: Household/Maid-Servant; 95002: Cook; 952003: Gardener; 95004: Gate- Keeper/Chowkidar/Watchman; 95005: Governess/Baby-Sitter; 95009: Others.

Thus, the number of people in domestic service has fallen in accordance with NIC-1998, as against the earlier classification, which clubbed all domestic services into one Section 960.

Urban Maharashtra Level

The 43rd Round depicts that 23 per thousand people are involved in domestic service in both, principal status, and principal and subsidiary status. This figure is five times higher in both the categories for female domestics due to the large amounts of especially migrant women, who are generally forced into this activity due to either lack of alternate employment opportunities or low skill and educational status.

Similar results are also found in case of the 50th Round. Almost nil or negligible figures are observed for all workers due to the bifurcation explained earlier, in case of the subsequent Round.

Mumbai Level

The 43rd Round shows even higher figures of 31 for total domestic servants in both the groups of principal status, and principal and subsidiary status. They stood at 178 and 172 respectively, for female domestic workers, and total domestic workers, respectively. Women workers were found to be six times higher than the total.

Similar results, with large figures observed in case of female workers are documented by the 50th Round. The subsequent round shows negligible or zero workers. Thus, the number of female domestics has risen over the years, as their per centage ranges in-between 2-3 in recent years in comparison with barely one per cent in the earlier decade of 1990's. This is a result of numerous factors like poor agricultural performance due to uncertain rainfall and inadequate irrigation, worsened by lack of alternative non-farm jobs, sub-division and fragmentation of land, thereby making cultivation unviable and increasing migration of women from rural areas.

(4) Growing of Vegetables

Maharashtra State level

The three-digit 43rd Round shows four per thousand total workers in both the categories, with similar amounts for females in the principal status, and a slightly lower figure in the principal, as well as principal and subsidiary status category together. The amounts are negligible at the 50th Round, with just about 0.1 per cent at the subsequent round.

Urban Maharashtra State Level

Data for the 43rd Round demonstrates that only 0.1 per cent at the total worker level in both the statuses is found, with a doubling of these figures in case of women. The 50th Round shows negligible figures at all levels and for all workers. Subsequently, these figures are observed to remain at low levels of barely 1 per thousand in case of total and female worker categories.

Mumbai Level

Information at all the rounds in case of all the workers depict negligible or nil figures, thus pointing to the absolute low priority accorded to this primary activity in urban areas.

(5) Retail Trade of Fresh Fruits and Vegetables

Maharashtra State Level

The 55th Round gives a five-digit code, viz.52202 to the Retail Sale of Fresh Fruits and Vegetables, which belonged to Division 52 or 522 or 5220 at the 2, 3, and 4-digit levels respectively. Unfortunately, data is not available for these digits except the latest 5-digit one.

A total of 2449 workers were found in this Section, out of which women account for a little over 1/5th. Thus, less than 1 per cent of the total working people sell vegetables with females comprising over half of these figures.

Urban Maharashtra State Level

Nearly 2 per cent retail vegetable and fruit sellers are found amongst total workers with a female majority.

Mumbai Level

Data shows an improvement in the figures of total workers and more so, in case of females. This point to the importance of retailing due to a rise in demand for fresh fruits and vegetables in daily diet.

Concluding Remarks on NSS Data

The NSS contributes to the assessment of the volume and structure of employment and unemployment through its various surveys since the 9th round of 1955 to the ongoing 61st one from July 2004-June 2005. Few flaws in NSS's data source can be enlisted as under:

- Data is collected at all-India level, thus making it too general and alien to the realities of lower levels of Mumbai or the ward;
- The survey or sample size of NSS is restricted to a few blocks, thereby questioning the generalization of block-level results;
- The concepts of NSS's 'usual', 'weekly', 'daily' status of work are peculiar to this data source only, thus, making it difficult to compare it with other secondary sources of the Census or Annual Survey of Industries;
- The invisibility and peculiar nature of women's work cannot be adequately captured by NSS questionnaires, thereby leaving an important source of female employment unreported or under-reported;
- Unfortunately, the probes used by the NSS are misleading, thus resulting in many women continuing to think that they are not workers;
- The NSS source has proved to be a major failure in accounting for female employment in the unorganized sector, despite the upsurge in both, informal sector employment, as well as women's work in this area;
- The comparability of NSS data with Census becomes obscure, especially in case of females, as the former has higher estimates in comparison with the latter. This occurs due to the agency difference in capturing women's participation in economic activities, and the concept of economic activity adopted for enumeration. The very

definition of work differs due to lack of consensus of the treatment of activities related to non-market output of the primary sector other than cultivation, as the NSS considers them as 'work', while the Census does not;

- The NSS schedule uses a separate block to collect particulars of marginal workers among women, who constitute one-fourth of female work force. The NSS contends that the chance of missing these workers is the least in its approach. However, its own 55th Survey shows a fall in this estimate;
- The NSS definition excludes some of the activities defined in the UN System of National Accounts. Further, adoption of a 'time criterion' by the NSS excludes some of the activities considered to be economic in nature because the time spent on them is nominal. Women usually pursue this work as a part of and along with their household chores, resulting in the subsidiary status of women who are 'usual status' workers (Sarvekshana, 2001, pp.1-5).

The detailed secondary data analysis of livelihoods at various geographic levels, especially, with respect to our chosen activities of fieldwork brings out divergent trends in the post-reform period. A more focused view of labour market trends can be gauged from the Work Force Participation Rates that is directly impacted by employment reforms, as discussed in the subsequent section.

WORK PARTICIPATION RATES

Here, we look at the meaning of Work Participation Rates (WPR's) and its estimates by gender in Section 3.6.1, followed by WPR's at different levels of All-India, Maharashtra, and Brihan Mumbai in the subsequent section.

Meaning of Work Participation Rates

The WPR is an important economic indicator that shows the economically active population of a nation lying in the age group of 15-59 years. It helps depict the dependency load, along with the gender component of labour force. Thus, it represents an important tool in the hands of policy-makers to enrich and strengthen human resources for attaining economic development.

However, the Indian experience is quite contrary to general development patterns and experiences of developed nations, as the very definition of 'economically active population' of 15-59 years is evaded due to the prevalence of child labour and people working beyond 60 on account of poverty on one hand, and lack of old age security or social welfare, on the other.

The Central Statistical Organization (1998, p. 22) states that, "The NSS via its various rounds from 1977 to 1993-94, show the working population of 63 per cent of males in rural areas and 60 per cent in urban areas, along with 27 per cent females in rural areas and only 14 per cent in urban areas in 1993-94, thus depicting low participation among females, constituting nearly 1/3rds of their male counterparts. The child-age group of 5-14 years shows 6 per cent males and females in rural areas and about 2-3 per cent in the urban areas as working. Similarly, the old-age group also depicts 60 per cent males and 17 per cent females in rural areas and 43 per cent males and 9 per cent females in urban areas to be employed".

Work Participation Rates at Different Geographic Levels

WPR's are seen at different geographic levels ranging from the National to State, and District as seen in the subsequent sections.

All-India Work Participation Rates

Table 3.14
Work Participation Rates by Gender for Rural and Urban Areas at All-India level: 1983 to 1999-2000

Year	*Rural*		*Urban*	
	Male	*Female*	*Male*	*Female*
1983	54.7	34.0	51.2	15.1
1987-88	53.9	32.3	50.6	15.2
1993-94	55.3	32.8	52.1	15.5
1994-95	56.0	31.7	51.9	13.6
1999-00	53.1	29.9	51.8	13.9

Source: Central Statistical Organization, 1998.

The above table shows us the following:

- Male WPR's are higher than their female counterparts in both rural and urban areas;
- Males in the countryside have a slightly higher WPR than their urban counterparts;

- Females in the rural areas have WPR's half the size of their male counterparts;
- Urban WPR's of females are one-fourth of their male counterparts;
- The time-span analysis from 1983-1995 points to the marginal rise in male WPR's in the rural and urban areas, along with a marginal fall in case of females. The decline is more for rural females, contrasted by a marginal rise in case of their urban counterparts.

A better representation of the WPR's can be observed from the age-group analysis and concentration on the economically active group of 15-59 years, as seen from the following table.

Table 3.15
Work Participation Rates by Age-Group for Rural and Urban Areas at All-India level: 1983 to 1999-2000

Year	*Rural*		*Urban*	
	Male	*Female*	*Male*	*Female*
1983	92.2	41.0	88.1	21.1
1987-88	91.3	42.2	87.1	21.4
1993-94	90.9	38.3	86.4	21.1
1994-95	90.7	38.0	85.2	18.3
1999-00	90.0	49.5	83.0	22.1

Source: Government of India, 1998.

We have taken an average of the three age groups of 15-29, 30-44, and 45-59 to arrive at the 15-59 figures. The following observations can be made:

- There has been a marginal decline in the WPR's in all categories and areas, more in case of females, particularly, urban ones. However, a reversal was observed at the end of nineties, especially in case of rural women;
- The gap between the WPR's of working women and men has increased from half to one-third in the rural areas, while it has widened in urban areas, from one-fourth to one-fifth over the twelve year time period;
- Rural female WPR's are double that of their urban counterparts;
- Rural male WPR's are marginally higher than their urban counterparts;

- The working age group of 15-59 years gives a better and more realistic picture, than the all-ages data, especially, in case of men. The economically active male population has over 60 per cent higher contribution in comparison to the total male category. Similarly, the economically active females are also 10 per cent higher than the total females of all ages in the case of WPR's.

Table 3.16
Work Participation Rates by Age-Group for Rural and Urban Areas in Maharashtra: 1981-1991

Year	*WPR by Gender*					
	Total Workers			*Main Workers*		
	Male	*Female*	*Persons*	*Male*	*Female*	*Persons*
1981	53.7	30.6	42.5	52.5	23.9	38.7
1991	52.1	33.1	42.9	51.2	26.4	39.3

Source: Dewan, 2000.

The above table shows us the following trends:

- A surprising development emerged over the decade of 1981-91, as total and female WPR's have risen marginally, while that of male workers has fallen in case of total, as well as main workers;
- Male WPR's are the highest and nearly double of their female counterparts;
- The WPR's of female main workers are 20 per cent lesser than the total female workers, while the difference is negligible in case of males.

Table 3.17
Work Participation Rates by Age-Group for Rural and Urban Areas in Brihan Mumbai: 1981-91

Year	*WPR by Gender*					
	Total Workers			*Main Workers*		
	Male	*Female*	*Persons*	*Male*	*Female*	*Persons*
1981	55.4	8.9	35.2	54.8	8.5	34.7
1991	55.0	11.0	35.2	54.3	10.5	34.6

Source: Dewan, 2000.

The following observations can be made at the Mumbai level:

- WPR's for males and persons have remained somewhat constant, while that of females has risen in the ten year period;
- WPR's of males are the highest and five times those of females;
- The gap between the WPR's of total and main workers in case of males, females and total persons is negligible.

After an analysis of labour participation, it becomes imperative to also review the effect of industrial reform on enterprises in the manufacturing sector, as it has immediate bearings on livelihoods. Thus, we evaluate employment data of Own-Account Manufacturing Enterprises and Non-Directory Manufacturing Establishments for our chosen field segment of plastics, which is clubbed with other industries like Rubber, Petro Products, Coal, and Nuclear Fuel at the secondary level.

OWN-ACCOUNT MANUFACTURING ENTERPRISES (OAME'S) AND NON-DIRECTORY MANUFACTURING ESTABLISHMENTS (NDME'S)

The informal sector in India is largely manifested in terms of OAME's and NDME's that makes their analysis vital for the purpose of this thesis. We have looked at the definitional concepts in Section 3.7.1, followed by total NDME Employment in 'Rubber, Plastic, Petro Products' at Greater Mumbai, and R/S Ward levels in the next section. Sub-section 3.7.3 covers total NDME's and Employees in 'Manufacture of Rubber, Plastic, Petroleum and Coal Products; Processing of Nuclear Fuel' at Maharashtra, and Urban Maharashtra State level. Total OAME's and Employees in 'Manufacture of Rubber, Plastic, Petroleum and Coal Products; Processing of Nuclear Fuel' at Maharashtra, Urban Maharashtra State, and Mumbai levels for the same activity, as analyzed for NDME's are dealt with in the last sub-section.

Definitional Concepts

At the outset, let us look at the connotations of various concepts of enterprise and establishment in order to analyze the growth of OAME's and NDME's in India's industrial development and their contribution to employment and entrepreneurship. Sarvekshana, (1995, p.2) gives us the following definitions:

An enterprise is defined as, "An undertaking engaged in the production and/or distribution of some goods and/or distribution of some goods and/or services meant mainly for the purpose of sale, whether fully or partly, is termed as an enterprise. An enterprise may be owned and operated by a single household or by an institutional body. There are two types of enterprises, household and non-household; the former being run by one or more members of the household irrespective of whether the enterprise is located in the same premises as the household or not; while the latter, are institutionalized, owned and run by the public sector".

An Own-Account Enterprise (OAE) is classified as, "An enterprise, which is run without any hired worker employed on a fairly regular basis. If such an enterprise is engaged in manufacturing and/or repairing activities, it is termed as 'Own-Account Manufacturing Enterprise' (OAME)".

The meaning of an establishment is, "An enterprise, which is employing at least one hired worker on a fairly regular basis".

The Non-Directory Manufacturing Establishment (NDME) is, "An establishment employing less than six workers (household and hired taken together). If such an establishment is engaged in manufacturing and/or repairing activities, it is termed as a 'Non-Directory Manufacturing Establishment' (NDME)".

Total NDME Employment in 'Rubber, Plastic, Petro Products' at Greater Mumbai, and R/S Ward levels

Let us look at the plastic industry, which forms a part of the industry code 30 represented by 'Rubber, Plastic, Petro Products' in terms of total employment in Maharashtra (already seen in the earlier section on ASI data), Greater Bombay and the R/S Ward level:

Table 3.18
Total NDME Employment in 'Rubber, Plastic, Petro Products' in Greater Bombay: 1980-81 to 1990-91

	1980-81	*1990-91*	*Annual Compounded Growth Rate 1981-91*
	26371 (4.3)	44553 (10.2)	5.38
Grand Total	603069	433640	-3.25

Source: ASI, Special Data, 2000-01.

The available data shows us that employment in industry code 30 has nearly doubled over the 1980-90 decade. Also, as a per cent of total employment, its contribution has risen from 4 to 10 per cent; i.e. two and a half times. Most important is the 5 per cent decadal growth rate, despite the overall negative growth rates. The figures for 2001 are yet to be released, thus making the comparative analysis of the decadal variation incomplete.

Table 3.19
Total NDME Employment in 'Rubber, Plastic, Petro Products' in R/S Ward: 1980-81 to 1990-91

Years	*Employment*		*Establishments*	
	R/S Ward	*Greater Bombay*	*R/S Ward*	*Greater Bombay*
1980-81	90643	2199524	13910	284205
	(4.1)	(100.0)	(4.9)	(100.0)
1990-91	123902	2425881	27385	423418
	(5.1)	(100.0)	(6.4)	(100.0)

Source: ASI, Special Data, 2000-01.

The above table shows us the following trends:

- Employment over the decade has risen at the Greater Bombay and R/S ward level, by about 15 per cent in the former and nearly 50 per cent in the latter;
- The R/Sward level employment as a per cent of total has increased marginally by a per centage point over the decadal variation of 1980-90;
- The number of establishments have risen in case of Greater Mumbai and the R/S Ward, nearly double in case of the former and by 75 per cent in case of the latter;
- As a per cent of the total, the Ward level establishments have increased marginally by about a per cent and a half over the ten-year period. Thus, the R/S ward has performed well in absolute and relative terms on the dual fronts of employment and establishments.

NSS's 51st Round Results on OAME's and NDME's for the Industry Code 313 of "Manufacture of Rubber, Plastic, Petroleum and Coal Products; Processing of Nuclear Fuels" is analyzed with the help of special data generated for our study by the Directorate of Economics and Statistics, Maharashtra; at the following four levels:

Total NDME's and Employees in 'Manufacture of Rubber, Plastic, Petroleum and Coal Products; Processing of Nuclear Fuel' at Maharashtra, and Urban Maharashtra State level

In this section, we look at data on number of enterprises and employees at the State, Urban State, and Mumbai level in the category of, 'Manufacture of Rubber, Plastic, Petroleum and Coal Products; Processing of Nuclear Fuel' as under:

Table 3.20
Total NDME's and Employees in 'Manufacture of Rubber, Plastic, Petroleum and Coal Products; Processing of Nuclear Fuel' in Maharashtra: 2000-01

Industry Division	*No. of Enterprises*		*Total Employees*		
	Sample	*Estbs.*	*Male*	*Female*	*Total*
313	92	1896	7087	347	7434
	(4.8)	(100.0)	(95.3)	(4.7)	(100.0)
As % of all industries	(3.0)	(1.2)	(1.4)	(1.5)	(1.4)
All	2968	155164	493131	22561	515692

Source: ASI, 2000

The above table shows us that 313-industry division barely represents 5 per cent of the estimated enterprises and forms just 3 per cent of all enterprises. On the employment front, there is a male-majority, greater than the one seen for OAME's; as barely 5 per cent are females. But, the situation is different on the per centage front as females in this segment form 1.5 per cent of total female employment, which is marginally higher than the male and total employees' figures in this section.

Table 3.21
Total NDME's and Employees in 'Manufacture of Rubber, Plastic, Petroleum and Coal Products; Processing of Nuclear Fuel' in Urban Maharashtra: 2000-01

Industry Division	*No. of Enterprises*		*Total Employees*		
	Sample	*Estbs.*	*Male*	*Female*	*Total*
313	88	1771	6640	333	6974
	(4.9)	(100.0)	(95.2)	(4.7)	(100.0)
As % of all industries	(3.8)	(1.4)	(1.6)	(2.8)	(1.6)
All	2284	120497	399766	11565	411332

Source: ASI, 2000

In case of NDME's of industry code 313, Urban Maharashtra shows a better representation in terms of per centage of total enterprises and employees. The sample accounts for 5 per cent of estimated enterprises and a little lesser (4 per cent) of all enterprises. A majority of the employees are males, with barely 5 per cent females. An interesting fact is a reversal of this trend, as females form nearly double of their male counterparts when considered as a per centage of all employees.

Table 3.22
Total NDME's and Employees in 'Manufacture of Rubber, Plastic, Petroleum and Coal Products; Processing of Nuclear Fuel' in Mumbai: 2000-01

Industry Division	*No. of Enterprises*		*Total Employees*		
	Sample	*Estbs.*	*Male*	*Female*	*Total*
313	0	0	0	0	0
All	6	263	785	135	920

Source: ASI, 2000

The Mumbai data for NDME's portrays a similar negligible trend as the OAME's seen earlier in case of both enterprises and employees. Also, the figures for 'all' are at 1/3rd of OAME's data; thereby showing the reduced importance of NDME's vis-à-vis OAME's (NSS, 2001, Schedule 2.2; Table 8).

Total OAME's and Employees in 'Manufacture of Rubber, Plastic, Petroleum and Coal Products; Processing of Nuclear Fuel' at Maharashtra, Urban Maharashtra State, and Mumbai levels

Information on number of enterprises and employees in the industry of 'Manufacture of Rubber, Plastic, Petroleum and Coal Products; Processing of Nuclear Fuel' at Maharashtra, Urban Maharashtra State, and Mumbai levels is analyzed as follows:

Table 3.23
Total OAME's and Employees in 'Manufacture of Rubber, Plastic, Petroleum and Coal Products; Processing of Nuclear Fuel' in Maharashtra State: 2000-01

Industry Division	*No. of Enterprises*		*Total Employees*		
	Sample	*Estbs.*	*Male*	*Female*	*Total*
313	24	403	1126	110	1237
	(5.6)	(100.0)	(91.0)	(8.9)	(100.0)
As % of all industries	(0.3)	(0.0)	(0.1)	(0.0)	(0.1)
All	6152	647653	910692	246898	1157591
	(100.0)	(100.0)	(100.0)	(100.0)	(100.0)

Source: ASI, 2000.

At the State level, the sample represents barely 6 per cent of the estimated enterprises (code 313) and less than half a per cent of all enterprises. On the work front, industry code 313 has a male bias, with 90 per cent male majority. As a per centage of total employment, men in this segment account for merely 0.1 per cent of total male employees, while females for a still lower per cent of 0.04.

Table 3.24
Total OAME's and Employees in 'Manufacture of Rubber, Plastic, Petroleum and Coal Products; Processing of Nuclear Fuel' in Urban Maharashtra: 2000-01

Industry Division	*No. of Enterprises*		*Total Employees*		
	Sample	*Estbs.*	*Male*	*Female*	*Total*
313	19	277	808	31	839
	(6.8)	(100.0)	(96.3)	(3.7)	(100.0)
As % of all industries	(0.7)	(0.1)	(0.2)	(0.0)	(0.2)
All	2602	196586	286158	52539	338697

Source: ASI, 2000

The above data shows that industry code 313 accounts for 7 per cent of estimated enterprises and $1/10^{th}$ of total enterprises. In terms of employment, there is male-domination to the tune of 96 per cent, which is barely over quarter of a per cent in terms of per centage of total employees. The female employment scenario is still more skewed with a negligible 0.05 per cent of all employees figure. Thus, it is clear that this industry is not very important from the Urban Maharashtra level.

Table 3.25
Total OAME's and Employees in 'Manufacture of Rubber, Plastic, Petroleum and Coal Products; Processing of Nuclear Fuel' in Mumbai: 2000-01

Industry Division	*No. of Enterprises*		*Total Employees*		
	Sample	*Estbs.*	*Male*	*Female*	*Total*
313	0	0	0	0	0
All	59	7077	9326	1513	10840

Source: ASI, 2000

The Mumbai level data demonstrates that a nil or negligible number of enterprises and employees are seen in the industry code 313. Even at the level of 'all' enterprises (OAME's), the figures are about 5 per cent of the Urban Maharashtra level.

CONCLUSION

We have looked at the detailed analysis of secondary sources to enrich our macro economic base. Unfortunately, few comparisons can be made between different agencies or sources due to variations in methodology, sample size, time periods, and geographical coverage. Nevertheless each of these represents a rich collection of information that is vital for mapping the general trend of labour markets, and acceleration or deceleration experienced by enterprises on account of the 'New Economic Policy'. Thus, data mining has enabled us to get a rough picture of aggregative economic repercussions of the process of globalization. The shortcomings of secondary data and their vastness in terms of size, coverage, and collation clearly put forth a case for detailed and minute evaluation of people's livelihoods as impacted by restructuring. The lack of gender disaggregated information, along with the invisibility; undercounting, misreporting and under-representation in official national statistics make individual research work imperative and vital. Personal experiences and life histories bring out aspects and dimensions of policy effects and lags that no secondary source can tap. In the three subsequent Chapters, we have attempted to focus exhaustively on the ground reality via detailed fieldwork analysis at the micro economic level of Charkop in the city of Mumbai.

4

BACKGROUND OF AREA OF STUDY

INTRODUCTION

In this chapter, we shall look at the background of area of our study. Section 4.2 analyzes the rationale of studying Mumbai, which is a crucial and highly topical area. Subsequently, the next connected aspect of the choice and transition of the city is studied, as the metropolis has gone through various economic and extra-economic changes. Section 4.4 deals with the selection of the field study area of Charkop, popularly called 'Charkop Village' by the residents, in order to focus on the micro-economic aspect. In the concluding part to the chapter we have tried to locate fieldwork analysis in the larger context of the mega city.

RATIONALE OF STUDYING MUMBAI

There are many reasons for studying Mumbai, ranging from the more general causes to the specific ones. The metropolis is chosen for our field survey due to its recognition as a Class I city since the first Census of 1872 (Dewan, 2000, pp. 26-27). Over the years, various changes have occurred in the occupational activities of the metropolis, ranging from the traditional ones of fishing, farming, livestock, and mining, to textiles till the mid-eighties. Later, new areas like construction, manufacturing, petrochemicals, and services have emerged. There has been a great deal of resilience and tenacity seen through all this transition and Mumbai, even today, remains the commercial capital of India. All these unique features make the mega city an interesting case study.

India's development has been facilitated by the processes of urbanization and industrialization in major cities like Mumbai. This has also increased migration into the state due to vast employment opportunities generated in the ports, mills, construction sites and factories; on the one hand, as well as poor economic performance or perpetuation of natural calamities like floods, famines and droughts in neighbouring states; on the other. Thus, migration becomes an essential characteristic of urbanization (Bose, 1973, p. 20).

Mumbai, apart from being the financial capital of the nation, is also the state capital of Maharashtra. It provides numerous employment opportunities to migrants. In 2001, the population of the metropolis accounted for 12 per cent of the state's total population and 29 per cent of its urban population, thus bringing out the pivotal role of the city. All this makes the mega city a melting pot for different people, internally as well as internationally. Therefore, Mumbai is relevant on account of its key position in India's development process. It is rightly characterized as the nation's most modern city, thereby making any study of India incomplete without the analysis of its nerve centre (See Patel, S. and Alice Thorner, 1996, p. xii).

AN ANALYSIS OF THE TRANSITION OF MUMBAI

As seen in the earlier section, the transition of the metropolis into the nation's commercial capital has been interesting, as well as, heterogeneous in nature. The period from 1961-91 marks a rise and shift in population into the suburbs, accommodating two-thirds of the people (Economic Census of Greater Mumbai, 1991, pp. 18-21).

The city has accommodated various spatial changes too, thereby making its transition dynamic. This functional change of Mumbai is universally found in case of many urban economies like the United States of America and the United Kingdom in the seventies, followed by Japan. This involves the decline in manufacturing and a shift to service-dominated employment, which is accentuated by globalization and increased mobility of labour and capital (Lever, 1991, pp.983-999). A deceleration in industry in the seventies was worsened by a slowdown in urbanization in the eighties. Thus, a continued sluggishness in the industrial sector led to a further cut in organized sector jobs

(Gugler, 1976; pp. 102-103). A majority of workers from Mumbai and the neighbouring regions sought employment in the urban industrial sector. Despite the rising share of the manufacturing sector, a major sub-sector; namely, textile and textile products suffered a sizeable decline in its workforce from 35 per thousand in 1961 to 26 per thousand in 2000. In terms of absolute number of labourers, between 1994 and 2000, less than 1.5 lakh workers were added to this segment. All increases in employment in this sub-sector took place in the rural areas with a general fall in urban jobs by about 93,000, and 1, 43,000, particularly in case of women.

Thus, a decline in selective industrial sub-sectors with high employment potential, coupled with a sharp fall in agriculture and allied segment workforce from 73 per cent in 1961 to less than 60 per cent in nineties has worsened the plight of labour (Sundaram, 2001, p. 3045).

There has been deterioration in the quality of work as shown by the labour market trends in the post-reform period. This decade has witnessed a decline in the organized sector jobs from 8.7 per cent to 8.1 per cent; along with an increase in wage employment in the unorganized segment from 6.6 per cent to 7 per cent. The emerging trend of informalization and casualization is seen to accelerate, as it provides livelihoods to nearly 95 per cent of workers, especially women. There has also been a downtrend in self-employment from 56.5 per cent to 51.7 per cent, coupled with a rise in casual jobs from 28.2 per cent to 33.2 per cent in the nineties with respect to the earlier decade (Nagraj, 2000, pp. 3707-3715).

The pre-reform period is known to be characterized by the phenomenon of 'jobless growth', followed by a restructuring of employment from the organized public sector manufacturing enterprises to small and medium-sized firms in the private sector, especially in the decade of nineties. This has resulted in industrial restructuring and sub-contracting, which in turn led to a decrease in production, as well as opportunities in the organized segment in favour of the unorganized. The on-going decade portrays a majority of 92 per cent of workers and 59 per cent of GDP are generated in the unorganized sector in India (Dyson *et al.*, 2003, pp.108-129; 158-177). Thus, the 'New Economic Policy' of 1991 along with the 'New Industrial Policy' has led to restructuring of state-directed industrialization in India. Thus, it altered the earlier regulatory and restrictive pattern, which used stringent work laws to market driven policies of output and work. New practices of sub-contracting, retrenchment; temporary, casual, and on-site labour norms have emerged as labour market institutions remained outside the reform process (Ramaswamy, 1999, pp. 363-368). Macro changes have ramifications at all levels, ranging from the state to the district. This is also true for Mumbai, the financial capital of the nation. The metropolis has attracted migrants due to its varied employment opportunities in the past. However, the nature of work has undergone rapid changes in the post-reform era, which is probably more pronounced and visible in the mega city. Thus, Mumbai presents an interesting case study to analyze the impact of reforms on work, livelihoods, and earnings.

Micro or grass root level research in the city would help us focus on a select population for observation and analysis of reforms. We found that very few scientific studies have been conducted in the past in this area, especially with respect to globalization and gender. Researchers have documented that despite industrial deceleration in the seventies and eighties, there was an improvement in the status of main workers that benefited women more than men at the All-India level. This is evident from a 4 per centage points increase for female main workers vis-à-vis a mere 1 per cent rise experienced by their counterparts. Thus, the contention that urbanization leads to an upsurge in women's employment holds true. This is ratified by the case of urban Maharashtra, where despite retrogression in output and jobs in industry; growth rates of female labour more than doubled in the four-decade period of 1960 to 2000, and also represents two times that of men. Women's participation in specific sectors like construction, trade, household industry, and 'other services' has shown an uptrend at the national and urban state levels. However, the position of Mumbai in terms of total urban population and total main workers as a proportion of Maharashtra has experienced a fall over the decades. This is evident from a fall in urban population of the metropolis as a per centage of the state's urban grouping from one-third to barely one-twentieth. Also, the share of main workers of the mega city as a proportion of the state's has decreased by 5 per cent (Dewan, 2000, pp. 33-38).

Surprisingly, the trends have been quite contrary for men and women, which justify the incorporation of gender analysis to make any study scientific and relevant. The decline in case of males is 3 times that of their counterparts. Also, the pattern of change for both these genders differs, as the contribution of female workers has risen despite a fall in their counterparts' share to the state's ration in the 60's and 70's; after which they decreased. However, the extent of reduction is lesser for women with respect to men in Mumbai in comparison to Maharashtra's urban population. This is clear from the figures portraying a downtrend in the share of male workers in the metropolis to the state's urban labourers from over 45 per cent to about 36 per cent covering the 3 decades of 60's to 90's. Contrastingly, the share of female workers in Mumbai to the state's urban women ratio has increased by 10 per cent over the same period. Thus, females have gained from the 'de-development' process of the metropolis in the eighties; and their ratio nearly equals that of men, which is one-thirds of the state's share of urban workers. However, the above data needs to be carefully interpreted in order to avoid generalizations. A deeper insight would show that a rising proportion of women in manufacturing do not necessarily increase their status, as this sector also includes the informal and household segments. Unfortunately, both of these are not stringent about labour laws or workers protection; with virtually non-existent trade union activity. In fact, all this could worsen the condition of women labourers. Another trend that needs to be examined with the gender lens is the emergence and domination of the unorganized sector since the eighties. Males in Mumbai and Maharashtra constitute a majority of marginal workers, as the city's men account for two-fifths of the state's secondary labour. Females continue to account for a steady 15 per cent over the period 1960-61 to 1990-91 (Dewan, 2000, pp. 33-38).

The 2001 Population Census also depicts similar trends as the earlier decade, with an increase in the main and marginal workers at almost all levels. Female main and marginal workers have risen nearly 3 per centage points over the previous decade in the metropolis. The respective figures in case of males have been slightly higher at a per centage point for main workers and about 2 points more for marginal ones. The trend towards marginalization of work is accelerating, and is higher in case of the city's males in comparison to females (Census of India, 2001, pp. 54-55).

The Work Participation Rates (WPR's) at the All-India level have risen by a little over a per centage point for rural male workers and remained almost the same for urban men over the decades of eighties and nineties. But, the WPR's for the state's male workers have fallen by a per centage point, while it increased by 3 points for females. However, these rates have dropped by over 2 points for the same time span in case of both urban and rural female workers in Maharashtra. Contrastingly, the 2001 Census portrays a rise in the ratios for males and females in Mumbai by nearly 3 points (Census of India, 2001, pp. 59-60; CSO, 1998, p. 25). Thus, the metropolis continues to provide livelihoods and earnings to people despite a general slowdown at the national or state levels.

BACKGROUND OF AREA OF STUDY OF CHARKOP

We have chosen Charkop in the city of Mumbai for our fieldwork analysis to capture the grass-root level impact of reforms. The resident locals popularly call the field study area as 'Charkop Gaothan/Village'. It is located at the northern tip of Mumbai and lies at the southwest end of the R-South ward of Kandivali, a western suburb of the metropolis. The R-South ward is approximately 17.76 square kilometers with a population of 3,67,832 according to the 2001 census. Charkop Village is approximately 12 square kilometers with a population of about 850; excluding the residents of private buildings and Maharashtra Housing and Area Development Authority (Brihan Mumbai Corporation, 2002-03; 2003-04; 2004-05, pp. 4-7).

There are about 200 households constituting local fisher folk and migrants, which we intend to study in the following chapter on fieldwork analysis in detail. The reason for choosing Charkop is to bring out the micro-economic aspect of reforms and their impact on women's employment in the informal sector. This, in turn, would help us to establish linkages if any with macro-economic policies. Charkop provides an excellent case study as it mirrors the cosmopolitan nature of the metropolis, representing a mix of the local population of Kolis or the fisher folks, and the migrants from other states in consonance with Mumbai's development pattern.

Apart from the general similarity between Mumbai and Charkop, there are strong economic reasons governing the choice of our field area. Like Mumbai being impacted by the New Economic Policy at the macro level, Charkop too is at the micro level especially in terms of unemployment; fall in the share of organized sector work, coupled with increased joblessness amongst men due to a shift from command to demand policies. These developments have repercussions on the gender dimension, as it results in an upsurge in female employment, especially in the unorganized sector. Women have been evolving different coping strategies and survival mechanisms to deal with the effect of reforms that make an exclusive case study.

CONCLUSIONS

The above analysis clearly justifies the choice of the metropolis of Mumbai, which represents a microcosm of the emerging national picture; especially in terms of employment and gender relations. Similarly, our fieldwork analysis of the chosen area of Charkop in the subsequent chapters would help to capture the grass root level experiences. Thus, an attempt to look at the micro-foundations of macro-economic policies via our fieldwork is made. We would also be in a position to bring out contrasts and comparisons at different levels of analysis, like macro and micro; secondary and primary; and local and non-local responses within the primary level itself. Most importantly, we can focus on the gender analysis; which is gaining importance as the share of women workers is rising as a consequence of reform.

Therefore, the global processes of economic restructuring and deregulation have led to informalization and feminization of labour in many countries. At present, there is little information on the number of third world women working in the informal sector. It is generally seen that females tend to be concentrated in the informal sector. Despite this, the problems of measurement have made it difficult to estimate the exact size of informal sector women workers (Greenhalgh, 1991, p. 6).

We need to also look at different methods of analysis, as the labour markets in the developed countries are different from those in the developing ones. They are heterogeneous, with differing sectoral composition; which is predominantly agrarian and self-employed in nature in case of developing world. Also, a majority of people are compelled to find jobs for themselves due to dualism at work places created by its formal and informal components. Export-led growth strategies worsen this dichotomy and accelerate informalization. The World Development Report of 1995 sites labour market distortions, like trade unions and government policies to create inflexibilities of employment. Other researchers cite capital market distortions as possibly leading to informalization. Whatever the cause, it leads to an increase in the number of women workers into this sector, as they are losing foothold in the formal segment. They are seeking new jobs in informal enterprises, as globalization, export zones, sub-contracting, ancilliarisation, and relocation of plants from the West to the East is intensifying (as quoted in Unni, 2001, pp. 2360-2361).

In the subsequent two chapters, we attempt to focus exhaustively and exclusively on the groupings of Kolis and migrants of Charkop for a detailed field analysis. Thus, various techniques and methodologies are used to gather, analyze, and collate micro level information to study the impact of change in macro policies from command to demand.

5

FIELDWORK ANALYSIS OF RESIDENT LOCAL POPULATION

INTRODUCTION

The process of globalization has differing effects on various sections of the population. It is obvious that this mega process is not confined to macro-economic levels, but has also seeped to the grassroots. Our study tries to capture this cross-cutting nature of the new economic order by looking at the case study of an urban centre in the metropolis of Mumbai, called Charkop, which is a peculiar mix of resident locals, i.e Kolis, and migrants.

Fieldwork analysis helps to link the micro level with the macro. The survey largely uses structured, as well as unstructured questionnaires to collect information, supplemented by personal interviews, and several life histories. A number of issues focused on include employment changes from formal to informal, different kinds of informal activities of women, effect of declining male livelihoods on female employment, and changes in the expenditure patterns. The thesis examines various parameters like employment, income, expenditure, assets, and levels of living. The impact of the New Economic Policy of 1991 has been analyzed separately for the local and migrant population, attempting to draw a comparison and contrast between the two. We have tried to focus on differing impacts of reform on the resident locals and migrant population, as well as the resulting survival strategies adopted to cope with change. The breakup into resident local and migrant households portrays the general picture of the metropolis, which represents a mixture of both groupings. The non-migrant households account for two-thirds of population and the migrants for one-third. It must be pointed out that we deliberately surveyed all the non-resident locals, as they were very eager to be interviewed, as well as extremely co-operative. Their survey is also statistically important because of relatively small numbers. As the migrant analysis is being carried in the subsequent chapter, we focus here on the non-migrant/original settlers. The study has not accounted for the 5000 residents in privately owned and constructed buildings, as they largely characterize middle class population. The field survey covered same questions for the groupings, except that aspects relating to migration were not asked to the resident local population, as they claimed to be the original settlers of Charkop, and had no other native place. Similarly, aspects relating to electricity and the duration of its use were exclusively analyzed for only the migrants, as their counterparts were seen to have this facility throughout the day. We did not field the asset ownership questions to the non-Kolis, as they did not own any substantial assets worth mentioning.

The thesis attempts to link the grassroots level experiences to the macro one to get a holistic picture on one hand, and highlight the missing policy links in case of an emerging area like the urban informal sector, on the other. This chapter is divided into various parts, as seen below, wherein Section 5.2 deals with the socio-economic profile covering various aspects like the sample size of households, distribution of respondents by gender, relationship of members with the head of household, age composition, and literacy levels of respondents. Subsequently, the focal areas of occupational distribution, skill status, and women's employment are analyzed. Section 5.4 highlights the employment status of women covering aspects like conditions and intensity of work and occupational changes. The income, asset, and expenditure analysis has been carried out in next segment. The concluding section analyzes respondents' perceptions of globalization. An attempt to tabulate the entire findings of our field work for Kolis is attempted in Section 5.7.

SOCIO-ECONOMIC PROFILE

In this section, different aspects of the socio-economic profile of resident local population have been analyzed. At the start, total sample size has been covered, along with demographic details like the sex ratio, age-group analysis, and relationship with the head of the household and literacy levels. The above details are seen from the set of tables from 5.1 to 5.11.

Our analysis begins with the sample size of total households of resident locals. These are the Kolis or the native fisher folk, who are the Soan Kolis or the farming community, representing the upper caste. However, with the passage of time and increasing unemployment, they shifted to the 'Scheduled Tribe' category of Mahadev Kolis. Traditionally, they were involved in farming, fishing, and toddy tapping. Various changes have surfaced in the occupations and shall be analyzed later in this chapter. The total number of households in Charkop Village is 220. Originally, we had planned to take 100 per cent sample, however only 180 are covered, as the remaining were either not available for interviews at the time of survey or were unwilling to spare their time.

Out of these 180, 120 households belong to the Kolis and 60 to the migrants. Thus, in Charkop, two-thirds of the total households have been surveyed, comprising a similar proportion of people. The migrant grouping represents one-third of the resident local population and roughly a quarter of the total population of Charkop village (Table 5.1: Sample Size of Total Households Surveyed).

The 120 Koli households comprise of a population of 465 people, of which 241 are males, and 224 are females, representing an almost equal gender distribution. We have defined the head of the household in economic terms, in contrast with the traditional cultural one. Thus, income becomes the deciding factor and not patriarchy or family headship governed by societal norms or mores.

The majority of households are Male Headed, accounting for two-thirds of heads of households. The same is true when we consider household members, as seen from 331 versus 134 members of Male Headed and Female Headed Households respectively. Female Headed Households have largely emerged due to death, disability, or divorce in a few cases, with the common trend of loss of employment of the male head for almost all groupings (Table 5.2: Gendered Distribution of Surveyed Households).

The survey focuses on the relationship with the head of the household of Total Local Heads of Households, Male Heads of

Households, and Female Heads of Households. We have drawn a distinction between the economic head and cultural head. The former shows family headship in terms of earning, while the latter, in terms of societal norms, which vests the headship in males in a patriarchal society.

Male Headed Households were found to have 60 per cent male majority, coupled with a breakup of joint families due to the impact of urbanization and changing social structures. This largely occurs due to changing value systems based on materialism and marketization of human relations, which in most cases leads to a break-up of the traditional joint family.

The survey found an increasing tendency towards nuclearization, governed by economic compulsions in case of Female Headed Households, as women were generally found to fend for themselves in the absence of the male head, or were not supported by the husband's family in case of death or divorce (See Table 5.3: Relationship of Respondents with the 'Cultural' Head of the Household of Total Households, Table 5.4: Relationship of Respondents with the 'Cultural' Head of Male Headed Households, and Table 5.5: Relationship of Respondents with the 'Cultural' Head of Household of Female Headed Households).

An age-group analysis for Total Heads of Households, Male Headed Households, and Female Headed Households is also studied. It portrays the highest concentration in the 40 plus group as it accounts for about 25 per cent of the sample with an almost equal gender balance. The second highest concentration is found in the 21-25 year group, followed by the next slot of 26-30 years, thus, showing a higher proportion of economically active people. Barely one-sixth of the population comprises the child-age group, with an approximately similar proportion of the aged, thereby denoting an apparently lesser dependency burden (See Table 5.6: Age-Group Analysis of Total Households).

We observe lesser females in comparison to males, especially in the marriageable and childbearing age group of 16-40, due to maternal mortality and morbidity. The life experiences of Veena, Shobha, and other young mothers are quite similar, as almost all of them have delivered their first child within the first year of marriage, followed by the second baby in the next two years. This is largely due to societal pressures and ignorance of family planning, along with low levels of contraception. Often, young mothers were seen to have a history of miscarriages and abortions leading to severe hemorrhage, anemia, maternal morbidity, and mortality in extreme cases. Also, the survival of women is seen to worsen in the later years due to the stress of double burden of reproduction and production. Almost all of them seem to be perpetually busy with their household chores; coupled with drudgery of caring for young kids, the sick, and aged. Vaishali and Kamini shared their experiences of increased pressures of domestic work, coupled with their new income-augmenting roles due to the 'voluntary retirement schemes' generally forced on their husbands working in the ports and docks. Women are increasingly resorting to multi-tasking to maintain a balance between their roles of production and reproduction, as clearly brought out by our time-use surveys. This has long run repercussions on their physical and mental health, as they suffer from 'unexplained' aches and pains, along with general anemia in their middle ages. All these emerging situations are a result of over-work and lack of sharing of the domestic burden by their male counterparts.

Patriarchal trends are seen through the domination of Male Headed Households comprising nearly two-thirds of total households. However, these are also associated with an apparently higher dependency burden, as one-fourth of the population is comprised of children and aged. The reality is quite different, especially in the post-reform period due to loss of jobs of younger men, compelling the older members to work (See Table 5.7: Age-Group Analysis of Male Headed Households).

One-third of the largest concentration of population lies in the 16-40 years group, obviously representing the majority amongst both males and females. This trend seems to be in conformity with the emerging national trend of a majority of 'young population'. Thus, our survey brings out the increasing presence of economically productive people. The sex ratio is particularly adverse in the two age groups of 6-15 and over 40 years. Male Headed Households are found to reinforce male prominence, as men constitute about 60 per cent of total household members.

A reversal of this is seen in Female Headed Households, clearly showing us a favourable sex ratio, as females constitute almost 60 per cent of household members. A similar proportion of women are found in the age group of 16-60 years, thus, denoting an increasing trend of their productive contribution. Unfortunately, there are few females above 60 years, pointing to lower life expectancy. This could probably be explained by rising stress on account of multi-tasking, coupled with income-augmenting activities, and the strains of maintaining balance between productive and reproductive roles. Majority of males are found in the age group of 16-40 years, with a lesser proportion of elderly men, showing a lesser longevity among them mainly due to alcoholism (Table 5.8: Age Group Analysis of Female Headed Households).

The literacy component is brought out by Table 5.11: Literacy of Total Local Households, Table 5.12: Literacy of Male Headed Households, and Table 5.13: Literacy of Female Headed Households. Total households show over one-thirds of their members to be illiterate, excluding 26 infants, indicating a literacy rate of barely 60 per cent. A similar majority of people are observed at the middle (5th to 8th standard), and higher levels (9th and 10th). Illiteracy among women, especially middle-aged in Female Headed Households is more in comparison with men in Male Headed Households, possibly due to lower priority accorded to women' education, that is reinforced by patriarchy. Thus, there is a clear indication that education is a recent phenomenon and the figures of women illiterates are almost double of males, pointing towards 'feminization of illiteracy'.

The literacy graph, particularly for women is skewed at higher levels, thus portraying the gender bias. The number of graduates comprising barely 8 males and 2 females brings out the disparity in higher education. This may be due to a number of reasons like poverty, ignorance, economic compulsions of taking up a job at the cost of studying, along with a dearth of or an absence of nearness to higher educational institutions. Most of the resident locals are seen to lack the vision of education due to the comfort provided by hereditary occupations such as fishing and toddy tapping. Elders confessed this to be a mistake of not investing in education that has prompted a few visionaries like Shri Vinayak to start a private school and a computer institute for the village. Surprisingly, only one person is found to be technically qualified and that too a woman belonging to a Female Headed Household. The head of this household, Radhabai, is a widow selling dried fish and provides an inspiring case of progress. She narrated the hardships faced as a sole bread-earner while imparting technical education to her daughter to ensure a better job (See Table 5.9: Literacy Levels of Total Households).

However, primary education shows unsatisfactory results, as only a quarter of the population was educated up to the fourth standard. Recently, primary schooling, being free and easily accessible is gaining importance as observed from the case of about 15 per cent of population below 10. The government-run municipal school in the village is attracting children from nearby slums primarily due to the mid-day meal programme that provides nutritious meals of biscuits and milk for snacks, along with 'khichadi' for lunch. Recently, the school has also tied up with the newly formed Rotary Club of Kandivali West for the supply of free books and uniforms, thereby encouraging additional students.

As observed earlier, the literacy graph is found to be increasingly asymmetrical at higher levels of education. Illiteracy is observed to rise with age and is almost double in case of Female Headed Households vis-à-vis Male Headed ones. A higher incidence is found among females in comparison to males, with greater inequity among females of Female Headed Households vis-à-vis their counterparts in Male Headed Households (See Table 5.10: Literacy Levels of Male Headed Households and Table 5.11: Literacy Levels of Female Headed Households). This represents 'feminization of illiteracy', as women are denied education due to their domestic responsibilities and socially constructed gender roles. It also highlights the additional disadvantage that the poorest of poor women suffer.

OCCUPATIONAL DISTRIBUTION OF POPULATION

This represents a key part of our analysis as it studies the focal area of the thesis that deals with the impact of reforms on employment. We have attempted to study the intertwined triple issues of occupational distribution and skill status of the resident locals in Section 5.3.1, subsequently focusing on women's employment to enable us to view the gendered impact of the State-led change from a command to a demand economy.

Women's Employment and Occupational Distribution of Households

We have divided the information on occupational activities into 2 categories, namely, worker and non-worker. The non-worker grouping includes people who are studying, too old, disabled, and unemployed, as well as housewives. It has been extremely difficult for us to classify people into these categories due to problems of overlapping that are worsened by women's multi-tasking. Thus, we submit that this data interpretation is carried out against various definitional and practical difficulties. Over 94 per cent of the total resident local population accounting for 438 people are involved in some or the other economic activity ranging from traditional ones like fishing and cropping to modern ones like plastic enterprises and rickshaw driving (See Table 5.12: Occupational Activity of Total Households).

The most important occupation continues to be fishing; the change being that retail selling of fish has replaced traditional fishing from the creek, thereby providing a means of livelihood to one-fourth of the population. Actual fishing by the men has reduced due to a host of factors like acquisition of land by the Government in 1960's for the formation of it industrial estate, along with the reclamation of land by private and government authorities for housing since the mid-eighties. Apart from public policy impacts on major livelihood sources like fishing, resultant man-made factors like the dumping of waste from these industrial units into the creek has polluted water, thereby adversely affecting the fish catch. We also came across a reversal of the earlier trend of selling a major proportion of fish in wholesale markets and residual in the local market, as the Kolis have switched over to retail selling in Charkop itself by mainly buying from wholesale markets of the adjacent suburb of Malad, as well as the distant Ferry Wharf in the city due to a depletion of the catch from the creek. This ironical situation of transition over a decade-and-a-half from wholesale suppliers of fish from the Charkop creek for the Malad market to now, retail purchasers of fish from the Malad wholesale market to be sold in Charkop is caused by several factors. First, over-fishing even during the spawning period governed by the survival needs of Kolis has resulted in disturbance of the reproductive cycle of fish. This causes the vicious circle of present consumption being preferred to future catch even at the cost of current smaller yields.

Second, destruction of marine life has been a result of continuous dumping of industrial waste and effluents into the creek since the formation of the industrial estate by the government in the eighties. This is seen to increase over the years as new industries emanating toxins and dangerous chemicals and gases have been set up on account of relatively simpler entry and exit norms in the region. However, these industrial wastes have proved to be fatal to the ecology, as well as economy due to the resultant pollution for humans, and also, the marine life that chokes the fish, thereby harming the reproductive process. Various pollutants like lead, mercury, and arsenic have depleted the oxygen content that is harmful for marine life, as well as leads to the rusting of boat joints, thereby increasing unnecessary expenditures for the fisher folk. Pollution is also caused by dumping of garbage, sewage, plastic bags, immersion of religious idols, etc. Third, the entry of local large mechanized trawlers and Multi-National Corporations' 'factory ships' have hastened the destruction of the marine life as they are involved in deep-sea fishing that cause irreparable damage. These private players have been creating havoc amongst the locals, as fisher folk's livelihoods and incomes were at stake. Although, these trawlers were later withdrawn and a few licenses cancelled due to nationwide protests by the fishing community under the banner of the National Fish Workers Forum in 1997, deep-sea fishing continues to threaten the Kolis. This native community faces survival problems even in a reforming and 'shining' India, as their marginalization and exclusion is documented to rise. Thus, a series of natural, manmade, domestic policy reforms and globalization have cumulatively deteriorated the status of Mumbai's 'original' residents.

The Kolis have been resorting to new avenues of earning for income augmentation. One such practice noticed since the last five to six years is selling gold-fish, crabs and other exotic fish to fish-tank shops. We came across a peculiar trend of female-domination in the local retail market, characterized by a total absence of men, as barely one-tenth of the males sell fish in non-local markets in the adjacent suburbs of Malad and Borivali. This brings out the gender based division of work. Interestingly, the retail market retained its local nature, as fisher-women from outside Charkop were denied entry. Thus, fish retailing has changed in its nature and composition due to a variety of factors.

Industrial restructuring has led to job cuts in the formal sector and informalization of labour relations within the formal segment, along with a surge in informal sector activities. People are being pushed back into primary sector activities of fishing and farming due to the emerging capital-intensive pattern of industrialization and globalization. These policies are governed by markets and thus, prove to be gender-blind, as economic efficiency gains priority over concerns of equity and social justice. One-fourths of the local residents in total, as well as Male Headed Households are involved in retailing of fish, 90 per cent of which is undertaken by females.

The field study documents over one-tenth of the men fish, while a majority of 25 per cent have shifted to factory or casual labour in the nearby industrial estate or enterprises owned by the government. About 10 per cent of men of all households work on temporary basis or as contract workers, with a similar proportion take to auto-rickshaw driving for commercial purposes, mainly in the night due to higher remuneration. Males are also involved in the sale of illicit liquor during the day to augment incomes. Thus, they represent the work category of 'others', which have primarily lost their jobs in formal enterprises and public sector undertakings due to reform, industrial restructuring, and change from a command to a demand economy. A few private sector units, especially in the government's industrial estate are closing down on account of undue political interference, coupled with high taxes and rents, as well as militant trade union activities. This category of underemployed face an additional burden of the educated unemployed youth due to the de-reservation policy being followed in case of certain scheduled tribes like the 'Mahadev Kolis' to which the resident locals belong. The unemployed youth is increasingly taking to self-employment like rickshaw driving, or selling of illicit liquor.

Male Headed Households account for the highest number of fisher folk, as well as casual factory workers in comparison with total households. Surprisingly, no women are seen to work in industries in case of all local residents, be they Male Headed or Female Headed, largely on account of socio-cultural factors and patriarchy that hinder the economic agency of women (Table 5.13: Occupational Activity of Male Headed Households).

Non-worker categories depict more than 10 per cent students with similar proportions of unemployed, old, and disabled, thereby collectively representing a large dependency burden in case of total resident local households.

Almost one-third of the households are Female Headed, in the economic sense, as they are the sole or major earners of family income. We have not considered the additional 24 households that can probably be taken as Female Headed, but continue to be termed, 'Male Headed' in the cultural sense. Most of the men in these households are occupationally inactive or earn lesser than the earning women members. Female Headed Households show the predominance of retail sale of fish employing one-thirds of people, majority of who are females. Labourers and vegetable-sellers also follow this occupational segregation by gender, characterized by total absence of women in case of the former, and men in case of the latter. In Female Headed Households, a peculiar observation needs mention, as we came across a single man selling fish in the neighbouring markets and not in the local one to avoid competition, thereby retaining female-domination at home. Labourers constitute the most important category of work employing half of the men folk. Few males have started enterprises, mainly of plastic products, with a handful venturing into varied activities classified as 'others' in our survey like steel vessel polishing, retail sale of cameras, poultry farming, and ironing of clothes. Relatively new occupations of auto-rickshaw driving and leasing of these vehicles to migrants is undertaken by the resident locals.

Nearly half of the women sell fish, while one-fourth are involved in kitchen gardens growing only vegetables and seasonal flowers for festivals like Dassera and Diwali. This is a recent trend, as these kitchen garden areas were paddy fields and toddy farms about two decades ago. The shift in land use is seen to subsequently alter occupations, and is largely on account of urbanization and economic compulsions of falling family incomes due to rising male unemployment and inflation that compel women to sell their property to private builders (most of the property is owned by women, as it is a major form of dowry). Over one-fourth of women are vegetable sellers or gets plastic products home. New occupations emerging for them are domestic service, getting products home or 'others' that include fall beeding or making decorative items like garlands and lamps for festivals. A negligible percentage of females are found to own enterprises such as a laundry and alcohol stalls started by their husbands or brothers, to help salvage a financial crisis either due to debility or loss of jobs of male family members (Table 5.14: Occupational Activity of Female Headed Households).

The major areas of livelihood in Charkop are fish retail, kitchen gardens, assembling of plastic products, and domestic service undertaken by women in Total, Male Headed, and Female Headed Households.

Skill Status

A look at the skill status of employed people shows a majority of Kolis, particularly women to be unskilled. This ratio becomes adverse in case of Female Headed Households, as three-fourths of women lack skills. Most of the people, especially females have no formal training, and account for 80 per cent amongst the resident local employed population. The skill graph is absolutely lop-sided in case of Male Headed Households, as only 2 per cent of the workers with formal skills are males. This is contrasted by the sole case of a woman belonging to a Female Headed Household. Half of the men and one-fourth of women are semi-skilled in case of Total, as well as Male Headed Households. Female Headed Households depict a higher amount of semi-skilled women with the male skill status remaining the same as other households. Less than 5 per cent of the employed are trained on the job, with a majority of such cases found among men in Total and Male Headed Households, with a reversal in Female Headed Households. In conclusion, we can easily correlate the low levels of literacy and skill of women that result in their low employability and incomes (See Table 5.15: Skill Status of Total Households, Table 5.16: Skill Status of Male Headed Households, and Table 5.17: Skill Status of Female Headed Households).

EMPLOYMENT STATUS OF WOMEN

The focal areas of our thesis are discussed in a detailed manner in this section. Section 5.4.1 looks at conditions of work, followed by intensity of work, working profile, and job change in the subsequent part.

Conditions of Work

This refers to the kind of remuneration and whatsoever benefits received by the workers. There are three different kinds of wage payments, namely, piece-rate, daily-rate, and monthly-rate. The four major occupations surveyed among Koli women carry differing wages. About 85 per cent earn daily wages with nearly 10 per cent drawing piece-rates, and barely 5 per cent monthly incomes.

Piece-rate wages are generally found among females assembling plastic products at home, or selling vegetable and flowers, for example, Rs. 2 for a set of 5 small brinjals, or a bunch of raddish or Rs. 3 for a bunch of spinach, and Rs. 0.50 for a small size garland of flowers or Rs. 2-3 for a string of jasmine flowers. These prices vary in accordance with the season, as higher rates are charged during the summer months and festive seasons of Dassera and Diwali. Similarly, greater prices are levied on richer customers, specially, the ones staying in buildings and bungalows. Thus, lack of uniformity in prices lead to variations in personal, as well as, inter-personal earnings.

About 85 per cent of females, mostly fisherwomen, earn daily wages. Some piece-rate earnings in case of vegetables and flower vendors are considered as daily incomes by a few. Similarly, women retailing fish regard their earnings as piece-based, as they sell it on an individual basis like Rs. 100-150 for a pair of white pomfrets or Rs. 30-35 for small size 15-18 shrimps, called 'vatta' locally or just Rs. 5 for a single black mackarel or Rs.20 for 5 of them. Thus, it is not easy to arrive at an absolutely accurate earning due to a thin dividing line between the two wage rates.

This obscurity is obviously not present in case of occupations governed by the monthly mode of payment, as found in case of domestic servants, as they are paid on a monthly basis, irrespective of differing tasks performed, like Rs.200 for washing clothes, Rs.150 for cleaning utensils or for sweeping. Only 8 women were found to undertake this kind of work due to its menial nature. There are hardly any perquisites offered, as these activities belong to the informal sector, where no labour laws or benefits prevail. The same is true in case of self-employed women in fish retail or vegetable and flower vending as they have no employer.

In case of Male Headed Households, nearly half are piece-wage earners, with a slightly lesser proportion of daily wage, and hardly any monthly earners largely on account of the varying nature of their jobs. They receive insignificant benefits in kind like old clothes and furniture. Earnings of Female Headed Households are almost equally distributed into piece and daily wages due to the intrinsic nature of occupations and their importance. Thus, majority of women sell vegetables and fish that make their incomes daily, as well as piece based, as most of their customers belong to poor households. Surprisingly, we have not come across any case of monthly wages or kind benefits, mainly due to the self-employed nature of occupations (See Table 5.18: Conditions of Work of Total Households, Male Headed Households, and Female Headed Households).

Intensity of Women's Work

It is essential to measure women's work in order to bring out their contribution to economic and extra-economic activities, an area that is highly under-represented, under-valued, and ignored in national income accounts. Women's multi-tasking further blurs the demarcation between market and non-market activities. Thus, we have tried to apply the time-use method to bring out the contribution of productive and reproductive work of females. This helps to estimate the intensity of women's work at home and outside. Time schedules enable us to break up the entire day into 10 sub-groups of 2 hours each, starting at 4 a.m. in the morning and ending at 12 a.m. Various activity codes are assigned to different tasks performed, which have been observed during data collection via structured questionnaires and life histories. Most of the women combine two to three activities together in their various time slots of 2 hours, thereby trying to optimize time management (Table 5.19: Intensity of Work of Total Households).

Male Headed Households depict three-fourths of women members wake up in the wee hours of dawn at around 4-6 a.m., while the rest between 6-8 a.m. primarily due to lack of toilet facilities. They also get up very early to finish routine chores like cooking lunch for the men and children.

Other early morning jobs mostly concern drawing of water from the nearby well or other private sources / taps of better-off Kolis. Barely 5 per cent of the households employ domestic servants for washing, cleaning and mopping. Some women defer this work to a late afternoon slot. Only a handful visit the market in the morning due to their pre-occupation with other chores that make purchases of vegetables, fruits, and even groceries an evening activity. Often, girls are seen to assist their mothers in this area.

Barely 5 per cent of women drop their children to school, as only small children below 5 years need help. Groups of older children generally walk to school or use the school/ Brihan Mumbai Electricity Supply and Transport Undertaking (BEST) bus facility available in the vicinity. Thus, hardly one-tenth of females allocate exclusive time slots for children or the aged or sick in the earlier part of the day and usually multi-task these care activities with other domestic work like cooking or cleaning.

We found that one-fifth of the females go to work or the wholesale market for buying fish, vegetables, and flowers in the morning, while only about a per cent of them in the evening (Table 5.20: Intensity of Work of Male Headed Households).

About one-thirds of women in Female Headed Households get up as early as 4 o'clock for ablutions and water-related activities like fetching drinking water, washing clothes and utensils. Most of the remaining women carry out their daily chores in the next time slot of 6-8 o'clock. The fisherwomen are the only ones setting out of their homes for the wholesale markets at this early time, as they begin fish retailing at 8 a.m. and normally wind up at 8 p.m. Some are even found to work longer due to a dearth of storage facilities, especially in case of perishables like fish, vegetables and flowers. An emerging positive trend is that half of the women have begun to realize the importance of spending time with their children and nursing the sick. However, due to time constraints, these activities are generally undertaken in the evenings, along with the routine purchases of vegetables and fish (Table 5.21: Intensity of Work of Female Headed Households).

Only one-thirds of women get up very early for their morning ablutions and chores in case of Male Headed Households, in contrast with three-fourths of them in case of all households. This clearly shows that women in Female Headed Households are compelled to get up earlier, as they have no help in domestic or economic activities. Their work and rest schedules are also similar, the only difference being in lesser time being spent with children due to economic compulsions, along with late household purchases, as well as cooking. Unfortunately, the question of caring for the aged or sick seems to be missing from this grouping. This is a very important aspect of the fieldwork analysis, as it deals with women's work that covers both, the productive and reproductive sphere/care economy, which is generally neglected or masked due to multi-tasking.

INCOME, EXPENDITURE, AND ASSET ANALYSIS

We now analyze key aspects of income and the nature of women's work in Section 5.5.1. The subsequent sub-section deals with the expenditure analysis, where we cover different outlays like food, clothing, shelter, education, health, and others. Section 5.5.3 analyses asset holdings of Total, Male, and Female Headed Households.

Income Analysis

This section is sub-divided into an analysis of the nature of women's work, wherein aspects like time span of work, job change, and duration of job change are looked into. The subsequent section discusses average monthly income, along with earning months in a year. We decided not to include agricultural income in our study, as this source of revenue is found only in a handful of rich families, besides being seasonal and highly irregular in nature.

Nature of Women's Work

The nature of women's work for Total, Male Headed, and Female Headed Households is analyzed in this section. This is discussed in terms of time span of women's work, change of job, and duration of job change of women.

Time Span of Work of Women

Over three-fourths of working women are found in the age group of 14-45 years with about half of them employed for over the past decade. A similar proportion is also seen to be working for less than a decade, with no new entrants in the last one-year. This brings out an interesting facet of females lives, wherein they get busy on the home front after marriage, and after about 7 to 8 years find time for productive activities; as their reproductive role is over. Working women over 45 years constitute about one-fourth of all employed women. A majority of them are found to work for over a decade (Table 5.22: Time Span of Work of Women of Total Households, Male Headed Households, and Female Headed Households).

Job Change of Women

The analysis of occupational change shows about 90 per cent of women in Total, Male Headed, and Female Headed Households not change their jobs, probably because they are original residents of Charkop. Only 10 per cent of women have changed their jobs, majority of who lie in the 14-45 years grouping.

Occupational changes in women over 45 generally show that they have been working since the last decade. We observe that barely 5 females working for both; more, as well as less than a decade are prone to shift jobs vis-à-vis fresh entrants. This behaviour pattern is particularly noticed among women working over 10 years, which is largely governed by better monetary remuneration. We also find a certain degree of caution that females take while changing jobs, especially in terms of the time of switching. Most of them are noted to change at a juncture when their earnings do not create uncertainty to the family's income. In case of Male Headed Households, only one-tenth of the ones changing jobs have been working for over a decade. Thus, a majority of changes are seen among women working for over two years, but less than a decade.

On the other hand, less than 10 per cent of members of Female Headed Households depict an occupational switch-over, which is largely confined to elders working for over a decade. This group of women portrays maximum occupational changes, as they have grown-up children; and thus, comparatively lesser responsibilities vis-à-vis their younger counterparts (Table 5.23: Job Change of Women of Total Households, Male Headed Households, and Female Headed Households).

Women's Activity Change

This section focuses on the duration of job change for all households, and also studies changes in women's occupational activities for all resident local households. In case of Male Headed Households, two-thirds of women have been working for over a decade, primarily in the age group of over 45 years. This shows a tendency of older women working, which could be on account of reproductive roles getting priority over the productive ones. A variety of reasons explain higher work participation among elder women due to greater spare time as their children grow up, or due to the loss of male head, coupled with the break-up of the joint family system. Thus, females largely begin to work out of no choice, and to augment family incomes.

Barely, one-tenth of Koli women have switched their occupations. These changes are mainly noticed in case of 75 per cent of females working for over a decade, with the remaining employed for about 2 to 10 years. A peculiar trend is seen among the few who have changed jobs, as most of them continue with their earlier activities, while taking new ones, thus bringing out the income-augmenting nature of women's occupational change. Also, only a few have switched jobs due to higher monetary rewards, thereby focusing the non-market behaviour of female labour market participation that largely arises out of socio-cultural constraints.

Similar results, as those of Male Headed Households are seen even in case of Female Headed Households, except that one-fourth of those changing their jobs have worked for about 2 to 10 years and lie in the age group of 14-45 years. Thus, a majority of women over 40 are switching occupations, thereby symbolizing a direct relation between mobility and age. Again, like the Male Headed Households, less than one-tenth of the women had changed their jobs; particularly in the category of 14-45 years. As observed earlier, women in this grouping are relatively more mobile, compared to younger ones.

Male Headed Households show a mixed trend, as women in these families have changed various occupations, showing a higher degree of flexibility and mobility, probably due to the fact that females are not the heads of household or main earners upon whose income family survival depends. They constitute secondary earners and serve as income augmenters. On the other hand, Female Headed Households depict a lesser degree of flexibility due to socio-cultural compulsions, compounded by economic roles (Table 5.24: Duration of Job Change of Women of Total Households, Male Headed Households, and Female Headed Households).

Surprisingly, in terms of activities changed to, only one fisherwoman has given up her job to become a housewife. Another case of change-over to the care economy is cited in case of a vegetable grower now spending more time at home, due to the breakup of her former joint family. On the other hand, her sister-in-law has also given up her economic activities to focus on extra-economic ones at home. In another case, a fisherwoman has taken to domestic service due to loss of her husband's job as a result of the company's closure. Two fisherwomen have started teaching primary school children at home. Also a shift from fish retail to vegetable growing is observed in case of an elderly woman due to health problems. We came across an innovative lady, who has started fall beeding at home, along with assembling plastic pins to augment the family income. Two former housewives have taken to fish retail in one case, and domestic service, in the other, due to loss of their husband's jobs. These varied cases of occupational shifts clearly portray the vulnerability of women, as their market behaviour or worker status is largely influenced by crisis in the family due to rising male unemployment and loss of jobs. This has been a result of a change from a command to a demand economy, particularly after the implementation of industrial and labour market reforms (See Table 5.25: Activity Change of Total Households, Table 5.26: Activity Change of Male Headed Households, and Table 5.27: Activity Change of Female Headed Households).

Income Analysis

In this section, the earnings of Total, along with Male and Female Headed Households have been analyzed. Different aspects like the average monthly income and earning months in a year are studied in detail. Fieldwork analysis shows that about half the families still draw incomes from agricultural sources, mostly comprising of vegetable retailing, fruit and flower selling, milk, and barter transactions in case of rice only. We have decided not to tabulate or include agricultural income in our data analysis, as it mostly found among a few affluent families, apart from being seasonal and irregular in nature.

Average Monthly Income

Average monthly income is sub-divided into six divisions. The first group covers people earning less than Rs. 500 per month, where a sole woman worker was found. Subsequently, people earning between Rs. 500-1000 have been covered, which accounts for nearly 15 per cent of workers, one-thirds of who are male, and two-thirds female. Thus, we find that less than 0.5 per cent draw low levels of income, and that women are always located at the lower end of the spectrum, thus, reiterating the trend of 'feminization of poverty'. This is seen to continue even in the subsequent income division of Rs.1001-2000 that accounts for a 42 per cent majority, more than half of which are women.

However, at the relatively higher end of the spectrum accounting for a quarter of the resident locals, as demonstrated by the income grouping of Rs.2001-3000, men form a 60 per cent majority, contrasted by only 40 per cent of women. Income distribution tends to get skewed at higher levels, as seen from the subsequent income slab of Rs.3001-4000 accounting for just over 8 per cent of total resident locals, two-thirds of which are males. The asymmetry in earnings gets pronounced in the highest income grouping of over Rs.4000, as it accounts for less than 10 per cent of Kolis, of which men constitute 90 per cent.

The above analysis clearly shows the universality of disparity in earnings, which gets more acute in the higher income slabs. This gender gap generally arises due to market and non-market forces. At the workplace, discrimination against female workers is found in terms of relatively lower income or wage rates. Extra-economic factors are largely responsible for the lack of time commitment of women that arises on account of role clashes between their productive and reproductive roles (Table 5.28: Average Monthly Income of Total Households).

In case of Male Headed Households, no income-earners below Rs. 500 are seen, as a 60 per cent majority is located in the slot of up to Rs. 2000. Thus, it portrays a predominantly lower middle-class population, especially, comprising of women workers. After this cut-off point, male earnings are found to exceed those of females, along with increasing gaps between the two. This is due to greater availability of time in case of men, coupled with higher wages earned due to the inherent gender-bias against women. The stark contrast is found at the highest level of over Rs.4000, where we notice about one-fifth of males and a sole female earner (See Table 5.29: Average Monthly Income of Male Headed Households).

Female Headed Households show women's incomes exceed their counterparts at all levels due to their sole or main earner status. A majority of these households are observed to be lower middle-class, along with a narrowing of the wage differentials between male and female earnings at higher levels, except the highest one of above Rs.4000, where they tend to get equalized

(Table 5.30: Average Monthly Income of Female Headed Households).

Earning Months in a Year

We have divided the earning months into 2 parts, namely, less than 6 months and more than 6 months. In case of all households, we came across barely 5 per cent of people who work for less than 6 months, with an 80 per cent of majority constituted by men. This is largely due to the seasonal nature of male-dominated occupations like fishing, coupled with the temporary nature of jobs due to labour restructuring in the post-nineties. Male Headed Households show a similar result, the only difference being that all the 5 per cent of people who work for less than 6 months are men. This conclusion automatically arises from the intrinsic nature of male occupations, as mentioned earlier (See Table 5.31: Earning Months in a Year for Total Households, and Table 5.32: Earning Months in a Year for Male Headed Households).

Female Headed Households show a majority of 98 per cent of people, comprising two-thirds of women working for over 6 months. A negligible proportion of people are found to work for less than 6 months, all of who are men. This is due to the same reasons cited above in case of males. Women are compelled to take to employment due to their head of household status. We observe females to be highly flexible, as the fisherwomen are seen to sell vegetables and flowers during the monsoons or festive season due to the fact that people generally avoid a non-vegetarian diet, which in turn has reduced the demand for fish. This clearly brings out the aspect of 'women as target earners' and also portrays multi-tasking of female workers (Table 5.33: Earning Months in a Year for Female Headed Households).

Expenditure Patterns

Expenditure patterns are analyzed in total and percentage terms for various items ranging from essentials like food, clothing, shelter, health, education, including non-essentials like drinking, rituals and other miscellaneous items. Obviously, accurate income and expenditure data are hard to extract from any household survey, yet the information we have collected reveals interesting trends that cannot be neglected. We also came across reservations of people, especially in case of sources like illicit sale of alcohol that constitute primary earnings of women, who generally use the cover of selling vegetables and flowers to evade police authorities, as well as, social ostracism.

Expenditures on a monthly basis of 118 local resident households have been collected via fieldwork with the exception of 2 families not willing to comment on their outlays. The following interesting facts are brought out by our surveys:

- The first expenditure group of less than Rs.1000 shows only 5 households, accounting for less than 5 per cent of total households;
- The second group of expenditures between Rs. 1001-2000 covers about one-thirds of people;
- The next sub-group deals with expenses of Rs. 2001-3000, and accounts for over one-thirds, thus representing a majority of households;
- The fourth group covers one-fifths of households that are found to spend between Rs. 3001-4000 per month;
- The subsequent sub-group covers spending in the range of Rs. 4001-5000, accounting for less than one-tenth of households;
- Lastly, about one-tenth of households are seen to incur over Rs. 5000 for monthly expenses.

The above analysis clearly shows that less than 5 per cent of people are found in the lower expenditure groups, contrasted by over 60 per cent that spends large amounts of money. However, barely one-tenth of members of all Koli households allocate over Rs. 5000, generally depicted by their lifestyles. Our field surveys show over 85 per cent, constituting majority lie between these two extreme income groupings; thus portraying a pre-dominantly middle class population. Male Headed Households, show that nearly 80 per cent spend up to Rs. 4000 per month, with a little more than 10 per cent over Rs. 5000. Thus, these households were seen to have lesser people at the lowest level of expenditure, along with comparatively larger proportions at the higher end of the expenditure spectrum, in comparison with total Koli households (See Table 5.34: Total Expenditure as a Share of Income of Total Households, and Table 5.35: Total Expenditure as a Share of Income of Male Headed Households).

Contrastingly, Female Headed Households depict a majority incur up to Rs. 3000, with a negligible proportion of large spenders. This can be easily explained by comparatively lower incomes earned vis-à-vis Male Headed Households (Table 5.36: Total Expenditure as a Share of Income of Female Headed Households).

The field survey undertakes a detailed analysis of various items of expenditure, ranging from food, clothing, shelter, transport, health, education, to drinking, rituals, and others. Turning to the food outlay, we came across some interesting results. Only a single household was seen to allocate less than 25 per cent of income to this item, with over 90 per cent of the resident locals spend up to 75 per cent on the same. Also, less than 10 per cent was observed to allocate over 75 per cent to food. During fieldwork, we came across a poor widow, Nanda with a small 3-year-old child represent the only exceptional case of a meager outlay on this outlay (Table 5.37: Expenditure on Food as a Share of Income of Total Households).

Again, in case of Male Headed Households, we observed a single case allocating less than 25 per cent to food, with a majority of over 90 per cent of households spending up to 75 per cent. At the higher end, less than 5 per cent spent over 75 per cent on this outlay. Female Headed Households also show a similar trend as the Male Headed ones, as we came across a majority spent about 75 per cent on this outlay, with just about 10 per cent allocating above that proportion. The only difference was that nobody spent less than 25 per cent on food (See Table 5.38: Expenditure on Food as a Share of Income of Male Headed Households, and Table 5.39: Expenditure on Food as a Share of Income of Female Headed Households).

We notice half of the households allocate negligible amounts of Rs. 500 per annum in terms of clothing, closely followed by shelter and transport outlays as most of them pay small amounts of municipal tax as maintenance, and almost nothing on conveyance as their work places are mostly in proximity with their homes, and also because they generally walk to work to avoid expenses on bus fares.

Clothing expenditures denote a mixed trend, as over one-third were seen to allocate less than Rs. 100 per month, with a slightly higher number now spending over Rs. 400 on the same outlay. This is clearly evident as most of the older people continue to dress in their simple traditional attire. The earlier figure portrays a simple lifestyle of the elders, while the latter shows the impact of urbanization, modernization, globalization, and the demonstration effect on the younger generation (See Table 5.40: Total Outlay on Clothing of Total Households, Table 5.41: Total Outlay on Clothing of Male Headed Households and Table 5.42: Total Outlay on Clothing of Female Headed Households).

Low allocations of almost nil amounts by half of the Koli households are seen in case of housing and transport due to reasons cited earlier. Similar observations have been made from field tabulations in case of Male and Female Headed Households for items like clothing, shelter, and transport.

Outlays on health, education, drinking, rituals, and others bring out the following trends. Almost all households report nil expenditure on health, despite our indirect probing questions that portray a different trend, as over 60 per cent spend about Rs.100 per month and barely one-tenth over Rs. 250. Medical camps on vaccination, family planning, tuberculosis, and Hepatitis-B are held by the local ward office on a regular basis. Personal interviews with the doctors and senior ward personnel highlight low levels of literacy and awareness, along with the prevalence of home-based remedies to be some of the causes of low health care allocations.

Relatively smaller expenditures on education by the Kolis should not be perceived as a major cause of concern, as most of the children go to the nearby municipal school, where education is free up to standard VII, or is highly subsidized in the private 'Ekvera' school started by a resident local. Also, affluent Kolis affiliated to various political parties along with the newly formed Rotary Club of Kandivli West generally provide notebooks and stationery. Still, over 20 per cent of the population spends about Rs. 250 per month on this outlay due to the belief that investment in education would contribute to their children's future. Parents prefer to send children to English medium or Convent schools, and have started keeping private tuitions for them (See Table 5.43: Expenditure on Health, Education, Transport, and Shelter as a Share of Income of Total Households, Table 5.44: Expenditure on Health, Education, Transport, and Shelter as a Share of Income of Male Headed Households, and Table 5.45: Expenditure on Health, Education, Transport, and Shelter as a Share of Income of Female Headed Households).

Drinking seems to be a universal expense among Kolis, as two-thirds of them spend at least Rs. 100 per month on alcohol, while the remaining one-thirds even more than Rs. 150. Surprisingly, during personal interviews, a majority of men justified this as a 'necessary' outlay due to the strenuous and monotonous nature of their occupational activities of fishing and rickshaw driving. This justification has an economic basis, as our study finds the indirect submission of majorities of women being involved in illicit liquor sales. In fact, this possibly forms a substantially large part of family incomes, which is never accounted for.

A majority of 95 per cent claims to allocate almost nothing to rituals, but when asked about other outlays, we found that over one-thirds spend anything between Rs. 50 and Rs.250 on items like marriage, birth, and festivals like Lord Dingeshwar's (the village deity of Charkop) birth anniversary celebrations in the month of July every year.

Outlays on health, rituals, and education have been accorded low priority, vis-à-vis items like drinking, and 'others' in both, Male, as well as Female Headed Households. Unfortunately, education is a lower priority area in Female Headed Households due to low incomes. This seems to be in conformity with the universal trend of feminization of poverty and illiteracy (See Table 5.46: Expenditure on Drinking, Rituals, and 'Others' as a Share of Income of Total Households, Table 5.47: Expenditure on Drinking, Rituals, and 'Others' as a Share of Income of Male Headed Households, and Table 5.48: Expenditure on Drinking, Rituals, and 'Others' as a Share of Income of Female Headed Households).

Analyses of percentage distribution on the above outlays give us varied conclusions. 94 per cent of respondents of all Koli households claim to spend less than 1 per cent of their income on drinking. However, the figures turned out to be the reverse in case of Male Headed Households, as barely one per cent of households spend up to a per cent of income on drinking, contrasted by 5 per cent allocation of one-thirds of households. Almost half of the Female Headed Households are observed to allocate less than a per cent of income on drinking, with the exception of a few accounting for over 5 per cent. This brings out the prominence of alcoholism among Kolis, especially in Male Headed Households and also among men in Female Headed ones. However, there are discrepancies in information, as the trends of

Total Households do not add up to those of Male and Female Headed Households. Similar data gaps are seen in case of expenses on rituals, as one-thirds of people spend over 5 per cent, inspite of being a low priority area for Male, as well as Female Headed Households. However, this observation should not be taken at face value, as many confuse rituals with 'other' outlays, and these finally taken together present the same picture as observed in case of Total Households. Expenses on health and education are generally seen to be less than one per cent of income in almost 90 per cent of all Koli households, including Male and Female Headed, and should not be considered as less important, as these are generally provided free by public authorities. Similar low outlays on transport and shelter arise, as most of the resident locals have inherited property, and do not require traveling to far-off places to work.

Ownership of Non-Productive Assets

The Kolis possess both, productive, as well as unproductive assets. Generally, landed property in Charkop, and distant areas of Vrajreshwari is held by the resident locals either for personal or commercial uses like kitchen gardens/farms or industrial galas/ workshops. Fisher folks also own boats and fishing equipments. The non-productive category ranges from ordinary kitchen items like gas, stove, and chul or firewood burner in case of the only young widow Meenakshi, contrasted by plush sofas, fancy chairs, and wall-units complete with the latest electronic items in the living room to huge antique teakwood and rosewood beds and wardrobes in the bedrooms of the better-off homes. Over 10 per cent of all households also have sewing machines, along with cars in a few cases and vast expanses of land in the backyards. Total Koli households show that almost all possess basic necessities comprising of cots or beds, cupboards, stove or gas, and television sets. Similar observations can be made for Male Headed Households, as larger numbers own refrigerators, sewing machines, and motorcycles. Female Headed Households hardly have any assets, as bare necessities like cooking gas, cupboards, refrigerators, and the like were missing. All these observations confirm the asset-less status of a majority of women.

Repeated meetings with the village elders helped to get an insight into the undisclosed assets lying in safe deposit vaults in a few cases and in land holdings outside Mumbai, like Vajreshwari, which is cultivated seasonally. Kolis are also involved in the construction of buildings and galas/industrial workshops, as it is considered to be a safe investment. This land holding is equally matched by women's asset holding in the form of gold ornaments considered to be the best and most liquid asset. However, we do not estimate it in economic terms (market value), as most females consider it to be their personal belonging, which is not to be added to the list of family possessions. Nevertheless, they tend to sell these personal items in case of family crisis and debt. This leads to their further impoverishment, as they continue to be asset-less (See Table 5.49: Ownership of Assets of Total Households, Male Headed Households, and Female Headed Households).

CONCLUSIONS

In this section, concluding remarks on field work analysis of Kolis is attempted. Various aspects of the income, expenditure, and levels of living are discussed. The impact of globalization and effects of a change from command patterns to demand oriented policies is highlighted. The most pertinent question of the impact of globalization on resident locals had differing responses from various households surveyed, but almost all admitted to experience a decline in their living status. A few confess to use unscrupulous means like charging heavy rents or selling kerosene, water, and electricity to the tenant migrants. Some Kolis were seen to trade in illicit liquor that mainly involved their wives, as police authorities least suspect women. This clearly brings out the vulnerability of females, as most of them took the cover of vegetable selling as they carried hooch to avoid suspicion. The 'New Economic Policy' has practically affected all aspects of livelihoods, ranging from occupations and incomes to expenditures and asset holdings. This was especially true in case of Koli men in government service and organized employment, as the 'Exit Policy' forced many to accept 'Voluntary Retirement Schemes'. Thus, a majority was pushed from formal to informal sector, thereby reducing incomes, benefits, and certainty of employment. Besides, new entrants were denied jobs due to industrial restructuring in the post-reform period, and also on account of de-reservation of their status as a 'Scheduled Tribe' pushing them into the informal sector. All this had its bearing on incomes, expenditures, and asset holdings. Falling male incomes forced women to take to income augmenting activities that are largely home-based in nature. This resulted in an increase in women's burden, as they switched between productive and reproductive work. Despite their additional economic roles, most of them received no help from their counterparts in extra-economic activity, thereby adversely impacting their health. Also, the burden, especially of girls increased, as they tend to help their working mothers in household chores. This resulted in increasing absenteeism and dropout rates in schools in many cases. Women also cut expenditures by buying cheaper foodstuffs, mixing vegetable stalks in daal, added potatoes to almost all vegetables, mixing maida to expensive wheat dough for chapattis; and reducing their own consumption. They also mortgaged or sold gold ornaments in times of family crisis and indebtedness. All this increased the 'lack of assets' status and poverty of females. Women in Female Headed Households were worst affected, being sole earners; and were characterized by illiteracy, poverty, and low skills.

TABULAR ANALYSIS OF FIELDWORK RESULTS OF RESIDENT LOCAL POPULATION

In this section, we look at the set of tables from 5.1 to 5.49 that deal with the results of our fieldwork of the non-migrants with respect to different pre-determined parameters covering the socio-economic analysis, detailing patterns of women's employment; along with an income, expenditure, and asset data sheet.

Table 5.1
Sample Size of Total Households

(in actuals & %)

				% to Total		
Sample	*Kolis*	*Migrants*	*Total*	*Kolis*	*Migrants*	*Migrants*
Households	160	60	220	70	30	100.0
Surveyed	120	60	180	67	33	100.0
Population	625	225	850	70	30	100.0
Surveyed	465	225	690	68	32	100.0

Table 5.2
Gendered Distribution of Surveyed Households

(in actuals & %)

Gender	*TH*		*MHH*		*FHH*	
	No.	*%*	*No.*	*%*	*No.*	*%*
Male	241	51.9	184	55.6	57	42.5
Female	224	48.1	147	44.4	77	57.5
Total	465	100.0	331	100.0	134	100.0

Notes: TH: Total Households
MHH: Male Headed Households
FHH: Female Headed Households

Table 5.3
Relationship of Respondents with the 'Cultural' Head of Total Households

(in actuals & %)

Relationship	*No.*	*%*
Self	120	25.8
Wife	77	16.5
Husband	15	3.2
Brother/Brother-in-law	18	3.9
Sister/Sister-in-law	16	3.4
Son/Son-in-law	115	25
Daughter/Daughter-in-law	79	17.0
Mother/Mother-in-law	9	1.9
Father/Father-in-law	6	1.2
Others	10	2.1
Total	465	100.0

Table 5.4
Relationship of Respondents with 'Cultural' Head of Male Headed Households

(in actuals & %)

Relationship	*No.*	*%*
Self	79	23.9
Wife	75	22.7
Brother/Brother-in-law	11	3.3
Sister/Sister-in-law	15	4.6
Son/Son-in-law	83	25
Daughter/Daughter-in-law	48	14.5
Mother/Mother-in-law	6	1.8
Father/Father-in-law	5	1.5
Others	9	2.7
Total	331	100.0

Table 5.5
Relationship of Respondents with 'Cultural' Head of Female Headed Households

(in actuasl & %)

Relationship	*No*	*%*
Self	41	30.6
Husband	17	12.7
Brother/Brother-in-law	7	5.2
Sister/Sister-in-law	1	0.8
Son/Son-in-law	32	23.8
Daughter/Daughter-in-law	31	23.1
Mother/Mother-in-law	3	2.2
Father/Father-in-law	1	0.8
Others	1	0.8
Total	134	100.0

Table 5.6
Age Composition of Total Households

(in actuals & %)

Age Group	*M*		*F*		*Total*	
(yr.)	*No*	*%*	*No*	*%*	*No.*	*%*
≤ 5	10	40.0	15	60.0	25	100.0
6 to 15	30	57.6	22	42.3	52	100.0
16 to 40	137	51.9	127	48.1	264	100.0
> 40	64	51.6	60	48.4	124	100.0
Total	241	51.9	224	48.1	465	100.0

Table 5.7
Age Composition of Male Headed Households

(in actuals & %)

Age Group	*M*		*F*		*Total*	
(yrs.)	*No*	*%*	*No*	*%*	*No.*	*%*
≤ 5	8	40.0	12	60.0	20	100.0
6 to 15	25	56.9	19	43.1	44	100.0
16 to 40	99	55.0	81	45.0	180	100.0
> 40	52	59.7	35	40.2	87	100.0
Total	184	55.6	147	44.4	331	100.0

Table 5.8
Age Composition of Female Headed Households

(in actuals & %)

Age Group	*M*		*F*		*Total*	
(yrs.)	*No*	*%*	*No*	*%*	*No.*	*%*
≤ 5	2	40.0	3	60.0	5	100.0
6 to 15	5	62.5	3	37.5	8	100.0
16 to 40	38	45.2	46	54.8	84	100.0
> 40	12	32.4	25	67.5	37	100.0
Total	57	42.5	77	57.5	134	100.0

Table 5.9
Literacy Levels of Total Households

(in actuals & %)

Literacy Level	*M*		*F*		*Total*	
	No	*%*	*No*	*65.2*	*No.*	*%*
Illiterate (including infants)	66	34.8	124	62.5	190	100.0
Literate	3	37.5	5	48.0	8	100.0
Primary (Std. I to IV)	27	52.0	25	43.9	52	100.0
Middle (Std. V to VIII)	46	56.1	36	27.0	82	100.0
High Std. (IX to X)	62	73.0	23	21.6	85	100.0
H.S.C. (Std. XI to XII)	29	78.4	8	20.0	37	100.0
Degree (Std. XIII to XV)	8	80.0	2	100.0	10	100.0
Technical	0	0	1	465	1	100.0
Total	241	51.9	224	48.1	465	

Table 5.10
Literacy Levels of Male Headed Households

(in actuals & %)

Age (yrs.) *Literacy* *Level*	*No.*	*%*	*5 to 15* *No.*	*%*	*Total*	*No.*	*%*	*16 to 40* *No.*	*%*	*Total*
Illiterate	0	0	0	0	0	9	25.7	26	74.3	35
Literate	0	0	0	0	0	1	50.0	1	50.0	2
Primary (Std. I to IV)	17	54.9	14	45.1	31	5	62.5	3	37.5	8
Middle (Std. V to VIII)	6	66.7	3	33.3	9	22	50.0	22	50.0	44
High (Std. IX to X)	2	66.7	1	33.3	3	36	66.7	18	33.3	54
H.S.C. (Std. XI to XII)	0	0	1	0	1	22	81.5	5	18.5	27
Degree (Std. XIII to XV)	0	0	0	0	0	4	66.7	2	33.3	6
Technical	0	0	0	0	0	0	0	1	100.0	1
Total	25	56.9	19	43.1	44	99	55.0	81	45.0	180

Table 5.11
Literacy Levels of Female Headed Households

(in actuals & %)

Age (yrs.)	*5 to 15*					*16 to 40*				
Literacy Level	*No.*	*%*	*No.*	*%*	*Total*	*No.*	*%*	*No.*	*%*	*Total*
Illiterate	0	0	1	100.0	1	2	6.9	27	93.1	29
Literate	0	0	0	0	0	0	0	1	100.0	1
Primary (Std. I to IV)	0	0	2	100.0	2	1	20.0	4	80.0	5
Middle (Std. V to VIII)	3	100.0	0	0	3	8	47.0	9	53.0	17
High (Std. IX to X)	1	100.0	0	0	1	19	82.6	4	17.4	23
H.S.C. (Std. XI to XII)	0	0	0	0	0	6	85.7	1	14.3	7
Degree (Std. XIII to XV)	0	0	0	0	0	2	100.0	0	0	2
Technical	0	0	0	0	0	0	0	0	0	0
Total	4	57.0	3	42.0	7	38	45.2	46	54.8	84

Table 5.12
Occupational Activity of Total Households

(in actuals & %)

Occupational Activity	*M*		*F*		*Total.*	
	No.	*%*	*No.*	*%*	*No*	*%*
Creek Fishing	26	100.0	0	0	26	100.0
Retailing Fish	7	8.8	73	91.2	80	100.0
Crop Growing	6	85.8	1	14.2	7	100.0
Retailing Vegetables	0	0	21	100.0	21	100.0
Casual Labour	42	100.0	0	100.0	42	100.0
Entrepreneurship of Plastic Enterprises	15	88.2	2	11.8	17	100.0
Working in Factories	19	100.0	0	100.0	19	100.0
Getting Work Home/Home Working	2	14.3	12	85.7	14	100.0
Domestic Service / Outwork	0	0	6	100.0	6	100.0
Others	26	83.9	5	16.1	31	100.0
Retailing Fish & Crop Growing	0	0	2	100.0	2	100.0
Retailing Fish & Retailing Vegetables	0	0	2	100.0	2	100.0
Crop Growing & Retailing Vegetables	0	0	1	100.0	1	100.0
Retailing Fish & Others	0	0	2	100.0	2	100.0
Retailing Fish, Retailing Vegetables, & Others	0	0	1	100.0	1	100.0
Crop Growing & Getting Work Home / Home Working	0	0	1	100.0	1	100.0
Crop Growing, Domestic Service/Outwork	0	0	1	100.0	1	100.0
Retailing Vegetables & Others	0	0	1	100.0	1	100.0
Getting Work Home / Home Working & Domestic Service	0	0	1	100.0	1	100.0
Domestic Service / Outwork & Others	0	0	1	100.0	1	100.0
TOTAL	143	45.0	175	55.0	318	100.0

Table 5.13
Occupational Activity of Male Headed Households

(in actuals & %)

	M		*F*		*Total*	
	No.	*%*	*No.*	*%*	*No.*	*%*
Creek Fishing	22	100.0	0	0	22	100.0
Retailing Fish	6	12.5	42	87.5	48	100.0
Crop Growing	5	0	1	0	6	100.0
Retailing Vegetables	0	0	7	100.0	7	100.0
Casual Labour	27	100.0	0	0	27	100.0
Entrepreneurship of Plastic Enterprises	15	88.2	2	11.8	17	100.0
Working in Factories	16	100.0	0	0	16	100.0
Getting Work Home/Home Working	2	18.1	9	81.9	11	100.0
Domestic Service/Outwork	0	0	1	100.0	1	100.0
Others	19	0	1	100.0	20	100.0
Others & Domestic Service/Outwork	1	100.0	0	0	1	100.0
Retailing Fish & Crop Growing	0	0	2	100.0	2	100.0
Retailing Fish, Retailing Vegetables & Others	0	0	1	100.0	1	100.0
Crop Growing & Others	0	0	1	100.0	1	100.0
Crop Growing & Retailing Vegetables	0	0	1	100.0	1	100.0
Getting Work Home/Home Working & Domestic Service/Outwork	0	0	1	100.0	1	100.0
Total	113	62.0	69	38.0	182	100.0

Table 5.14
Occupational Activity of Female Headed Households

(in actuals & %)

Occupational Activity	*M*		*F*		*Total*	
	No.	*%*	*No.*	*%*	*No.*	*%*
Creek Fishing	4	100.0	0	0	4	100.0
Retailing Fish	1	3.1	31	96.9	32	100.0
Crop Growing	1	100.0	0	0	1	100.0
Retailing Vegetables	0	0	14	100.0	14	100.0
Casual Labour	15	100.0	0	0	15	100.0
Working in Factories	3	100.0	0	0	3	100.0
Getting Work Home/Home Working	0	0	3	100.0	3	100.0
Domestic Service/Outwork	0	0	5	100.0	5	100.0
Others	6	66.7	3	33.3	9	100.0
Others & Domestic Service/Outwork	0	0	1	100.0	1	100.0
Getting Work Home/Home Working & Domestic Service	0	0	1	100.0	1	100.0
Retailing Fish & Others	0	0	1	100.0	1	100.0
Retailing Fish	0	0	1	100.0	1	100.0
Crop Growing & Getting Work Home/Home Working	0	0	1	100.0	1	100.0
Retailing Vegetables & Others	0	0	1	100.0	1	100.0
Total	30	32.2	63	67.8	93	100.0

Table 5.15
Skill Status of Total Households

(in actuals & %)

Skill Status	*M*		*F*		*Total*	
	No.	*%*	*No.*	*%*	*No.*	*%*
Unskilled	98	43.3	128	56.7	226	100.0
Semi-skilled	81	77.1	24	22.9	105	100.0
Skilled-on-the-job	15	77.1	24	22.9	105	100.0
Formally Trained	4	80.0	1	20.0	5	100.0
Total	198	56.0	155	44.0	353	100.0

Table 5.16
Skill Status of Male Headed Households

(in actuals & %)

Skill Status	*M*		*F*		*Total*	
	No.	*%*	*No.*	*%*	*No.*	*%*
Unskilled	38	48.9	55	59.1	93	100.0
Semi-skilled	59	82.0	13	18.0	72	100.0
Skilled-on-the-job	14	93.3	1	6.7	15	100.0
Formally Trained	2	100.0	0	0	2	100.0
Total	113	62.0	69	38.0	182	100.0

Table 5.17
Skill Status of Female Headed Households

(in actuals & %)

Skill Status	*M*		*F*		*Total*	
	No.	*%*	*No.*	*%*	*No.*	*%*
Unskilled	8	13.3	52	86.7	60	100.0
Semi-skilled	19	65.6	10	34.4	29	100.0
Skilled-on-the-job	3	75.0	4	25.0	4	100.0
Formally Trained	0	0	1	100.0	1	100.0
Total	30	32.0	64	68.0	94	100.0

Table 5.18
Conditions of Work of Total Households, Male Headed Households, & Female Headed Households

(in actuals & %)

Skill Status	*Total*		*MHH*		*FHH*	
	No.	*%*	*No.*	*%*	*No.*	*%*
Piece-rate	11	10.4	8	14.6	3	7.3
Daily-rate	87	82.9	44	80.0	35	85.4
Monthly-rate	7	6.7	3	5.4	3	7.3
Total	105	100.0	55	100.0	41	100.0

Table 5.19
Intensity of Work of Total Households

(in hrs.)

	Time Schedule										
Occupational Activity	*4 to 6*	*6 to 8*	*8 to 10*	*10 to 12*	*12 to 2*	*2 to 4*	*4 to 6*	*6 to 8*	*8 to 10*	*10 to 12*	*Total*
1	63	8	0	0	0	0	0	0	0	0	71
1, 11	4	1	0	0	0	0	0	0	0	0	5
1, 10	0	0	0	0	0	0	0	0	0	0	0
1, 12	5	1	0	1	0	0	0	0	0	0	7
1, 2	29	7	0	0	0	0	0	0	0	0	36
1, 2, 3	4	2	0	0	0	0	0	0	0	0	6
1, 2, 11	1	0	0	0	0	0	0	0	0	0	1
1, 3	8	5	0	0	0	0	0	0	0	0	13
1, 3, 4	16	4	0	0	0	0	0	0	0	0	20
1, 3, 11	1	0	0	0	0	0	0	0	0	0	1
1, 3, 4, 5	1	0	0	0	0	0	0	0	0	0	1
1, 4	2	2	0	0	0	0	0	0	0	0	4
1, 4, 5	2	1	0	0	0	0	0	0	0	0	3
1, 5	5	0	0	0	0	0	0	0	0	0	5
13	38	0	4	8	30	124	31	7	61	177	480
2	0	24	1	0	0	0	0	0	0	0	25
4	0	1	1	1	0	0	0	0	0	0	3
5	0	4	7	1	3	0	0	0	1	0	16
11	0	3	22	15	8	0	1	16	17	0	82
12	0	33	76	118	102	29	104	104	39	0	607
1, 14	0	2	0	0	0	0	0	0	0	0	2
2, 3	0	11	3	0	0	0	0	0	0	0	14
2, 3, 4	0	11	0	0	0	0	0	0	0	0	11
2, 3, 5	0	0	1	0	0	0	0	0	0	0	1
2, 4, 5	0	5	0	0	0	0	0	0	0	0	5
2, 5	0	12	1	0	0	0	0	0	0	0	13
2, 5, 11	0	3	0	0	0	0	0	0	0	0	3
2, 6	0	1	0	0	0	0	0	0	0	0	1
2, 11	0	4	0	1	0	0	0	0	0	0	5
3	0	0	1	0	0	0	0	0	0	0	1
3, 5	0	0	0	0	1	0	0	0	0	0	1
3,8	0	0	1	0	0	0	0	0	0	0	1
3, 4	0	15	4	0	0	1	0	0	0	0	20
3, 4, 5	0	8	6	1	5	2	0	0	0	0	24
3, 11	0	1	0	0	0	0	0	0	0	0	1
4, 5	0	6	5	2	0	0	0	0	0	0	13
4, 5, 11	0	1	2	1	1	0	0	0	0	0	5
4, 5, 6	0	0	1	0	0	0	0	0	0	0	1
4, 6	0	0	1	0	0	0	1	0	0	0	2
8, 11	0	1	2	0	0	0	0	0	0	0	3
5, 6	0	2	0	0	0	0	0	0	0	0	2
5, 11	0	0	0	1	0	0	0	0	0	0	1
5, 12	0	0	5	1	0	0	0	0	0	0	6
5, 8	0	0	2	0	0	0	0	0	0	0	2

contd. table 5.19

Occupational Activity	Time Schedule 4 to 6	6 to 8	8 to 10	10 to 12	12 to 2	2 to 4	4 to 6	6 to 8	8 to 10	10 to 12	Total
5, 6, 11	0	0	2	0	0	0	0	0	0	0	2
5, 13	0	0	1	0	0	0	0	0	0	0	1
6	0	0	0	0	0	1	0	0	0	0	1
6, 8	0	0	1	4	0	0	11	10	1	0	27
6, 8, 9	0	0	0	1	0	0	1	0	0	0	2
6, 11	0	0	11	7	3	1	7	27	37	0	93
6, 13	0	0	0	0	0	1	0	0	0	0	1
6, 12	0	0	0	0	0	0	3	1	0	0	4
7	0	0	0	1	3	0	0	0	0	0	4
7, 8	0	0	0	1	2	0	0	0	0	0	3
7, 11	0	0	1	0	0	0	0	0	0	0	1
7, 12	0	0	1	0	0	0	0	0	0	0	1
8	0	0	3	9	16	14	13	6	15	1	77
8, 9	0	0	0	3	3	1	3	2	4	0	16
8, 11	0	0	2	0	0	0	3	5	2	0	12
8, 13	0	0	0	0	0	1	0	0	0	0	1
9	0	0	0	0	0	1	0	0	1	1	3
9, 11	0	0	1	0	0	0	0	0	1	0	2
9, 12	0	0	0	0	0	1	1	0	0	0	2
10	0	0	0	1	1	1	0	0	0	0	3
11, 12	0	0	10	1	0	0	0	0	0	0	11
13, 8	0	0	0	0	0	1	0	0	0	0	1
Total	179	179	179	179	179	179	179	179	179	179	179

Codes: 1-Creek Fishing, 2-Retailing Fish, 3-Crop Growing / Cultivation, 4-Retailing Vegetables, 5-Casual Labour, 6-Entrepreneurship of Plastic Enterprises, 7-Working in Factories, 8-Getting Work Home/Home Working, 9-Domestic Service / Outwork, 10-Others (specify)

Table 5.20
Intensity of Work of Male Headed Households

(in hrs.)

Occupational Activity	Time Schedule 4 to 6	6 to 8	8 to 10	10 to 12	12 to 2	2 to 4	4 to 6	6 to 8	8 to 10	10 to 12	Total
1	35	5	0	0	0	0	0	0	0	0	40
1, 11	2	0	0	0	0	0	0	0	0	0	2
1, 12	3	0	0	1	0	0	0	0	0	0	4
1, 2	16	5	0	0	0	0	0	0	0	0	21
1, 2, 3	4	1	0	0	0	0	0	0	0	0	5
1, 3	5	2	0	0	0	0	0	0	0	0	7
1, 3, 4	11	2	0	0	0	0	0	0	0	0	13
1, 3, 11	1	0	0	0	0	0	0	0	0	0	1
1, 4	2	4	0	0	0	0	0	0	0	0	6
1, 5	4	0	0	0	0	0	0	0	0	0	4
13	23	0	4	6	16	72	24	3	32	104	284
2	0	13	1	0	0	0	0	0	0	0	14

contd. table 5.19

Occupational Activity	*Time Schedule* 4 to 6	6 to 8	8 to 10	10 to 12	12 to 2	2 to 4	4 to 6	6 to 8	8 to 10	10 to 12	Total
4	0	1	0	1	0	0	0	0	0	0	2
5	0	4	4	1	3	0	0	0	0	0	12
11	0	3	15	10	5	0	0	12	9	0	55
12	0	11	35	62	50	14	48	53	21	0	294
2, 3	0	7	2	0	0	0	0	0	0	0	9
2, 3, 4	0	10	0	0	0	0	0	0	0	0	10
2, 5	0	0	1	0	0	0	0	0	0	0	1
2, 4, 5	0	5	0	0	0	0	0	0	0	0	5
2, 5	0	8	1	0	0	0	0	0	0	0	9
2, 5, 11	0	3	0	0	0	0	0	0	0	0	3
2, 6	0	1	0	0	0	0	0	0	0	0	1
2, 11	0	1	0	0	0	0	0	0	0	0	1
3	0	0	1	0	0	0	0	0	0	0	1
3, 5	0	0	0	0	1	0	0	0	0	0	1
3, 4	0	7	3	0	0	0	0	0	0	0	10
3, 4, 5	0	5	4	0	4	1	0	0	0	0	14
3, 5	0	1	0	0	0	0	0	0	0	0	1
3, 4	0	4	1	2	0	0	0	0	0	0	7
3, 4, 11	0	1	1	0	1	0	0	0	0	0	3
3, 4, 6	0	0	1	0	0	0	0	0	0	0	1
3, 6	0	0	1	0	0	0	1	0	0	0	2
3, 11	0	0	2	0	0	0	0	0	0	0	2
5, 6	0	0	0	1	0	0	0	0	0	0	1
5, 11	0	0	3	0	0	0	0	0	0	0	3
5, 11	0	0	1	0	0	0	0	0	0	0	1
5, 8	0	0	2	0	0	0	0	0	0	0	2
5, 6, 11	0	0	1	0	0	0	0	0	0	0	1
5, 13	0	0	0	0	0	1	0	0	0	0	1
6	0	0	1	3	0	0	8	7	0	0	19
6, 8	0	0	0	1	0	0	0	0	0	0	1
6, 8, 9	0	0	0	1	0	0	0	1	0	0	2
6, 11	0	0	8	4	3	0	5	19	22	0	63
6, 12	0	0	0	0	0	0	3	0	0	0	3
7	0	0	0	1	3	0	0	0	0	0	1
7, 8	0	0	0	1	2	0	0	0	0	0	3
7, 11	0	0	1	0	0	0	0	0	0	0	1
7, 12	0	0	1	0	0	0	0	0	0	0	1
8	0	0	3	7	14	13	12	6	14	1	70
8, 9	0	0	0	3	3	1	3	2	4	0	16
8, 11	0	2	1	0	0	0	2	3	2	0	10
8, 13	0	0	0	0	0	2	0	0	0	0	2
9	0	0	0	0	0	1	0	0	1	1	3
9, 11	0	0	1	0	0	0	0	0	1	0	2
9, 12	0	0	0	0	1	1	0	0	0	0	2
11, 12	0	0	6	1	0	0	0	0	0	0	7
Total	106	106	106	106	106	106	106	106	106	106	1060

Codes: 1-Creek Fishing, 2-Retailing Fish, 3-Crop Growing / Cultivation, 4-Retailing Vegetables, 5-Casual Labour, 6-Entrepreneurship of Plastic Enterprises, 7-Working in Factories, 8-Getting Work Home / Home Working, 9-Studying, 10-Home Making / House Wife, 11-Domestic Service / Outwork, 12-Too Old, 13-Disabled, 14-Unemployed, 15-Others (specify)

Table 5.21
Intensity of Work of Female Headed Households

(in hrs.)

	Time Schedule										
Occupational Activity	*4 to 6*	*6 to 8*	*8 to 10*	*10 to 12*	*12 to 2*	*2 to 4*	*4 to 6*	*6 to 8*	*8 to 10*	*10 to 12*	*Total*
1	27	2	0	0	0	0	0	0	0	0	29
1, 11	2	1	0	0	0	0	0	0	0	0	3
1, 12	2	1	0	0	0	0	0	0	0	0	3
1, 2	13	2	0	0	0	0	0	0	0	0	15
1, 2, 5	1	0	0	0	0	0	0	0	0	0	1
1, 3	3	3	0	0	0	0	0	0	0	0	6
1, 3, 4	5	2	0	0	0	0	0	0	0	0	7
1, 3, 4, 5	1	0	0	0	0	0	0	0	0	0	1
1, 4, 5	2	1	0	0	0	0	0	0	0	1	4
1, 5	1	0	0	0	0	0	0	0	0	0	1
13	12	0	0	0	11	49	5	4	26	69	176
2	0	10	0	0	0	0	0	0	0	0	10
4	0	0	1	0	0	0	0	0	0	0	1
5	0	0	3	0	0	0	0	0	0	1	4
11	0	0	5	4	3	0	1	3	7	0	23
12	0	22	40	55	52	15	55	50	18	0	307
2, 3	0	4	1	0	0	0	0	0	0	0	5
2, 3, 4	0	1	0	0	0	0	0	0	0	0	1
2, 3, 5	0	0	0	0	0	0	0	0	0	0	0
2, 4, 5	0	0	0	0	0	0	0	0	0	0	0
2, 5	0	4	0	0	0	0	0	0	0	0	4
2, 5, 11	0	0	0	0	0	0	0	0	0	0	0
2, 6	0	0	0	0	0	0	0	0	0	0	0
2, 11	0	3	0	1	0	0	0	0	0	0	4
3, 4	0	0	1	0	0	0	0	0	0	0	1
3, 8	0	0	1	0	0	0	0	0	0	0	1
3, 4, 5	0	3	2	1	1	1	0	0	0	0	8
4, 5	0	1	3	0	0	0	0	0	0	0	4
4, 5, 11	0	0	1	1	0	0	0	0	0	0	2
4, 11	0	1	0	0	0	0	0	0	0	0	1
8, 11	0	0	1	0	0	0	1	2	0	0	4
5, 11	0	0	2	1	0	0	0	0	0	0	3
5, 12	0	0	1	0	0	0	0	0	0	0	1
6	0	0	0	1	0	0	3	2	1	0	6
6, 8	0	0	0	0	0	0	1	0	0	0	1
6, 11	0	0	3	3	0	1	2	7	15	0	31
6, 13	0	0	0	0	0	1	0	0	0	0	1
6, 12	0	0	0	0	0	0	0	0	1	0	1
8	0	0	0	2	2	1	1	0	1	0	1
11, 12	0	0	0	0	0	0	0	0	0	0	4
Total	69	69	69	69	69	69	69	69	69	69	690

Codes: 1-Creek Fishing, 2-Retailing Fish, 3-Crop Growing / Cultivation, 4-Retailing Vegetables, 5-Casual Labour, 6-Entrepreneurship of Plastic Enterprises, 7-Working in Factories, 8-Getting Work Home / Home Working, 9-Studying, 10-Home Making / House Wife, 11-Domestic Service / Outwork, 12- 15-Others (specify)

Table 5.22
Time Span of Work of Women of Total Households, Male Headed Households, & Female Headed Households

(in actuals & %)

Age Group (yrs.)	Time Span of Work: ≤1						1 to 10						> 10						Total		
	TH		MHH		THH		TH		MHH		FHH		TH		MHH		FHH		TH	MHH	FHH
	No.	%	No.	%	No.	%	No.	%	No.	%	No.	%	No.	%	No.	%	No.	%			
< 14	0	0	0	0	0	0	2	100.0	1	100.0	1	100.0	0	0	0	0	0	0	2	1	1
14 to 45	0	0	0	0	0	0	47	51.7	28	60.9	19	42.2	44	48.3	18	39.1	26	57.8	91	46	45
> 45	0	0	0	0	0	0	2	4.7	1	4.6	1	5.6	41	95.3	21	95.4	17	94.4	43	22	18
Total	0	0	0	0	0	0	51	37.5	30	43.4	21	32.9	85	62.5	39	56.6	43	67.1	136	69	64

Table 5.23
Job Change of Women of Total Households, Male Headed Households, & Female Headed Households

(in actual & %)

Age Group (yrs.)	Job Change: TH				MHH				FHH			
	Yes		No		Yes		No		Yes		No	
	No.	%	No.	%	No.	%	No.	%	No.	%	No.	%
< 14	1	100.0	0	0	0	0	1	100.0	0	0	1	100.0
14 to 45	6	100.0	0	0	6	13.0	40	87.0	3	6.7	42	93.3
> 45	2	100.0	0	0	2	19.0	20	91.0	1	5.6	17	94.4
Total	9	100.0	0	0	8	11.6	61	88.4	4	6.2	60	93.8

Table 5.24
Duration of Job Change of Women of Total Households, Male Headed Households, & Female Headed Households

(in actuals & %)

Age Group (yrs.)	Duration of Job Change																	
	< 2						2 to 10						> 10					
	TH		MHH		FHH		TH		MHH		FHH		TH		MHH		FHH	
	No.	%	No.	%	No.	%	No.	%	No.	%	No.	%	No.	%	No.	%	No.	%
< 14	0	0	0	0	0	0	0	0	0	0	0	0	1	100.0	0	0	0	0
14 to 45	0	0	0	0	0	0	5	83.3	6	100.0	1	33.3	1	16.7	0	0	2	66.7
> 45	0	0	0	0	0	0	0	0	0	0	0	0	2	100.0	2	100.0	1	100.0
Total	0	0	0	0	0	0	5	55.6	6	75.0	1	25.5	4	44.4	2	25.0	3	75.0

Table 5.25
Activity Change of Total Households

(in actuals & %)

Activity	*Age Groups (yrs.)*						*Total*	
	< 14		*14 to 45*		*> 45*			
	No	*%*	*No*	*%*	*No*	*%*	*No*	*%*
Fall Beeding to Pvt. Tutions	1	100.0	0	0	0	0	1	100.0
Crop Growing to labourer (& Crop Growing)	0	0	1	100.0	0	0	1	100.0
Fishing to Fall Beeding	0	0	1	100.0	0	0	1	100.0
Selling Fish to Owner of Plastic Enterprise (& Selling Fish)	1	100.0	0	0	0	0	1	100.0
Fishing , Selling Fish to Owner of Plastic Enterprise	0	0	1	100.0	0	0	1	100.0
Fishing to Crop Growing (& Fishing)	0	0	1	100.0	0	0	1	100.0
Fishing to Owner of Plastic Enterprise (& Fishing)	0	0	1	100.0	0	0	1	100.0
Owner of Plastic Enterprise to Crop Growing	0	0	0	0	1	100.0	1	100.0

Table 5.26
Activity Change of Male Headed Households

(in actuals & %)

Occupational Activities	*Age Groups (yrs.)*						*Total*	
	< 14		*14 to 45*		*> 45*			
	No.	*%*		*No.*	*%*	*No.*	*No.*	*%*
Fishing to Selling Fish	0	0	0	0	1	100.0	1	100.0
Fishing, Selling Fish to Owner of Plastic Enterprises	0	0	1	100.0	0	0	1	100.0
Fishing to Owner of Plastic Enterprises (& Fishing)	0	0	1	100.0	0	0	1	100.0
Selling Fish to Owner of Plastic Enterprise (& Selling Fish)	0	0	1	100.0	0	0	1	100.0
Owner of Plastic Enterprises to Fishing	0	0	1	100.0	0	0	1	100.0
Owner of Plastic Enterprises to Crop Growing	0	0	0	0	1	100.0	1	100.0
Total	0	0	4	66.7	2	33.3	6	100.0

Table 5.27
Activity Change of Female Headed Households

(in actuals & %)

Occupational Activities	*Age Groups(yrs.)*						*Total*	
	< 14		*14 to 45*		*> 45*			
	No.	*%*	*No.*	*%*	*No.*	*%*	*No.*	*%*
Fishing to Owner of Plastic Enterprises (& Fishing)	0	0	0	0	1	100.0	1	100.0
Fishing to Owner of Plastic Enterprises	0	0	1	100.0	0	0	1	100.0
Fishing to Crop Growing (& Fishing)	0	0	1	100.0	0	0	1	100.0
Crop Growing to Owner of Plastic Enterprises (& Crop Growing)	0	0	1	100.0	0	0	1	100.0
Total	0	0	3	75.0	1	25.0	4	100.0

Table 5.28
Average Monthly Income (AMI) of Total Households

(in actuals & %)

AMI Group	*M*		*F*		*Total*	
(Rs. p.m.)	*No.*	*%*	*No.*	*%*	*No.*	*%*
<500	0	0	1	100.0	1	100.0
500 to 1000	11	25.6	32	74.4	43	100.0
1001 to 2000	51	44.0	65	56.0	116	100.0
2001 to 3000	44	62.9	26	37.1	70.0	100.0
3001 to 4000	15	68.2	7	31.8	22	100.0
> 4000	22	88.0	3	12.0	25	100.0
Total	143	51.7	134	48.3	277	100.0

Table 5.29
Average Monthly Income (AMI) of Male Headed Households

(in actuals & %)

AMI Group	*M*		*F*		*Total*	
(Rs. p.m.)	*No.*	*%*	*No.*	*%*	*No.*	*%*
<500	0	0	0	0	0	100.0
500 to 1000	9	34.6	17	65.4	26	100.0
1001 to 2000	38	48.1	41	51.9	79	100.0
2001 to 3000	33	78.6	9	21.4	42	100.0
3001 to 4000	13	92.9	1	7.1	14	100.0
> 4000	20	95.2	1	4.8	21	100.0
Total	113	62	69	37.9	182	100.0

Table 5.30
Average Monthly Income (AMI) of Female Headed Households

(in actuals & %)

AMI Group	*M*		*F*		*Total*	
(Rs. p.m.)	*No.*	*%*	*No.*	*%*	*No.*	*%*
<500	0	0	0	0	0	100.0
500 to 1000	2	11.8	15	88.2	17	100.0
1001 to 2000	15	38.5	24	61.5	39	100.0
2001 to 3000	9	34.6	17	65.4	26	100.0
3001 to 4000	2	25.0	6	75.0	8	100.0
> 4000	2	50.0	2	50.0	4	100.0
Total	30	32.0	64	68.0	94	100.0

Table 5.31
Earning Months in a Year of Total Households

(in actuals & %)

Months	*M*		*F*		*Total*	
	No	*%*	*No*	*%*	*No.*	*%*
< 6	12	80.0	3	20.0	15	100.0
> 6	131	50.0	131	50.0	262	100.0
Total	143		134		277	100.0

Table 5.32
Earning Months in a Year of Male Headed Households

(in actuals & %)

Months	*M*		*F*		*Total*	
	No	*%*	*No*	*%*	*No.*	*%*
< 6	7	100.0	0	0	7	100.0
> 6	106	60.6	69	39.4	175	100.0
Total	113	62.0	69	38.0	182	100.0

Table 5.33
Earning Months in a Year of Female Headed Households

(in actuals & %)

Months	*M*		*F*		*Total*	
	No.	*%*	*No.*	*%*	*No.*	*%*
< 6	2	100.0	0	0	2	100.0
> 6	28	30.4	64	69.6	92	100.0
Total	30	32.0	64	68.0	94	100.0

Table 5.34
Total Expenditure as a Share of Income of Total Households

(in actuals & %)

Expenditure Group (Rs. p.m.)	*Households*	
	No.	*%*
< 1000	5	4.2
1001 to 2000	30	25.5
2001 to 3000	42	35.6
3001 to 4000	23	19.5
4001 to 5000	8	6.8
> 5000	10	8.4
Total	118	100.0

Table 5.35
Total Expenditure as a Share of Income of Male Headed Households

(in actuals & %)

Expenditure Group (Rs. p.m.)	*Households*	
	No.	*%*
< 1000	2	2.5
1001 to 2000	16	20.3
2001 to 3000	31	39.2
3001 to 4000	16	20.3
4001 to 5000	5	6.3
> 5000	9	11.4
Total	79	100.0

Table 5.36
Total Expenditure as a Share of Income of Female Headed Households

(in actuals & %)

Expenditure Group (Rs. p.m.)	*Households*	
	No.	*%*
< 1000	3	46.7
1001 to 2000	14	36
2001 to 3000	11	28.2
3001 to 4000	7	18
4001 to 5000	3	7.6
> 5000	1	2.6
Total	39	100.0

Table 5.37
Expenditure on Food as a Share of Income of Total Households
(in actuals & %)

% Categories	*Households*	
	No.	*%*
< 25	1	0.9
25.1 to 50	19	16.1
50.1 to 75	89	75.4
75.1 to 100	9	7.6
Total	118	100.0

Table 5.38
Expenditure on Food as a Share of Income of Male Headed Households
(in actuals & %)

Expenditure Group	*Households*	
	No.	*%*
< 25	1	1.2
25.1 to 50	13	16.5
50.1 to 75	61	77.2
75.1 to 100	4	5.1
Total	79	100.0

Table 5.39
Expenditure on Food as a Share of Income of Female Headed Households
(in actuals & %)

Expenditure Group	*Households*	
	No.	*%*
< 25	0	0
25.1 to 50	6	15.3
50.1 to 75	28	71.7
75.1 to 100	5	13.0
Total	39	100.0

Table 5.40
Expenditure on Clothing of Total Households
(in actuals & %)

Outlay	*Households*	
	No.	*%*
0	3	2.5
< 100	40	34.0
101 to 200	14	12.0
201 to 300	10	8.5
301 to 400	4	4.0
401 to 500	27	23.0
> 500	20	17.0
Total	118	100.0

Table 5.41
Expenditure on Clothing of Male Headed Households

(in actuals & %)

Outlay	*Households*	
	No.	*%*
0	2	2.5
< 100	23	29.0
101 to 200	6	8.0
201 to 300	8	10.0
301 to 400	2	2.5
401 to 500	21	26.5
> 500	17	21.5
Total	79	100.0

Table 5.42
Expenditure on Clothing of Female Headed Households

(in actuals & %)

Outlay	*Households*	
	No.	*%*
0	1	2.5
< 100	17	43.6
101 to 200	8	20.5
201 to 300	2	5.1
301 to 400	2	5.1
401 to 500	6	15.3
> 500	3	7.8
Total	39	100.0

Table 5.43
Expenditure on Health, Education, Transport, & Shelter as a Share of Income of Total Households

(in actuals & %)

% Categories	*Households*								*Total No.*	*%*
	Health		*Education*		*Transport*		*Shelter*			
	No.	*%*	*No.*	*%*	*No.*	*%*	*No.*	*%*		
0	2	1.6	90	76.3	58	49.1	52	44.0	202	100.0
< 5	60	50.9	7	6.0	14	11.9	43	36.4	124	100.0
5.1 to 10	45	38.1	9	7.7	23	19.6	20	17.0	97	100.0
10.1 to 15	7	6.0	6	5.0	12	10	2	1.7	27	100.0
15.1 to 20	4	3.4	2	1.6	6	5.1	1	0.9	13	100.0
> 20	0	0	4	3.4	5	4.2	0	0	9	100.0
Total	118	100.0	118	100.0	118	100.0	118	100.0	472	100.0

Table 5.44
Expenditure on Health, Education, Transport, & Shelter as a Share of Income of Male Headed Households

(in actuals & %)

Expenditure Group	*Households* Health	Education	Transport	Shelter	*Total* No.	%
0	1	52	38	37	128	100.0
< 1	43	6	10	33	94	100.0
1 to 10	29	9	16	7	92	100.0
10.1 to 20	4	6	8	1	49	100.0
20.1 to 30	2	2	4	1	24	100.0
> 30	0	4	3	0	8	100.0
Total	79	79	79	79	395	100.0

Table 5.45
Expenditure on Health, Education, Transport, & Shelter as a Share of Income of Female Headed Households

(in actuals & %)

Expenditure Group	*Households* Shelter	Health	Education	Transport	*Total* No.	%
0	11	1	38	20	70	100.0
< 5	17	17	1	4	39	100.0
5.1 to 10	10	16	0	7	33	100.0
10.1 to 15	1	3	0	4	8	100.0
15.1 to 20	0	2	0	2	4	100.0
> 20	0	0	0	2	2	100.0
Total	39	39	39	39	156	100.0

Table 5.46
Expenditure on Drinking, Rituals & 'Others' as a Share of Income of Total Households

(in actuals & %)

% of Income	*Households* Drinking		Rituals		'Others'		*Total*	
	No.	%	No.	%	No.	%	No.	%
< 1	111	94.1	26	22.0	9	7.7	146	100.0
1.1 to 2	1	0.9	14	11.9	1	0.9	16	100.0
2.1 to 3	1	0.9	20	17.0	9	7.7	30	100.0
3.1 to 4	2	1.6	12	10.1	16	13.6	30	100.0
4.1 to 5	1	0.9	7	6.0	14	11.7	22	100.0
> 5	2	1.6	39	33.0	69	58.4	110	100.0
Total	118	100.0	118	100.0	118	100.0	354	100.0

Table 5.47
Expenditure on Drinking, Rituals & 'Others' of Male Headed Households
(in actuals & %)

Outlay	*Drinking*		*Rituals*		*Others*		*Total*	
	No.	*%*	*No.*	*%*	*No.*	*%*	*No.*	*%*
0	7	5.0	73	52.1	7	5.0	87	100.0
< 50	20	41.0	1	2.0	1	2.0	22	100.0
51 to 100	26	34.0	3	4.0	19	25.0	48	100.0
101 to 150	2	10.0	0	0	12	60.0	14	100.0
151 to 200	15	36.1	0	0	10	24.0	25	100.0
201 to 250	1	25.0	0	0	2	50.0	3	100.0
> 250	8	13.0	2	3.1	28	44.4	38	100.0
Total	79	0	79	0	79	0	237	100.0

Table 5.48
Expenditure on Drinking, Rituals & 'Others' of Female Headed Households
(in actuals & %)

Outlay	*Drinking*		*Rituals*		*Others*		*Total*	
	No.	*%*	*No.*	*%*	*No.*	*%*	*No.*	*%*
0	15	16.0	38	40	2	2.1	55	100.0
< 50	5	16.1	0	0	10	32.3	15	100.0
51 to 100	7	26.0	1	3.7	10	37.0	18	100.0
101 to 150	2	25.0	0	0	2	25.0	4	100.0
151 to 200	7	46.6	0	0	4	26.7	11	100.0
201 to 250	1	50.0	0	0	1	50.0	2	100.0
> 250	2	11.1	0	0	10	55.6	12	100.0
Total	39	0	39	0	39	0	117	100.0

Table 5.49
Ownership of Assets of Total Households, Male Headed Households, & Female Headed Households

(in actuals & %)

Assets	*Households*		*MHH*		*FHH*	
	No	*%*	*No*	*%*	*No*	*%*
Cot / Bed	102	85.0	69	87.3	33	80.4
Cupboard	89	74.1	66	83.5	23	56.1
Chair/Stool	60	54.1	43	54.4	23	56.1
Table/Vessel Rack	50	41.7	34	43.0	17	41.4
Stove / Gas	119	99.1	44	55.7	75	19.2
Cycle	32	26.7	47	59.4	5	12.2
Radio	47	39.1	26	33.0	11	27.0
T.V.	83	69.1	36	45.5	23	56.1
Refrigerator	47	39.1	60	76.0	14	34.1
Sewing Machine	14	11.7	33	41.7	3	7.3
Fan	23	19.1	11	14.0	6	14.6
Motor Cycle	2	1.7	18	22.7	0	0.0
Telephone	2	1.7	2	2.5	0	0.0
Auto Rickshaw	2	1.7	2	2.5	0	0.0
Car	3	2.5	2	2.5	0	0.0
Air-Conditioner	3	2.5	3	3.8	0	0.0
Chul	1	0.8	3	3.8	2	5.0

6

FIELDWORK ANALYSIS OF MIGRANTS

INTRODUCTION

In the previous chapter, we examined the situation of the resident local population of Charkop. The investigation of the impact of the changing nature of women's employment would be incomplete unless the issue of migration is incorporated into analysis. Although rural-urban migration is a historically on-going phenomenon, it becomes necessary to examine whether recent macro policies have changed their nature and characteristics, and whether female job patterns have altered over time.

This analysis is carried out in two specific contexts. One, that of changes in the causes of women's migration during the decade of our analysis, viz.1991-2001; two, in order to analyze the extent and depth of the differences in female employment patterns of migrants as compared to non-migrants due to changes in macro policies that have resulted in a shift from a command economy to a demand one.

The information gathered during fieldwork for both the groupings is necessarily identical, except for some extra data on migration and electricity consumption regarding the resident non-locals. This additional information includes aspects like time, reason, and place of migration; as well as number of years of stay in Charkop Village.

In order to make comparison simpler, we have carried analysis by way of the same logical structure as in the previous chapter.

Thus, we have used similar questionnaires with slight modifications both structured and unstructured to gather information, supplemented by personal interviews, and several life histories. The issues focused on are also the ones stressed in the last chapter like work changes from formal to informal, different kinds of informal activities of women, effect of fall in male employment, and changes in the labour market. These are covered in our various sub-sections dealing with the socio-economic profile, pattern of migration, occupational details, income, and expenditure analysis, along with asset holding.

SOCIO-ECONOMIC PROFILE

In this section, different aspects of the socio-economic profile of migrant population like the total sample size, along with the demographic details of sex ratio, age-group analysis, and relationship with head of the household, and literacy levels are covered. Also, additional details of the caste status, electricity consumption, and migration are analyzed. We have selected all the 60 households comprising of 225 persons for detailed investigation. It is interesting to note that the sex ratio among migrants is favourable, as there are marginally more number of females in comparison with the males, and also vis-à-vis the local population that portrays an adverse sex ratio. This is a result of an increasing number of women migrating to the city on account of poverty, sub-division of land holdings, coupled with the unavailability of non-farm jobs in the countryside. The plight of resident non-locals is worsened by continuous droughts, lack of adequate irrigation facilities in the neighbouring regions of Chiplun, Khed and Jalna to which the majority belongs. A few of them have shifted from the neighbouring slums of Malad-Malawani and Damu Nagar in Kandivali (East) and the adjacent Kandivali (West) slum of Bhabrekar Nagar due to demolitions and occupation by private builders for construction purposes in the last few years.

Women from the countryside have migrated to the city especially in the last decade, due to socio-economic compulsions, as well as natural calamities like droughts and famines. Another prominent reason cited is income augmentation being undertaken by women. A recent trend of migrating with children is seen to emerge due to better educational facilities available in the city.

This helps to reduce the frequency and expenses of rural trips in a few cases (See Table 6.1: Sample Size of Total Households Surveyed).

Of the 60 households surveyed, over 90 per cent are Male-Headed, remaining being Female Headed. Identification of the head of household has been determined in two ways. One, by directly probing the respondents through our field surveys, which show nearly 60 per cent of heads to be women. This is done to capture what we have termed as 'cultural heads'. Two, depending upon the income information, we managed to draw information on who in reality is the 'economic head'. Over one-tenth of total migrant households are headed by women; despite the fact that more than half consider themselves Male-Headed, as men represent the cultural heads. Thus, it creates a strange situation governed by socio-cultural reasons and not economic ones.

The above finding stands in contrast with the headship of Koli households, one-thirds of which are Female-Headed, thereby bringing out the significant contribution of resident local women to economic activity.

The gender analysis portrays an adverse ratio in case of Total Migrant Households, as they account for a 92 per cent male majority. Predominance of men is also seen in Female Headed Households, as males approximately represent 60 per cent of population. Surprisingly, a slightly favourable sex ratio is observed in case of Male Headed Households, as women constitute about 57 per cent of people (Table 6.2: Distribution of Respondents by Gender of Total Households, Male Headed Households, and Female Headed Households).

In case of Total Households, nearly two-thirds are found to be Hindu, along with the remaining being Buddhists, with a negligible proportion of Christians. Nearly half the Female Headed Households are Hindu, and about one-fourth each Christian and Buddhist. Surprisingly, no other religion is found, as a majority of migrants come from the state of Maharashtra itself that has a Hindu majority. Over three-fourths of the migrant Male Headed Households follow Hinduism, with the remaining practice Buddhism. Thus, Male Headed Households have a Hindu majority as compared to Female Headed Households and do not follow any other religion except Buddhism, unlike their counterparts (Table 6.3: Religious Status of Total Households, Male Headed

Households, and Female Headed Households). The religious diversity is found to be missing from the local resident community, as they are all Hindus.

An analysis of the caste structure shows similar observations for Male Headed, Female-Headed, and Total Households, as a little over ten per cent belong to the other backward classes (Table 6.4: Caste Status of Total Households, Male Headed Households, and Female Headed Households). Recently, the Kolis have changed from their original status of Soan Koli, an upper caste to the Schedule Tribe one of Mahadev Koli for employment in the reservation list pertaining to the state of Maharashtra.

Another aspect of relationship with the head of the household shows a majority of households to be Male Headed, as three-fourths of the men have migrated along with their wives. Barely one-tenth of the migrants have brought their distant relatives to the Charkop. This helps to avoid extra financial burden, and also to take care of their native farms and houses. The second aspect is of economic significance as the elders earn rural incomes, while, to a certain extent, the migrants take care of disguised unemployment due to better earnings in the city. They also often get food grains and cereals from their villages to reduce food outlays in the city.

Over 50 per cent of members of Female Headed Households are constituted of women. Despite being married, about half of them have come alone. The remaining households represent cultural headship of males, who generally earn less than their counterparts. On the other hand, Male Headed Households show gender parity. Approximately one-tenth of these are constituted by other than their immediate nuclear family members, an aspect missing in Female Headed Households, as they cannot afford to entertain relatives, other than their own husbands or children for economic reasons (See Table 6.5: Relationship of Respondents with 'Cultural' Head of the Household of Total Households, Table 6.6: Relationship of Respondents with 'Cultural' Head of Male Headed Households, and Table 6.7: Relationship of Respondents with 'Cultural' Head of Female Headed Households). The above pattern stands in contrast with the non-migrants; living in relatively larger families, which are extended and even joint in many cases, Charkop Village being their place of origin and settlement.

One-thirds of the total migrant population belongs to the child-age group, with a nearly non-existent old-age group of over 60 years, along with a 60 per cent majority of economically active people upto 40 years. This also shows a low dependency ratio, as two-thirds of the people are employed. A similar trend is observed in Female Headed and Male Headed Households, which depict a labour population of over 70 per cent. Thus, the productive work force ratio of Female Headed Households is the highest (See Table 6.8: Age Composition of Members of Total Households, Table 6.9: Age-Composition of Members of Male Headed Households, and Table 6.10: Age Composition of Members of Female Headed Households).

The above trend is not seen in case of non-migrants, due to a higher dependency load as the old or economically inactive also stay with them unlike migrants, where the aged are left behind in villages.

Nearly half of the non-Kolis are illiterate, the incidence being double in case of females. Over one-fifth of them, constituting 22 per cent of migrant household members have acquired primary education, with a larger concentration among women. A little more than one-third have reached the middle and high standard, two-thirds of which are men, as the dropouts among females is typically higher. The literacy graph gets even more skewed at higher levels, as barely 0.25 per cent is fortunate to have higher education. The concentration is obviously found among men, for reasons cited earlier and also due to poverty, as it seems better to educate a son, rather than a daughter, due to the traditional gender stereo-typing of roles of men as bread-earners and women as home-makers.

One-tenth of the Female Headed Households are illiterate, with a 75 per cent concentration found among female members. However, it is heartening to note that these households are now sending their daughters to school. Most of these girls are aged below 10 years, as a negligible proportion beyond 11 have primary education. Less than one-tenth of the people have acquired middle level education till Standard 8, of which two-thirds are females. A little over one-tenth of the population is found to have higher education, spread equally among males and females over 16 years. The literacy graph gets more asymmetrical at higher levels, as only one male is a graduate; with not a single person technically qualified. One-thirds of the members of Male Headed Households are illiterate with a higher incidence among females and in the present labour force or the 15+ age group for reasons already seen in the earlier section. However, girls are now seeking entry into primary education on account of its freeship, as well as the nearness to the municipal school located in the vicinity. Despite this, female literacy portrays a downtrend at higher standards due to poverty, male-bias that perpetuates sons' education, instead of daughters; as well as gender-stereotyping (See Table 6.11: Literacy Levels of Total Households, Table 6.12: Literacy Levels of Male Headed Households and Table 6.13: Literacy Levels of Female Headed Households).

Contrasting this with the literacy scenario of Kolis, we find about one-thirds to be illiterate, thereby showing a lesser proportion as compared to the migrants. The literacy graph gets skewed at higher levels, especially with respect to females; which is common to both the groupings.

MIGRATION PATTERNS

Reforms in India have led to restructuring of employment and livelihoods. Any investigation of the effect of labour market reforms on women's employment to be holistic in nature should incorporate the issue of migration. Migration is an on-going process, and more importantly, we must analyze the repercussions of restructuring on its nature and characteristics, specifically with reference to females. Thus, the dual contexts in which the analysis is carried out are provided by the time frame of the decade of nineties, and a comparative analysis of the impact of reforms on female work patterns of non-Kolis and Kolis. Migration is on the rise in the past 5 years vis-à-vis the last decade for various reasons cited earlier like the economic ones of rising poverty, sub-division of land holdings, and dearth of non-farm jobs in the countryside; along with natural causes of droughts and famines. Also, slum demolitions in the adjacent suburbs of Goregaon and Malad on account of land development or infrastructure projects of the government are responsible for the relocation of people into this area. Forceful evictions are commonplace, as private builders have been displacing people in order to build high rises and malls for huge private gains. A new group of evicted migrants are expected to be relocated to Charkop from the airport areas of Santacruz and Kalina, as the runway and adjacent areas are being cleared of slums. Thus, the interests of the poor and marginal segments are always compromised for a supposedly 'larger public good' that happens to be the 'Shangaization of Mumbai' in this particular case. The nation is replicate with many such examples of displacement of 35,000 working class families comprising 1,50,000 people, mainly daily wage-earners like headloaders, handcart and richshaw-pullers, domestic workers, and ragpickers, as is seen from the 2004 Delhi evictions to 'clean up' the banks of the river Yamuna to construct a 100 acres promenade to attract tourism. This creates a paradox in habitat patterns and urban housing as the rich are being housed by making the poor homeless, thereby sacrificing the welfare of the masses for the ostentatious consumption of the rich classes. Worst still, their livelihoods are also at stake, as the new places either lack jobs, or are far-away from places of work. Evictions have several socio-economic impacts, as people are displaced from their roots or places of origin, thereby feeling alienated and isolated. The economic impacts are disastrous, as jobs, livelihoods, and earnings fall, along with higher costs of transport, relocation, housing, and basic amenities like water and toilets. The 'legitimate' evicted residents of Yamuna Pushta were given relocation in far-away areas without any basic amenities of living or working. The most vulnerable segments were found to be women, as they were expected to manage rising household expenditures with falling male earnings, thereby compelling them to find income-augmenting activities (Menon-Sen, 2006, pp.1969-1974).

The migrants of Charkop did not face the immediate threat of livelihoods due to the employment avenues provided by the industrial area comprising 150 units. However, the nature of jobs and earnings are far from satisfactory due to the contractual and temporary aspects that are worsened by falling domestic demand due to globalization and the resultant flooding of Indian markets with cheap foreign goods. The classic cases in point are provided by Chinese goods like footwear, cheap watches, plastic toys, and imitation jewelry. Domestic producers find it difficult to cover basic costs, as these are generally higher than the imported low priced items. Therefore, marginalization on account of modernization, urbanization, and globalization has further deteriorated the standards of living of the resident non-locals.

Our fieldwork shows different patterns of migration for Male Headed and Female Headed Households. Over half of the Female Headed Households moved into Charkop since the last 10 to 20 years with one-thirds migrated in less than a decade ago. Contrasting this is the experience of Male Headed Households, wherein the shift is prominent in the last 6 to10 years, accounting for nearly half of the migrants. A similar trend is observed in case of all resident non-local households. We also find that one-tenth of this grouping has migrated since the last 15 to 20 years, and seem to be geographically less mobile in comparison their counterparts (Table 6.14: Migration Pattern of Total Households, Male Headed Households, and Female Headed Households).

OCCUPATIONAL DISTRIBUTION

Introduction

This section focuses on one of the major issues of our thesis of emerging problems of transition from a command to a demand economy. The inter-connected triple areas of occupational distribution and skill status in general, along with women's employment in the particular context of migrants are analyzed. The occupational distribution of households shows us that nearly, half of the resident non-locals work as labourers, 90 per cent of who are males. Assembling of plastic products at home provides the second largest source of livelihood. This is got from the nearby factories, and is undertaken mostly by females due to its home-based nature, thereby enabling them to balance productive as well as reproductive roles.

Women's Employment and Occupational Distribution of Households

Approximately, one-tenth of males have started driving rickshaws taken on hire from local residents, due to the current employment scenario of lay-offs and contract work. This in turn, forces females to take to domestic service or get plastic products at home, often combining these activities together to augment falling incomes. It is typical to see that areas like domestic service or getting work home are women-dominated, while entrepreneurship of small-time businesses like spoon-polishing and dye-making, along with rickshaw driving and contract labour on farms and construction sites are male-dominated. This gender-bias tends to provide an entry point to females into the labour market, as it enables them to multi-task market activities with the non-market ones. However, the nature of these jobs being exhaustive and exploitative questions the gains from employment. Similarly, the outdoor occupations that are traditionally stereotyped for males seem to hold good even in case of migrant men (Table 6.15: Occupational Activity of Total Households).

Turning to the occupational scenario of Male Headed Households, we find half of the migrants to be labourers with barely one-tenth of females. Over one-tenth of men have started driving rickshaws due to the dearth of wage employment, while a few have tried their skills of enterprise by way of setting small shops on roads, working in factories, and getting work home. Surprisingly, no male has made an entry into vegetable selling; as women in Charkop dominate it, thereby reinforcing the gender stereotyping of occupations. Similar is the situation with domestic service; as it is female-dominated, leaving no place for men. We have not come across a single male here, as they find it less lucrative in comparison to other jobs. Also, people residing in this suburb seem to prefer women to males; in contrast to the reverse trend in South Mumbai.

One-thirds of the women get work home and over one-tenth serve as domestics, along with a similar number of them combining the two. Also, one-tenth of the females work as labourers. Despite there being more number of women working, vis-à-vis, men, we find they do less skilled and remunerative jobs. Thus, the higher figure of women's participation in the labour market is on account of the increasing trend of home working, enabling them to balance their economic and extra-economic roles. However, this leads to an increase in the double burden and exploitation (See Table 6.16: Occupational Activity of Male Headed Households).

Looking at the occupational profile of Female Headed Households, one-third of women performs domestic work and also gets plastic products home. One-fifth of them sell vegetables and a similar proportion work as labourers in farms or on construction sites. The remaining combines the above-mentioned activities to augment family incomes. Migrant women have no fixed jobs and keep on switching jobs to make ends meet. This is primarily due to their migratory nature, as they tend to lose their jobs when they shuttle back and forth to their villages during summer vacations, for festivals like Holi or Ganesh Chaturthi, and mainly for economic reasons like cropping. Another reason responsible for their migratory behaviour in the last 5 to 6 years is the uncertainty in the labour market encountered by their husbands (See Table 6.17: Occupational Activity of Female Headed Households).

Half of the men in these Female Headed Households are working as labourers, with one-thirds employed in factories and only one found to drive an auto-rickshaw. All these occupations are uncertain in nature, compelling women to take to odd jobs. The scenario stands in total contrast with the local residents' situation, especially, with respect to females. A majority of two-thirds sell fish, which is absent in case of migrants as Kolis consider it to be their monopoly. They are found to resort to strong-arm tactics to throttle any kind of external threat or competition witnessed by us on two different occasions during fieldwork. Similarly, one-thirds of resident local women sell vegetables, with a restricted entry of 3 per cent of migrant women in this occupation. We have not tabulated the skill status of migrants unlike the non-migrants, as almost all of them are unskilled and untrained. We shall thus not elaborate on this aspect.

EMPLOYMENT STATUS OF WOMEN

In this section, the major issue relating to employment is discussed explicitly. Various aspects covering conditions of work, intensity of work, along with the working profile and job change are analyzed.

Conditions of Work

Working conditions deal with the type of remuneration earned, along with benefits of employment. Migrants draw different types of wages, depending upon the nature of activities undertaken. Majority of men are labourers and perform odd jobs like selling hooch or driving rickshaws. Thus, their incomes are highly erratic, mostly daily earnings with no benefits. Similarly, migrant women mainly work as domestic servants or assemble plastic products at home, and thus get either monthly wages that carry no fixed terms, conditions, and perquisites like the formal segment jobs, or piece wages that are extremely uncertain without any fringe benefits in case of informal employment that is largely home-based. We have not been able to get appropriate infoımation on the conditions of work that can be tabulated for migrant households due to the ad hoc and temporary nature of employment either due to frequent village trips for economic reasons of cultivation, as well socio-cultural ones, or labour market changes on account of transition to a demand economy.

The major issues discussed in the thesis are explicitly brought out in this section. Different aspects like conditions of work, time span and intensity of women's work, as well as the working profile and job change with respect to Total, Male Headed, and Female Headed Households are analyzed.

One-thirds of migrant females get work home, which is double the corresponding figure for their local counterparts. This could be attributed to a higher incidence of poverty amongst the migrants. A negligible per cent of 0.25 per cent of Koli women do domestic work, as compared to 15 per cent of migrant females. This is because the former look down upon this activity and undertake it in no-choice situations, while the latter have to take recourse to it due to necessity.

Another interesting feature is that no labourers are found among resident women, unlike 5 per cent seen among migrant women. This is mainly due to the rigid and traditional society of the Kolis, which does not permit females to do menial outdoor jobs, in contrast to the non-Kolis who have to do them for survival. A majority is seen in numerical terms in the category of labourers for both resident local and migrant men, though it accounts for barely one-fourth in the earlier case, and over 60 per cent in the latter. These jobs seem to be available due to their inherently low educational and skill requirement.

The second largest source of livelihood amongst local men accounting for about 15 per cent of male employment is creek fishing and retail selling in nearby suburbs, totally absent among the migrants, mainly due to the monopoly of Kolis, restricting entry into this age-old activity. This is also found in case of other activities, never or less mentioned, like selling alcohol or hooch.

Rickshaw driving is gaining importance due to rising open and educated unemployment, especially among the local residents due to the general labour market scenario, and the de-recognition of Kolis as a Scheduled Tribe, thus denying them the traditionally reserved jobs. A recent trend we observe during our survey is that Kolis above 50 years are giving their rickshaws on hire to migrants on a monthly basis. This is being preferred to savings accounts, and fixed deposits due to the downward revision of rates of interest. In order to ensure fixed earnings, regular passengers like school children or office employees are preferred. This is seen to benefit the resident non-locals who find it difficult to get a remunerative job, and opt for this due to flexible working hours, along with no encumbrances in terms of tedious bank loan procedures, proof of residence, guarantors and regular repayment schedules, which they generally lack. We came across few migrants choosing steady and fixed incomes taking monthly passengers, while many others wanting to earn more money in lesser time tend to specialize in night shift due to the applicable double fares.

The dearth of availability of employment opportunities amongst migrants can be mainly attributed to their poverty, in contrast with one-tenth of the locals who are seen to venture into small-time businesses of mainly plastic products; along with more recent areas of retailing of groceries. Thus, the Koli men are highly flexible in changing the line of products in keeping with demand patterns, as space and investment is not a constraint. A miniscule proportion of resident local women are seen to start small provision stores or a laundry, as they possess the requisite capital unlike their migrant counterparts (See Table 6.15: Occupational Activity of Total Households, Table 6.16: Occupational Activity of Male Headed Households, and Table 6.17: Occupational Activity of Female Headed Households). Nevertheless, about 80 per cent of non-Kolis are included in the 'Worker' categories, as explained in the previous chapter; leaving only 20 per cent in the 'Non-Worker' grouping, that accounts for a students' majority, and hardly any aged or housewives. Only two people were unemployed. Interestingly, Female Headed Households did not have any Non-Workers, thereby depicting their economic contribution emerging on account of survival concerns.

Intensity of Women's Work

Valuation of women's work is essential to highlight their participation in economic and extra-economic activities. This is a difficult task due to the very definition of work, especially females' non-market contribution, which becomes complicated due to multi-tasking. Thus, it is imperative to measure the intensity of work via the device of time use pattern. We have divided the entire day into 10 time periods of 2 hours each that begin at 4 a.m. and end at 12 a.m. at midnight. Our analysis shows that majorities of people wake up as early as 4 a.m. as they used to in their villages for routine morning ablutions and females have to fetch water by standing in long queues. This portrays a dismal picture, as the migrant women have to go through the inconveniences of urban living in terms of basic toilet and water facilities.

Over one-thirds of women, most of who are home-based workers begins their work around 8 a.m. and generally combines it with cooking or washing clothes and utensils. The remaining two-thirds of women work outside the confines of their homes from 10 o'clock in the morning to about 6 p.m. Females usually undertake domestic purchases in the evening from the local market, after which they cook. This is a daily time-consuming activity due to lack of storage and refrigeration facilities, and also lack of sufficient daily incomes.

A negligible per centage of women spend time with their children or drop them to school as these concepts of nurturing children do not usually prevail, and are probably not required as the municipal school lies in the village itself. Similarly few females tend to the sick or aged or even rest in the afternoons, as they are always busy with household chores. The only source of entertainment is television, which is usually watched at their landlords' or own residences in a few cases. We find their lifestyles to be mundane and monotonous, generally governed by survival. A similar scenario is found in case of Male Headed Households (See Table 6.18: Intensity of Work of Total Households and Table 6.19: Intensity of Work of Male Headed Households).

A majority of members of Female Headed Households get up early, and continue to work till approximately 8 p.m. However, women do not find any separate time for themselves, or for care activities. This largely occurs due to a priority of economic roles over extra-economic ones (See Table 6.20: Intensity of Work of Female Headed Households).

INCOME, EXPENDITURE, AND ASSET ANALYSIS

Sub-section 6.6.1 examines income and nature of women's work, followed by an expenditure analysis in 6.6.2, where different outlays of food, clothing, shelter, education, health, and others are covered. Subsequently, asset holdings of Total, Male Headed, and Female Headed Households are studied.

Income Analysis

We deal with an analysis of the nature of women's work in this section, wherein aspects like time span of work, as well as job change are covered. In the following section, average monthly income and earning months in a year are discussed.

Nature of Women's Work

In this sub-section is analyzed the nature of women's work for all migrant households. The focal areas that are covered are time span of women's work, change of job, and duration of job change.

Time Span of Work of Women

We have tried to gather additional information on women's work due to various problems like definitional gray areas of the occupational status of women, worsened by the interspersion of their market and non-market activities, as well as rising home-based occupations further masking labour market participation are faced while collecting data on conditions of work. Thus, we tried to look at the time span of work, and found three-fourths of migrant women work since the past 1 to 6 years, with a majority of them in the age group of 19 to 35 years. This is mainly attributed to the constant drought situation in the last few years, forcing people to move out in the search of livelihoods. A negligible proportion of females have shifted to the city in the last one year, especially in the last decade, as the rural scenario is somewhat better due to good rainfall. Over 15 per cent migrated more than a decade ago along with their husbands. A similar situation is seen in case of Male Headed Households.

However, field investigation shows differing results in case of Female Headed Households, as a majority of them shifted over a decade ago accompanied by their husbands, and have eventually become heads of households due to loss of jobs or disability in case of the male member/head. One-thirds of the women have been working for the last 3 years to augment falling incomes or to support their children, in case of single-parent households (Table

6.21: Time Span of Work of Women of Total Households, Male Headed Households, and Female Headed Households).

Job Change of Women

We find one-thirds of women change their jobs, majority being in the 14-45 age groups, representing the youth that always strives for better options. Again, we notice occupational shifts particularly in the last few years. New employment avenues provided by recently set up plastic industries can probably explain this. Almost similar results are seen in case of Male Headed Households. Our survey depicts a reversal in case of Female Headed Households, as two-thirds are found to change their jobs. The ones that experienced an occupational change are found in the same age group of 14-45 years with the shift occurring in the same time-span as their counterparts in Male Headed Households. The reason behind a majority of them change is largely the constant need to earn more for their families, due to increasing needs of children, worsened by inflationary pressures (Table 6.22: Job Change of Women of Total Households, Male Headed Households, and Female Headed Households).

Most job changes occurred in the past decade, particularly in Male Headed Households. Also, very few changes are seen in the previous two years (See Table 6.23: Duration of Job Change of Women of Total Households, Male Headed Households, and Female Headed Households).

Women's Activity Change

Turning to the activity changes, we find that nearly half the women of total migrant households have moved from domestic service to plastic products due to the stigma attached to the former, as well as the home-based and flexible nature of the latter. One-fifth have shifted to assembling of plastic products from growing vegetables or factory employment due to the seasonal nature of primary sector occupations that results in low income, along with an uncertainty in industrial jobs, as well as rising competition from retrenched men folk in the formal sector. A reversal of the above is seen in case of a few, as they find more time to spare on account of grown-up children attending full-day schools.

In case of Male Headed Households, a major part of the shift is seen in case of plastic products, as females continue their prier activities of domestic service or vegetable selling to cushion uncertain incomes. On the other hand, with respect to Female Headed Households, one-thirds has moved to plastic products, along with earlier jobs of domestic services, factory jobs, or vegetable selling to augment incomes. The situation is quite different in case of non-migrant women's activity change, as it shows a mixed trend. Most of the Koli females have retained traditional occupations, while taking to income-augmenting activities like kitchen gardens, plastic products, and private tuitions; the exception being in case of domestic service. This activity is not accepted by the non-migrant community and is generally taken recourse to by women in distress; either due to sudden death, illness, or loss of job of the male head (See Table 6.24: Activity Change of Total Households, Table 6.25: Activity Change of Male Headed Households, and Table 6.26: Activity Change of Female Headed Households).

Income Analysis

The income of all households, along with Male Headed and Female Headed is analyzed in this section. A detailed study of average monthly income and earning months in a year is undertaken.

Average Monthly Income

The analysis of average monthly income of all migrants' shows three-fourths of the total population earning between Rs.500-3000 per annum, pointing to a predominant poor class. Investigations also portray a negligible proportion of people exist at both the higher and lower ends of the income spectrum, thereby pointing to a low incidence of inequalities (Table 6.27: Average Monthly Income of Total Households).

A look at the Male Headed Households, portrays barely one-fifth earn less than Rs.500, all of whom are females, while a similarly negligible proportion draw over Rs.4000 monthly, all of them being men. This skewed result clearly brings out the gender discrimination, particularly in opportunities and wages. A majority of females earn up to Rs.2000, while only one-tenth draw between Rs.2000-3000. On the other hand, over half of the males earn up to Rs.3000, and about a quarter earning above this level. This indicates income inequalities between the two genders, which get accentuated at higher slabs of income (Table 6.28: Average Monthly Income of Male Headed Households).

Female Headed Households have not a single person drawing less than Rs. 500 on the lower end of the spectrum and a negligible proportion earn over Rs.3000. The highest earner is a woman, which can be easily understood in case of such households. Females earn more than their counterparts with a majority drawing Rs.2000 or more, as most of them are into low paid jobs due to lack of skills and education (Table 6.29: Average Monthly Income of Female Headed Households).

A comparative analysis of the Kolis shows that a negligible proportion of people earn less than Rs.500, but about one-fourths draw over Rs.4000, 90 per cent comprised of self-employed men. More women earners are found in the income range up to Rs.2000, with a reversal at higher income levels. This clearly brings out the gender discrimination that appears to be almost universal.

Earning Months in a Year

A study of the actual duration of work is essential for a better picture of the job profile. Thus, the working months are divided into two parts, namely, less than 6 months and more than 6 months. An analysis of the earning months in a year in case of all migrants shows that one-tenth of the households usually have their male members employed for only half the year. The explanation given to us is the trans-area dilemma they face -viz. seasonal migration to and fro from the city to their villages, for cropping or harvesting of their village land on one hand, and resultant loss of jobs, along with lack of permanent jobs due to contractualisation of work on the other. This also represents one-fifth of the male population, as against four-fifth working throughout the year (Table 6.30: Earning Months in a Year for Total Households).

The scenario of women stands in total contrast, as they work throughout the year because they do not need to shuttle to and fro to their villages, and also due to children's education. In case of Male Headed Households, we find two-thirds of males and one-thirds of females employed for less than six months. On the other hand, the overwhelming proportion of females comprising 90 per cent of total migrant women work throughout the year; as against two-thirds of the remaining males. This can be explained by the reasons analyzed in the earlier section (Table 6.31: Earning Months in a Year for Male Headed Households).

On the other hand, our survey shows contrasting results in case of Female Headed Households, as we did not find a single person to work for less than six months. Two-thirds of women and one-third of men work for the entire year for reasons of survival (Table 6.32: Earning Months in a Year for Female Headed Households).

The scene with respect to the Kolis is quite different, as one-tenth of total men and a negligible proportion of women are employed for less than six months. The remaining population equally distributed between the two genders work all round the year. The ones who are found to be occupied for a lesser time did so either due to loss in job or break in service due to personal illness, or often, forceful voluntary retirements. Few people stayed away from the labour market due to reasonable levels of living, cushioned by inheritance.

Expenditure Patterns

This section discusses outlays on varied basic items of food, clothing, shelter, health, education, and also non-essentials like drinking, rituals, and miscellaneous allocations in total, as well as per centage terms. Expenditure details are difficult to get, as we realize that income information is even harder to extract. A negligible proportion of the migrants spend less than Rs.1000 at the lower end, and similarly so at the higher level of over Rs.5000. however, over 75 per cent are compelled to allocate up to Rs.5000 per month due to the high cost of living in the city (See Table 6.33: Total Expenditure as a Share of Income of Total Households, Table 6.34: Total Expenditure as a Share of Income of Male Headed Households, and Table 6.35: Total Expenditure as a Share of Income of Female Headed Households).

Data of all households show allocations of up to 75 per cent on food in case of all groupings. Also, a majority of Male Headed Households spent approximately Rs.4000 per month, primarily on this outlay. The allocation on food in case of Female-Headed Households follows the same pattern as of other migrants (See Table 6.36: Expenditure on Food as a Share of Income of Total Households, Table 6.37: Expenditure on Food as a Share of Income of Male Headed Households, and Table 6.38: Expenditure on Food as a Share of Income of Female Headed Households).

Allocations on clothing are low and we found negligible proportions spend over 30 per cent in this area. Thus, clothing remains a low priority item for the migrants into this city of fashion and fads (See Table 6.39: Expenditure on Clothing as a Share of Income of Total Households, Table 6.40: Expenditure on Clothing as a Share of Income of Male Headed Households, and Table 6.41: Expenditure on Clothing as a share of Income of Female Headed Households).

A combined analysis of items like shelter, health, education, and transport shows that three-fourths of the households spend about 15 per cent on shelter, as Mumbai continues to be an expensive place to live. None of the migrants own any dwellings and leases of at high deposits of Rs.2000 to 3000 and low rents of Rs.200 to 250 per month for a period of 11 months, or no deposits and high rents of Rs.500 to 550 per month. A majority of the dwellings are small huts with tin or tarpoleum roofs that further worsen their living conditions. Most of these are kutcha without any proper roof, floor, ventilation, and toilet facilities. Field work shows 75 per cent expend up to 10 per cent on medical treatment as malaria, diarrhea, and anemia are common ailments among migrants, particularly due to lack of hygienic conditions of existence, and also under-nourishment.

Majority spend less than 5 per cent on schooling like their non-migrant counterparts due to free primary education at the village municipal school up to Standard 7. Similarly, low allocations on transport are observed, as migrants work nearby and prefer to cover distances of up to 5 kilometers on foot to save money and time (See Table 6.42: Expenditure on Health, Education, Transport, and Shelter as a Share of Income of Total Households).

Outlays of Male Headed Households depict three-fourths allocate up to Rs.4000 per month with very few spend either less than Rs.1000 or more than Rs.5000. Our survey noted a single person take a loan of Rs.500 for meeting the sudden hospitalization charges of his son, as migrants generally avoid borrowing. An analysis of outlays on health, education, transport, and shelter portray the low priority nature of such expenses (Table 6.43: Expenditure on Health, Education, Transport, and Shelter as a Share of Income of Male Headed Households).

In case of Female Headed Households, smaller allocations can be explained by their low incomes and 'single earner' status. The essential difference is seen on outlays like health, education, and transport, which are lower than 5 per cent. Transport spending are almost nil, as they work nearby or are largely involved in home-based activities, especially in case of plastic products, generally preferred due to an ease of entry and exit, coupled with convenient and flexible timings (Table 6.44: Expenditure on Health, Education, Transport, and Shelter as a Share of Income of Female Headed Households).

Surprisingly, people claim to allocate very little to rituals as they have left their extended families in their villages, and may spend more on other outlays like sending money or gifts to their relatives in the countryside or entertaining them when they came to the city. Majority of all households admit to expend almost less than one per cent of their income on areas like drinking, rituals, and 'others'. But our fieldwork data and tabulations clearly show a larger amount being spent on 'other' outlays, as these are ambiguous and range from childbirth to marriages to festivals. Most of them are obviously reluctant to reveal actual outlays on drinking due to social ostracism.

Almost all households show low allocations in the dual areas of rituals and drinking, along with 'other outlays' comprising barely 5 per cent for one-fourth of Male Headed Households. Contrastingly, Female Headed Households portray smaller outlays on drinking, as women are usually not found to drink, unlike men. Relatively negligible amounts are spent on rituals, with the exception of 'other outlays', which are higher during festive months of Ganapati or Dassera or Diwali (See Table 6.45: Expenditure on Drinking, Rituals, and 'Others' as a Share of Income for Total Households, Table 6.46: Expenditure on Drinking, Rituals, and 'Others' as a Share of Income for Male Headed Households, and Table 6.47: Expenditure on Drinking, Rituals, and 'Others' as a Share of Income for Female Headed Households). The expenditure pattern of non-migrants, when contrasted with the migrants is similar in all aspects, except drinking and 'other' outlays, as these are accorded high priority due to the difficult and monotonous occupation of fishing, in case of Kolis.

Electricity Consumed

We decided to analyze this aspect separately, as this area is seen to be a necessity for the non-migrants, while it proves to be a luxury in case of most of the migrants. Over half of the households are found to have this essential service, while the remaining does not on account of poverty. This is a pointer of poor infrastructure not merely in the countryside, but also in pockets of highly advanced cities like Mumbai. In a few cases, we observe electricity being provided for less than half a day on the pretext of high power tariffs to be paid by the resident local owners. A higher proportion of electricity consumption is found among Female Headed Households to the tune of 60 per cent, vis-à-vis Male Headed ones that account for barely 40 per cent for reasons of safety, due to threats from anti-social elements, as well as snakes (See Table 6.48: Electricity Consumption of Total Households, Table 6.49: Electricity Consumption of Male Headed Households, and Table 6.50: Electricity Consumption of Female Headed Households). However, actual use in terms of hours show almost 90 per cent of all migrant households consume electricity for over 12 hours, with Male Headed Households constituting the majority of 95 per cent. Also, only three-fourths of Female Headed Households actually use electricity for over 12 hours, as most of them are working, and the prime use is during the late evening and night hours (See Table 6.51: Number of Hours of Electricity Consumption of Total Households, Table 6.52: Number of Hours of Electricity Consumption of Male Headed Households, and Table 6.53: Number of Hours of Electricity Consumption of Female Headed Households).

Electricity represents a basic necessity for all Kolis, and they consume it almost throughout the day, the only difference being in the units of consumption in accordance with incomes and electrical equipments possessed. Thus, electricity consumption for non-migrants is not tabulated.

Ownership of Assets

We are unable to tabulate asset holding for migrants, as most of them are assetless. Unfortunately, the ones who possess assets are hardly worth the mention, as they own just a few utensils, and table fans due to their meager incomes and migrant status of living. Only a few migrants, who have stayed for over 15 years possess small vessel racks, second hand radio and television sets. Women, under the influence of their non-resident counterparts, have started collecting gold and jewelry to a small extent, especially on festive occasions of Diwali and Dassera. No migrants are seen to own landed property due to basic lack of resources. However, a recently emerging trend of private builders buying land from Kolis has indirectly helped non-Kolis, as they seek cash compensation up to about Rs. 1 lakh, or alternative accommodation in newly constructed buildings in Charkop or elsewhere. Migrants mostly opt for cash settlement, and in many cases are going back to their native places. Thus, this new trend of de-migration would help to develop rural areas and boost incomes via spillover effects of these resources.

On the other hand, most of the Kolis own almost all items of modern living like cots or beds, cupboards, chairs, cooking gas, refrigerators, televisions, radios, and fans. The richer ones also have motorcycles, telephones, cars, rickshaws, and air-conditioners, along with fishing nets, oars, wooden, and fiber boats.

CONCLUSION

The impact of reforms has been quite adverse in case of migrant households, as their employment and incomes are jeopardized in an uncertain labour market. Migrant men are seen to face more competition from their own women, and largely from the Koli men, especially in the categories of labourers and home-based segments. Thus, migrants continued to face erratic employability worsened by low skills, illiteracy, and lack of resources; coupled with high costs of living in the city. Resident non-local men seem to be doubly disadvantaged due to their migratory status that causes several breaks in their jobs, as they are compelled to take to ad hoc employment. Most of the work they undertake is of an informal and temporary nature, as employers give compulsory breaks in service after every 11 months in order to avoid permanent labour due to the fear of trade unionism and collective bargaining. Thus, it reinforces their migratory status. Also, unlike the Kolis, these men face stiff competition from their own women who gain easy access to the unorganized sector; worsened by new male entrants of the resident local community due to retrenchment in formal employment.

These changes are accelerated due to the transition from a command economy to a demand one. Thus, male incomes become highly uncertain and temporary that largely impact women. Migrant females are compelled to join the labour market to augment family incomes and manage high costs of living in the city. This puts additional burdens of market activities on their non-market functions, thereby increasing the stresses and strains of urban living. Various coping strategies ranging from new jobs or extended hours of work to cutting expenses on self, extend to lowering of standards of living for the family, as well as withdrawal of girl children from private schools or beyond the freeship level of standard VII. This leads to the deterioration of the levels of well-being and health of the family, especially girls and women that further reduce their employability in future. Women are seen to fall sick very often, as they are under-nourished, anemic, and over-worked due to a fall in male incomes. We came across peculiar cases of older women working harder and longer by even doing extra jobs to enhance daily earnings due to unemployment or alcoholism of men folk. Migrants live in unhygienic conditions and lack general sanitation due to problems of water, as well as toilet facilities. Their housing conditions are deplorable as they live in tiny spaces without any amenities, despite paying high rents. Also, they continue to be exploited and harassed by the landlords, along with the local hoodlums. Women are often seen to return back from hectic daily schedules in the evenings, and still work for their landlords without any compensation for the fear of evacuation. Few, especially the ones who have stayed for over a decade, considered themselves lucky, as private builders had given them a lakh or two as compensation for evacuation. A few of them have taken the sum and gone back to their villages, which could probably provide resources for investment in their villages. Therefore, the migrant analysis brings out the perils of urban living and ramifications of reform that leads to the marginalization and exploitation of the poorest sections, especially the weaker ones constituted by women.

TABULAR REPRESENTATION OF RESIDENT NON-LOCAL DATA

Table 6.1
Sample Size of Total Households

(in actuals & %)

Gender	*Households*		*Pop.*	
	No.	*%*	*No.*	*%*
Males	23	38.3	112	49.8
Females	37	61.4	113	50.2
Total	60	100.0	225	100.0

Table 6.2
Gendered Distribution of Surveyed Households

(in actuals & %)

Gender	*TH*		*MHH*		*FHH*	
	No	*%*	*No*	*%*	*No*	*%*
Males	55	91.7	23	43.4	4	57.1
Females	5	8.3	30	56.6	3	42.9
Total	60	100.0	53	100.0	7	100.0

Table 6.3
Religious Status of Total Households, Male Headed Households, & Female Headed Households

(in actuals & %)

Religion	*TH*		*MHH*		*FHH*	
	No	*%*	*No*	*%*	*No*	*%*
Hindus	42	70.0	39	73.6	3	42.8
Christians	2	3.3	0	0	2	28.6
Buddhists	16	26.7	14	26.4	2	28.6
Total	60	100.0	53	100.0	7	100.0

Table 6.4
Caste Status of Total Households, Male Headed Households, & Female Headed Households

(in actuals & %)

Caste	TH		MHH		FHH	
	No	*%*	*No*	*%*	*No*	*%*
OBC	6	10.0	5	9.5	1	14.3
SC	17	28.3	15	28.3	2	28.6
General/Open	37	61.7	33	62.2	4	57.5
Total	60	100.0	53	100.0	7	100.0

Table 6.5
Relationship with 'Cultural' Head of Total Households

(in actuals & %)

Relationship	*Total*	%
Self	60	26.7
Wife	51	22.7
Husband	6	2.7
Brother/Brother-in-law	7	3.1
Sister/Sister-in-law	2	0.9
Son/Son-in-law	47	20.9
Daughter/Daughter-in-law	50	22.2
Mother/Mother-in-law	1	0.4
Others	1	0.4
Total	225	100.0

Table 6.6
Relationship with 'Cultural' Head of Male Headed Households

(in actuals & %)

Relationship	*Total*	%
Self	53	26.2
Wife	51	25.2
Husband	2	1.0
Brother/Brother-in-law	6	3.0
Sister/Sister-in-law	2	1.0
Son/Son-in-law	42	20.8
Daughter/Daughter-in-law	44	21.8
Mother/Mother-in-law	1	0.5
Father/Father-in-law	0	0
Others	1	0.5
Total	202	100.0

Table 6.7
Relationship with 'Cultural' Head of Female Headed Households

(in actuals & %)

Relationship	*Total*	%
Self	7	30.4
Husband	4	17.4
Sister/Sister-in-law	1	4.3
Son/Son-in-law	5	21.8
Mother/Mother-in-law	6	26.1
Total	23	100.0

Table 6.8
Age Composition of Total Households

(in actuals & %)

Age Group (yrs.)	*M*		*F*		*Total*	
	No	%	*No*	%	*No*	%
≤ 5	25	65.8	13	34.2	38	100.0
6 to 15	13	30.0	31	70.0	44	100.0
16 to 40	64	50.4	63	49.6	127	100.0
> 40	10	62.5	6	37.5	16	100.0
Total	112	49.8	113	50.2	225	100.0

Table 6.9
Age Composition of Male Headed Households

(in actuals & %)

Age Group (yrs.)	*M*		*F*		*Total*
	No.	%	*No.*	%	
≤ 5	21	67.6	10	32.4	31
6 to 15	15	33.3	30	66.7	45
16 to 40	58	51.3	55	48.7	113
> 40	8	61.6	5	38.4	13
Total	81	47.3	90	52.7	171

Table 6.10
Age Composition of Female Headed Households

(in actuals & %)

Age Group (yrs.)	*M*		*F*		*Total*
	No.	%	*No.*	%	
≤ 5	0	0	1	100.0	1
6 to 15	2	40.0	3	60.0	5
16 to 40	6	42.9	8	57.1	14
> 40	2	66.7	1	33.3	3
Total	10	45.4	12	54.6	22

Table 6.11
Literacy Levels of Total Households

(in actuals & %)

Literacy Level	*M*		*F*		*Total*
	No.	%	*No.*	%	
Illiterate	29	36.7	50	63.3	79
Literate	1	100.0	0	0	1
Primary (Std. I to IV)	17	40.5	25	59.5	42
Middle (Std. V to VIII)	19	63.3	11	36.4	30
High Std. (IX to X)	18	60.0	12	40.0	30
H.S.C. (Std. XI to XII)	3	75.0	1	25.0	4
Degree (Std. XIII to XV)	1	100.0	0	0	1
Technical	0	0	0	0	0
Total	88	47.0	99	53.0	187

Table 6.12
Literacy Levels of Male Headed Households

(in actuals &%)

Age (yrs.)	*5 to 15*					*16 to 40*					*> 40*				
Literacy Level	*No*	*%*	*No*	*%*	*Total*	*No*	*%*	*No*	*%*	*Total*	*No*	*%*	*No*	*%*	*Total*
Illiterate	0	0	6	100.0	6	27	42.9	36	57.1	63	1	20.0	4	80.0	5
Literate	0	0	0	0	0	1	100.0	0	0	1	0	0	0	0	0
Primary (Std. I to IV)	7	33.3	14	66.7	21	9	60.0	6	40.0	15	0	0	0	0	0
Middle (Std. V to VIII)	4	50.0	4	50.0	8	8	57.1	6	42.9	14	2	100.0	0	0	2
High (Std. IX to X)	0	0	1	100.0	1	11	64.7	6	35.3	17	5	83.3	1	16.7	6
H.S.C. (Std. XI to XII)	1	100.0	0	0	1	2	66.7	1	33.3	3	0	0	0	0	0
Degree (Std. XIII to XV)	0	0	0	0	0	0	0	0	0	0	0	0	0	0	0
Technical	0	0	0	0	0	0	0	0	0	0	0	0	0	0	0
Total	12	31	27	69	39	58	51	55	49	113	8	62	5	39	13

Table 6.13
Literacy Levels of Female Headed Households

(in actuals & %)

Age (yrs.)	*5 to 15*					*16 to 40*					*>40*				
Literacy Level	*No*	*%*	*No*	*%*	*Total*	*No*	*%*	*No*	*%*	*Total*	*No*	*%*	*No*	*%*	*Total*
Illiterate	0	0	0	0	0	1	25.0	3	75.0	4	0	0	0	0	0
Literate	0	0	0	0	0	0	0	0	0	0	0	0	0	0	0
Primary (Std. I to IV)	0	0	3	100.0	3	2	50.0	2	50.0	4	0	0	0	0	0
Middle (Std. V to VIII)	2	100.0	0	0	2	2	66.7	1	33.3	3	0	0	0	0	0
High (Std. IX to X)	0	0	0	0	0	1	33.3	2	66.7	3	0	0	0	0	0
H.S.C. (Std. XI to XII)	0	0	0	0	0	0	0	0	0	0	0	0	0	0	0
Degree (Std. XIII to XV)	0	0	0	0	0	0	0	0	0	0	0	0	0	0	0
Technical	0	0	0	0	0	0	0	0	0	0	0	0	0	0	0
Total	2	40.0	3	60.0	5	6	42.9	8	57.1	14	0	0	0	0	0

Table 6.14
Migration Pattern of Total Households, Male Headed Households, & Female Headed Households

(in actuals & %)

No. of years	*TH*		*MHH*		*FHH*	
	No.	*%*	*No.*	*%*	*No.*	*%*
< 1	0	0	0	0	0	0
1 to 10	39	65.0	36	67.9	3	42.8
11 to 20	15	25.0	13	24.5	2	28.6
> 20	6	10.0	4	7.6	2	28.6
Total	60	100.0	53	100.0	7	100.0

Table 6.15
Occupational Activity of Total Households

(in actuals & %)

Occupational Activity	*Male*		*Female*		*Total*
	Actual No.	*% of Total*	*Actual No.*	*% of Total*	
Selling/Cleaning of Vegetables	0	85.7	3	100.0	3
Labourer	54	100.0	9	14.3	63
Owner of Enterprise (Plastic Products)	2	100.0	0	0	2
Working in Factories	3	4.8	0	0	3
Getting Work Home	1	51.8	20	95.2	21
Studying	15	0.0	14	48.2	29
Housewife	0	0.0	5	100.0	5
Domestic service, too old	0	100.0	11	100.0	11
Disabled	1	100.0	0	0	1
Unemployed	2	0	0	0	2
Others	10	0	1	0	11
Selling /Cleaning of vegetables, Getting Work Home	0	0	2	100.0	2
Selling /Cleaning of vegetables, Domestic Service	0	0	2	100.0	2
Labourer, Getting Work Home	0	0	5	100.0	5
Labourer, Domestic Service	0	0	1	100.0	1
Getting Work Home, Studying	0	0	5	100.0	5
Getting Work Home, Domestic Service	0	0	16	100.0	16
Getting Work Home, Others	0	0	2	100.0	2
Getting Work Home, Labourer, Others	0	0	1	100.0	1
Studying, Domestic Service	0	0	1	100.0	1
Studying, Others	0	0	1	100.0	1
Total	88	47.0	99	53.0	187

Table 6.16
Occupational Activity of
Male Headed Households

(in actuals & %)

Occupational Activity	*Male*		*Female*		*Total*
	Actual No.	*% of Total*	*Actual No.*	*% of Total*	
Selling/Cleaning of Vegetables	0	0	1	100.0	1
Labourer	51	88.0	7	12.0	58
Owner of Plastic Enterprise	2	100.0	0	0	2
Working in Factories	1	100.0	0	0	1
Getting Work Home	1	4.8	20	95.2	21
Domestic service	0	0	11	100.0	11
Others	9	90.0	1	10.0	10
Domestic Service, Selling / Cleaning of Vegetables	0	0	1	100.0	1
Domestic Service, Getting Work Home	0	0	13	100.0	13
Domestic Service, abourer	0	0	1	100.0	1
Domestic Service, Studying	0	0	1	100.0	1
Others, Studying	0	0	1	100.0	1
Others, Getting Work Home	0	0	2	100.0	2
Selling/Cleaning of Vegetables, Getting Work Home	0	0	2	100.0	2
Labourer, Getting Work Home	0	0	5	100.0	5
Getting Work Home, Studying	0	0	4	100.0	4
Total	64	47.8	70	52.2	134

Table 6.17
Occupational Activity of
Female Headed Households

(in actuals & %)

Occupational Activity	*Male*		*Female*		*Total*
	Actual No.	*% of Total*	*Actual No.*	*% of Total*	
Selling/Cleaning of Vegetables	0	0	2	100.0	0
Labourer	3	60.0	2	40.0	5
Working in Factories	2	100.0	0	0	2
Others	1	100.0	0	0	1
Domestic Service, Getting Work Home	0	0	3	100.0	3
Domestic service, Selling/ Cleaning of Vegetables	0	0	1	100.0	1
Getting Work Home, Studying	0	0	1	100.0	1
Getting Work Home, Labourer, Others	0	0	1	100.0	1
Total	6	37.5	10	62.50	16

Table 6.18
Intensity of Work of Total Households

(in actuals & %)

Occupational Activity	*Time Schedule (hours)*										*Total*
	4 to 6	6 to 8	8 to 10	10 to 12	12 to 2	2 to 4	4 to 6	6 to 8	8 to 10	10 to 12	
1	33	5	0	0	0	0	0	0	0	0	38
1, 2	34	2	0	0	0	0	0	0	0	0	36
1, 2, 3	1	0	0	0	0	0	0	0	0	0	1
1, 3	1	2	0	0	0	0	0	0	0	0	3
1, 4	0	2	0	0	0	0	0	0	0	0	2
1, 3, 4	1	1	0	0	0	0	0	0	0	0	2
1, 8	0	1	0	0	0	0	0	0	0	0	1
2	0	13	0	0	0	0	0	0	0	0	13
2, 3	0	2	0	0	0	0	0	0	0	0	2
2, 4	0	1	0	0	0	0	0	0	0	0	1
2, 3, 4	0	3	0	0	0	0	0	0	0	0	3
2, 5	0	1	0	0	0	0	0	0	0	0	1
2, 4, 5	0	1	0	0	0	0	0	0	0	0	1
2, 11	0	1	0	0	0	0	0	0	0	0	1
3	0	5	1	0	0	0	0	0	0	0	6
3, 4	0	25	1	0	0	0	0	0	0	0	26
3, 5	0	1	0	0	0	0	0	0	0	0	1
3, 4, 5	0	2	0	1	1	0	0	0	0	0	4
3, 6	0	0	0	0	0	0	0	1	0	0	1
3, 4, 11	0	2	0	0	0	0	0	0	0	0	2
3, 9	0	0	0	0	0	0	0	0	0	0	0
3, 12	0	0	1	0	0	0	0	0	0	0	1
4	0	4	1	1	0	0	0	0	0	0	6
4, 5	0	0	0	0	0	0	0	0	0	0	0
4, 11	0	0	3	0	0	0	0	0	0	0	3
5	0	0	0	2	0	0	0	0	0	0	2
5, 6	0	0	0	0	0	0	0	0	0	0	0
5, 8	0	0	0	1	0	0	0	0	0	0	1
5, 11	0	0	3	0	0	0	0	0	0	0	3
6	0	0	1	4	0	0	10	23	1	0	
6, 11	0	0	2	0	0	1	0	16	3	0	22
6, 12	0	0	0	3	0	0	0	0	0	0	3
7	0	0	0	0	1	0	0	0	0	0	1
7, 11, 12	0	0	0	1	0	0	0	0	0	0	1
7, 12	0	0	1	0	1	0	0	0	0	0	2
8	0	0	2	2	9	5	3	0	6	0	27
8, 11	0	0	11	0	1	0	0	3	3	0	18
8, 12	0	0	0	1	0	1	3	0	1	0	6

Contd...

Occupational Activity	*Time Schedule (hours)*										*Total*
	4 to 6	6 to 8	8 to 10	10 to 12	12 to 2	2 to 4	4 to 6	6 to 8	8 to 10	10 to 12	
8, 13	0	0	0	0	0	8	1	0	5	1	15
9	0	0	0	0	0	0	1	0	1	0	2
10	0	1	5	5	8	4	2	1	0	0	26
11	0	3	17	3	1	1	0	18	17	0	60
11, 12	0	0	7	0	1	0	0	0	0	0	8
12	0	5	29	60	60	46	51	21	10	0	282
12, 13	0	0	0	0	1	1	1	0	0	0	3
13	12	1	0	1	1	18	13	2	36	84	168
13, 1	3	1	0	0	0	0	0	0	0	0	4
11, 13	0	0	0	0	0	0	0	0	2	0	2
Total	85	85	85	85	85	85	85	85	85	85	85

Codes: 1- Fishing (creek), 2-Retail/Selling Fish, 3-Crop Grower (Owner), 4-Selling/Cleaning of Vegetables (Crops), 5-Labourer, 6-Owner of Enterprise (Plastic Products), 7-Working in Factories, 8-Getting Work Home, 9-Studying, 10-House Wife, 11-Domestic Services, 12-Too Old, 13-Disabled, 14-Unemployed, 15-Others (specify).

Table 6.19
Intensity of Work of Male Headed Households

(in hours)

Occupational Activity	*Time Schedule*										*Total*
	4 to 6	6 to 8	8 to 10	10 to 12	12 to 2	2 to 4	4 to 6	6 to 8	8 to 10	10 to 12	
1	26	3	0	0	0	0	0	0	0	0	29
1, 2	31	2	0	0	0	0	0	0	0	0	33
1, 2, 3	1	0	0	0	0	0	0	0	0	0	1
1, 3	1	2	0	0	0	0	0	0	0	0	3
1, 3, 4	1	1	0	0	0	0	0	0	0	0	2
1, 13	3	1	0	0	0	0	0	0	0	0	4
1, 4	0	2	0	0	0	0	0	0	0	0	2
1, 8	0	1	0	0	0	0	0	0	0	0	1
2	0	12	0	0	0	0	0	0	0	0	12
2, 3	0	2	0	0	0	0	0	0	0	0	2
2, 3, 4	0	3	0	0	0	0	0	0	0	0	3
2, 4	0	1	0	0	0	0	0	0	0	0	1
2, 4, 5	0	2	0	0	0	0	0	0	0	0	2
2, 11	0	1	0	0	0	0	0	0	0	0	1
3	0	4	0	0	0	0	0	0	0	0	4

Contd...

Occupational Activity	*Time Schedule*										*Total*
	4 to 6	6 to 8	8 to 10	10 to 12	12 to 2	2 to 4	4 to 6	6 to 8	8 to 10	10 to 12	
3, 4	0	21	1	0	0	0	0	0	0	0	22
3, 5	0	1	0	0	0	0	0	0	0	0	1
3, 8	0	0	0	1	0	0	0	0	0	0	1
3, 6	0	0	0	0	0	0	0	1	0	0	1
3, 4, 5	0	2	0	1	1	0	0	0	0	0	4
3, 4, 11	0	2	0	0	0	0	0	0	0	0	2
4	0	3	1	1	0	0	0	0	0	0	5
4, 11	0	0	3	0	0	0	0	0	0	0	3
5	0	0	0	2	0	0	0	0	0	0	2
5, 11	0	0	3	0	0	0	0	0	0	0	3
6	0	0	1	4	0	0	9	22	1	0	37
6, 11	0	0	2	0	0	1	0	14	3	0	20
6, 12	0	0	0	3	0	0	0	0	0	0	3
7	0	0	0	0	1	0	0	0	0	0	1
7, 12	0	0	1	0	1	0	0	0	0	0	2
8	0	0	2	2	9	5	3	0	5	0	26
8, 11	0	0	1	0	1	0	0	3	3	0	18
8, 12	0	0	0	1	0	1	3	0	1	0	6
8, 13	0	0	0	0	0	8	1	0	5	1	15
9	0	0	0	0	0	0	1	0	0	0	1
10	0	1	5	5	7	3	1	1	0	0	23
11	0	3	16	3	1	1	0	17	17	0	58
11, 12	0	0	3	0	0	0	0	0	0	0	3
11, 13	0	0	0	0	0	0	0	0	1	0	1
12	0	4	26	51	52	39	45	16	8	0	241
12, 13	0	0	0	0	1	1	0	0	0	0	2
13	12	1	0	1	1	16	12	1	31	74	149
Total	75	75	75	75	75	75	75	75	75	75	750

Codes: 1- Fishing (creek), 2-Retail/Selling Fish, 3-Crop Grower (Owner), 4-Selling/Cleaning of Vegetables (Crops), 5-Labourer, 6-Owner of Enterprise (Plastic Products), 7-Working in Factories, 8-Getting Work Home, 9-Studying, 10-House Wife, 11-Domestic Services, 12-Too Old, 13-Disabled, 14-Unemployed, 15-Others (specify).

Table 6.20
Intensity of Work of
Female Headed Households

(in hours)

Occupational Activity	*Time Schedule*										*Total*
	4 to 6	6 to 8	8 to 10	10 to 12	12 to 2	2 to 4	4 to 6	6 to 8	8 to 10	10 to 12	
1	7	2	0	0	0	0	0	0	0	0	9
1, 2	2	0	0	0	0	0	0	0	0	0	2
1, 2, 3	1	0	0	0	0	0	0	0	0	0	1
2	0	1	0	0	0	0	0	0	0	0	1
2, 5	0	1	0	0	0	0	0	0	0	0	1
3	0	1	1	0	0	0	0	0	0	0	2
3, 4	0	2	0	0	0	0	0	0	0	0	2
3, 12	0	0	1	0	0	0	0	0	0	0	1
3, 8	0	0	0	0	0	0	0	0	0	1	1
3, 4, 11	0	0	0	0	0	0	0	0	0	0	0
4	0	1	0	0	0	0	0	0	0	0	1
6	0	0	0	0	0	0	1	2	0	0	3
6, 11	0	0	0	0	0	0	0	1	0	0	1
7, 11, 12	0	0	0	1	0	0	0	0	0	0	1
8	0	0	0	0	0	0	0	0	1	0	1
9	0	0	0	0	0	0	0	0	1	0	1
10	0	0	0	0	0	0	0	1	1	0	2
11	0	0	4	0	1	0	0	0	0	0	5
11, 12	0	0	0	0	0	0	0	0	1	0	1
11, 13	0	2	3	9	9	7	6	5	2	0	43
12	0	0	0	0	0	0	1	0	0	0	1
12, 13	0	0	0	0	0	0	1	0	0	0	1
13	0	0	0	0	0	2	1	1	4	9	17
Total	10	10	10	10	10	10	10	10	10	10	100

Codes: 1- Fishing (creek), 2-Retail/Selling Fish, 3-Crop Grower (Owner), 4-Selling/Cleaning of Vegetables (Crops), 5-Labourer, 6-Owner of Enterprise (Plastic Products), 7-Working in Factories, 8-Getting Work Home, 9-Studying, 10-House Wife, 11-Domestic Services, 12-Too Old, 13-Disabled, 14-Unemployed, 15-Others (specify).

Table 6.21
Time Span of Work of Women of Total Households, Male Headed Households, & Female Headed Households

(in years)

	Time Span of Work																		
	< 1						*1 to 10*						*< 10*						
	TH		*MHH*		*FHH*		*TH*		*MHH*		*FHH*		*TH*		*MHH*		*FHH*		*Total*
Age Group	*No.*	*%*	*No.*	*%*	*No.*	*%*	*No.*	*%*	*No.*	*%*	*No.*	*%*	*No.*	*%*	*No.*	*%*	*No.*	*%*	
< 14	0	0	0	0	0	0	12	0	11	0	1	0	0	0	0	0	0	0	24
14 to 45	1	1.5	0	0	0	0	52	78.8	49	0	3	0	13	19.7	10	17.0	6	0	134
> 45	0	0	0	0	0	0	2	100.0	2	0	0	0	0	0	0	0	0	0	4
Total	1	0	0	0	0	0	66	0	62	0	4	0	13	0	10	0	6	0	162

Table 6.22
Job Change of Women of Total Households, Male Headed Households, & Female Headed Households

(in actuals & %)

Age Group	Job Change														
	TH				MHH				FHH				Total		
	Yes		No		Yes		No		Yes		No		TH	MHH	FHH
(Yrs.)	No.	%	No.	%	No.	%	No.	%	No.	%	No.	%			
< 14	4	33.3	8	66.7	3	27.2	8	72.8	0	0	1	100.0	12	11	1
14 to 45	28	42.4	38	57.6	22	37.3	37	62.7	7	77.8	2	22.2	66	59	9
> 45	0	0	2	100.0	0	0	0	0	0	0	0	0	2	0	0
Total	3	0	48	0	25	0	45	0	7	70.0	3	30.0	80	70	10

Table 6.23
Duration of Job Change of Women of Total Households, Male Headed Households, & Female Headed Households

(in actuals & %)

	Duration of Job Change (years)																	
	< 2						2 to 10						< 10					
	TH		MHH		FHH		TH		MHH		FHH		TH		MHH		FHH	
Age Group	*No.*	*%*	*No.*	*%*	*No.*	*%*	*No.*	*%*	*No.*	*%*	*No.*	*%*	*No.*	*%*	*No.*	*%*	*No.*	*%*
< 14	0	0	0	0	0	0	2	100.0	2	100.0	0	0	0	0	0	0	0	0
14 to 45	3	9.7	3	10.0	0	0	27	87.1	26	86.7	5	83.3	1	3.2	1	3.3	1	16.7
> 45	0	0	0	0	0	0	0	0	0	0	0	0	0	0	0	0	0	0
Total	3	0	0	0	0	0	29	0	28	0	5	0	1	0	1	0	1	0

Table 6.24
Activity Change of Total Households

(in actuals & %)

	Age Groups (yrs.)						
	< 14		*14 to 45*		*> 45*		*Total*
Activity	*No.*	*%*	*No.*	*%*	*No.*	*%*	
Retailing Fish to Casual Labour	1	50.0	1	50.0	0	0	2
Crop Growing to Retailing Fish	0	0	2	100.0	0	0	2
Crop Growing to Retailing Vegetables	0	0	4	100.0	0	0	4
Crop Growing to Casual Labour	2	15.4	11	84.6	0	0	13
Retailing Vegetables to Crop Growing	0	0	1	100.0	0	0	1
Retailing Vegetables to Casual Labour	0	0	3	100.0	0	0	3
Casual Labour to Retailing Fish	0	0	1	100.0	0	0	1
Casual Labour to Entrepreneurship of Plastic Enterprises	0	0	3	100.0	0	0	3
Entrepreneurship of Plastic Enterprises to Crop Growing	0	0	2	100.0	0	0	2
Entrepreneurship of Plastic Enterprises to Casual Labour	0	0	1	100.0	0	0	1
Total	3	0	29	0	0	0	32

Table 6.25
Activity Change of Male Headed Households

(in actuals & %)

	Age Groups (yrs.)						
	< 14		*14 to 45*		*> 45*		*Total*
Activity	*No.*	*%*	*No.*	*%*	*No.*	*%*	
Crop Growing to Retailing Vegetables	0	0	1	100.0	0	0	1
Crop Growing to Casual Labour (& Crop Growing)	0	0	2	100.0	0	0	2
Crop Growing to Retailing Fish	0	0	2	100.0	0	0	2
Crop Growing to Retailing/ Entrepreneurship Fish (& Crop Growing)	0	0	1	100.0	0	0	1
Casual Labour to Entrepreneurship of Plastic Enterprises	0	0	1	100.0	0	0	1
Entrepreneurship of Plastic Enterprises to Crop Growing (& Casual Labour)	0	0	0	0	0	0	0
Total	1	2	2	1	1	0	7

Table 6.26
Activity Change of Female Headed Households

(in actuals & %)

	Age Groups (yrs.)						
	< 14		*14 to 45*		*> 45*		*Total*
Activity	*No.*	*%*	*No.*	*%*	*No.*	*%*	
Retailing Fish to Labourer (& Retailing Fish)	0	0	1	100.0	0	0	1
Crop Growing to Retailing	0	0	1	100.0	0	0	1
Crop Growing to Casual Labour (& Crop Growing)	2	0	9	0	0	0	11
Crop Growing to Retailing Vegetables (& Crop Growing)	0	0	1	100.0	0	0	1
Crop Growing to Retailing Vegetables (& Crop Growing)	0	0	1	100.0	0	0	1
Retailing Vegetables to Casual Labour (& Retailing Vegetables)	0	0	2	100.0	0	0	2
Retailing Vegetables to Crop Growing (& Retailing Vegetables)	0	0	1	100.0	0	0	1
Total	2	0	16	0	0	0	18

Table 6.27
Average Monthly Income (AMI) of Total Households

(in actuals & %)

AMI Group (Rs. p.m.)	*M*		*F*		*Total*
	No.	*%*	*No.*	*%*	
< 500	0	0	5	100.0	5
500 to 1000	8	17.0	39	83.0	47
1001 to 2000	14	33.3	28	66.7	42
2001 to 3000	29	80.6	7	19.4	36
3001 to 4000	15	100.0	0	0	15
> 4000	4	80.0	1	20.0	5
Total	70	46.7	80	53.3	150

Table 6.28
Average Monthly Income (AMI) of Male Headed Households

(in actuals & %)

AMI Group (Rs. p.m.)	*M*		*F*		*Total*
	No.	*%*	*No.*	*%*	
< 500	0	0	5	100.0	5
500 to 1000	6	14.3	36	85.7	42
1001 to 2000	12	33.3	24	66.7	36
2001 to 3000	28	84.9	5	15.1	33
3001 to 4000	14	100.0	0	0	14
> 4000	4	100.0	0	0	4
Total	64	47.8	70	52.2	134

Table 6.29
Average Monthly Income
(AMI) of Female Headed Households

(in actuals & %)

AMI Group (Rs. p.m.)	*M*		*F*		*Total*
	No.	*%*	*No.*	*%*	
< 500	0	0	0	0	0
500 to 1000	2	40.0	3	60.0	5
1001 to 2000	2	33.3	4	66.7	6
2001 to 3000	1	33.3	2	66.7	3
3001 to 4000	1	100.0	0	0	1
> 4000	0	0	1	100.0	1
Total	6	37.5	10	62.5	16

Table 6.30
Earning Months in a Year of Total Households

(in actuals & %)

Months	*M*		*F*		*Total*
	No.	*%*	*No.*	*%*	
< 6	14	100.0	0	0	14
> 6	56	41.1	80	58.9	136
Total	70	46.7	80	53.3	150

Table 6.31
Earning Months in a year of
Male Headed Households

(in actuals & %)

Months	*M*		*F*		*Total*
	No.	*%*	*No.*	*%*	
< 6	14	63.7	8	36.3	22
> 6	50	44.7	62	55.3	112
Total	64	47.8	70	52.2	134

Table 6.32
Earning Months in a year of
Female Headed Households

(in actuals & %)

Months	*M*		*F*		*Total*
	No.	*%*	*No.*	*%*	
< 6	0	0	0	0	0
> 6	6	37.5	10	62.5	16
Total	6	37.5	10	62.5	16

Table 6.33
Total Expenditure as a Share of Income of Total Households

(in actuals & %)

Expenditure Group (Rs. p.m.)	*No.*	%
< 1000	5	4.2
1001 to 2000	30	25.5
2001 to 3000	42	35.6
3001 to 4000	23	19.5
4001 to 5000	8	6.8
> 5000	10	8.4
Total	118	100.0

Table 6.34
Total Expenditure as a Share of Income of Male Headed Households

(in actuals & %)

Expenditure Group (Rs. p.m.)	*No.*	%
< 1000	3	5.6
1001 to 2000	13	24.5
2001 to 3000	20	37.7
3001 to 4000	12	22.6
4001 to 5000	4	7.6
> 5000	1	2.0
Total	53	100.0

Table 6.35
Total Expenditure as a Share of Income of Female Headed Households

(in actuals & %)

Expenditure Group (Rs. p.m.)	*No.*	%
< 1000	0	0
1001 to 2000	3	43
2001 to 3000	0	0
3001 to 4000	3	43
4001 to 5000	1	14
> 5000	0	0
Total	7	100.0

Table 6.36
Expenditure on Food as a Share of Income of Total Households

(in actuals & %)

% Categories	*Households*	
	No.	%
< 25	1	0.9
25.1 to 50	19	16.1
50.1 to 75	89	75.4
75.1 to 100	9	7.6
Total	118	100.0

Table 6.37
Expenditure on Food as a Share of Income of Male Headed Households
(in actuals & %)

% Categories	*Households* *No.*	*%*
< 25	1	2.0
25.1 to 50	17	32.0
50.1 to 75	33	62.2
75.1 to 100	2	3.8
Total	53	100.0

Table 6.38
Expenditure on Food as a Share of Income of Female Headed Households
(in actuals & %)

% Categories	*Households* *No.*	*%*
0 to 25	0	0
25.1 to 50	2	28.6
50.1 to 75	4	57.2
75.1 to 100	1	14.2
Total	7	100.0

Table 6.39
Expenditure on Clothing as a Share of Income of Total Households
(in actuals & %)

Expenditure Group	*Households* *No.*	*%*
0	3	2.6
1 to 10	50	42.3
10.1 to 20	45	38.1
20.1 to 30	19	16.1
> 30	1	0.9
Total	118	100

Table 6.40
Expenditure on Clothing as a Share of Income of Male Headed Households
(in actuals & %)

Expenditure Group	*Households* *No.*	*%*
0	2	3.8
1 to 10	12	22.6
10.1 to 20	31	58.5
20.1 to 30	6	11.3
> 30	2	3.8
Total	53	100

Table 6.41
Expenditure on Clothing as a Share of Income of Female Headed Households

(in actuals & %)

Expenditure Group	*Households*	
	No.	*%*
0	1	14.2
1 to 10	3	42.9
10.1 to 20	3	42.9
20.1 to 30	0	0
> 30	0	0
Total	7	100.0

Table 6.42
Expenditure on Health, Education, Transport, & Shelter as a Share of Income of Total Households

(in actuals & %)

	Households								
%	*Health*		*Education*		*Transport*		*Shelter*		*Total*
Categories	*No.*	*%*	*No.*	*%*	*No.*	*%*	*No.*	*%*	
0	2	1.6	90	76.3	58	49.1	52	44.1	202
< 5	60	50.9	7	6.0	14	11.9	43	36.4	124
5.1 to 10	45	38.1	9	7.7	23	19.6	20	17.0	97
10.1 to 15	7	6.0	6	5.0	12	10	2	1.6	27
15.1 to 20	4	3.4	2	1.6	6	5.1	1	0.9	13
> 20	0	0	4	3.4	5	4.2	0	0	9
Total	118	100.0	118	100.0	118	100.0	118	100.0	472

Table 6.43
Expenditure on Health, Education, Transport, & Shelter as a Share of Income of Male Headed Households

(in actuals & %)

Expenditure	*Households*				
Group	*Health*	*Education*	*Transport*	*Shelter*	*Total*
0	2	40	28	1	71
< 1	21	8	7	7	45
1 to 10	24	2	10	29	77
10.1 to 20	6	2	4	8	51
20.1 to 30	0	1	3	5	15
> 30	0	0	0	3	6
Total	53	53	53	53	265

Table 6.44
Expenditure on Health, Education, Transport, & Shelter as a Share of Income of Female Headed Households

(in actuals & %)

Expenditure Group	*Households*				
	Health	*Education*	*Transport*	*Shelter*	*Total*
0	0	1	3	6	10
< 5	1	4	2	1	8
5.1 to 10	2	1	0	0	3
10.1 to 15	3	0	0	0	3
15.1 to 20	0	0	1	0	1
> 20	1	1	1	0	3
Total	7	7	7	7	28

Table 6.45
Expenditure on Drinking, Rituals, & 'Others' as a Share of Income of Total Households

(in actuals & %)

	Households						
% of Income	Drinking		Rituals		'Others'		*Total*
	No.	*%*	*No.*	*%*	*No.*	*%*	
≤ 1	111	94	26	22.0	9	7.7	146
1.1 to 2	1	0.8	14	11.9	1	0.9	16
2.1 to 3	1	0.8	20	17.0	9	7.7	30
3.1 to 4	2	1.8	12	10.1	16	13.6	30
4.1 to 5	1	0.8	7	6.0	14	11.7	22
> 5	2	1.8	39	33.0	69	58.4	110
Total	118	100.0	118	100.0	118	100.0	354

Table 6.46
Expenditure on Drinking, Rituals, & 'Others' as a Share of Income of Male Headed Households

(in actuals & %)

	Households						
% of Income	Drinking		Rituals		'Others'		*Total*
	No.	*%*	*No.*	*%*	*No.*	*%*	
0	4	7.6	33	62.2	3	5.7	40
< 1	3	5.7	8	15	1	1.9	12
1.1 to 2	24	45.2	4	7.6	13	25	41
2.1 to 3	11	20.8	4	7.6	8	15	23
3.1 to 4	6	11.2	2	3.8	7	13.2	15
4.1 to 5	2	3.8	1	1.9	5	9	8
> 5	3	5.7	1	1.9	16	30.1	20
Total	53	100.0	53	100.0	53	100.0	459

Table 6.47
Expenditure on Drinking, Rituals, & 'Others' as a Share of Income of Female Headed Households

(in actuals & %)

	Households						
% of Income	Drinking		Rituals		'Others'		*Total*
	No.	%	*No.*	%	*No.*	%	
0	15	38.5	38	97.4	2	5.1	55
< 1	2	5.1	0	0	0	0	2
1.1 to 2	3	7.7	1	2.6	1	2.6	5
2.1 to 3	4	10.2	0	0	5	12.8	9
3.1 to 4	2	5.1	0	0	8	20.5	101
4.1 to 5	0	0	0	0	1	2.6	1
> 5	13	33.4	0	0	22	56.4	35
Total	39	100.0	39	100.0	39	100.0	117

Table 6.48
Electricity Consumption of Total Households

(in actuals & %)

Response	*No*	%
Yes	26	43.3
No	34	56.7
Total	60	100.0

Table 6.49
Electricity Consumption of Male Headed Households

(in actuals & %)

Response	*No*	%
Yes	22	41.5
No	31	58.5
Total	53	100.0

Table 6.50
Electricity Consumption of Female Headed Households

(in actuals & %)

Response	*No*	%
Yes	4	57.1
No	3	42.9
Total	7	100.0

Table 6.51
Number of Hours of Electricity Consumption of Total Households

(in actuals & %)

Duration (hrs.)	*No*	%
< 12	2	7.7
12 to 24	24	92.3
Total	26	100.0

Table 6.52
Number of Hours of Electricity Consumption of Male Headed Households

(in actuals & %)

Duration (hrs.)	*No*	%
< 12	1	4.6
12 to 24	21	95.4
22	100.0	

Table 6.53
Number of Hours of Electricity Consumption of Female Headed Households

(in actuals & %)

Duration (hrs.)	*No*	%
< 12	1	25.0
12 to 24	3	75.0
Total	4	100.0

7

CONCLUSIONS AND POLICY RECOMMENDATIONS

INTRODUCTION

A summary of conclusions of our exhaustive study of the gendered nature of restructuring and integration is brought out in this chapter. Findings of individual researchers and various data sources at the secondary level in Chapters two and three, respectively reiterate the growing importance of the informal sector and women workers on account of globalization and reforms at the macro level. Detailed field work analysis and results of the resident local and migrant population of Charkop are in conformity with these national trends of 'feminization of work, livelihoods, poverty, and the formal sector'. Thus, a synchronization and synthesis of the macro and micro levels is highlighted on account of the transition from a 'Command' to a 'Demand' economy which has its bearings on the grass roots. A revisit of the definitional aspects of the informal sector, along with policies that recognize the growing importance of women workers and empathize with their dual burdens of production and reproduction are suggested. Grass root findings on employment, income, expenditure, and ownership of assets, along with responses to globalization and emerging survival strategies are used to suggest micro level recommendations for gender-just development. Thus, we attempt to show the effect of national policies on the micro level, and put forth suggestions in the larger macro perspective. Simultaneously, we have also pointed out certain limitations of the study.

FINDINGS OF MACRO ANALYSIS

Introduction

We begin by briefly re-visiting the definitional aspects pertaining to the urban informal sector since Hart coined the term, to the UN-introduced changes in its classification system along with the contribution of individual researchers in the following Section. The next section summarizes findings of macro level studies carried out world over, followed by relevant national studies in India which we have already examined in Chapter 2.

Definitional Changes in the Concept of the Urban Informal Sector (UIS)

Definitional changes in the meaning of the informal sector have been discussed in detail in the chapter on review of literature. As seen earlier, the origins of the informal sector were associated with the post-World War II period that emphasized the 'trickle down theory' to solve problems of underdevelopment and dualism faced by UDC's. The growth of the modern industries was expected to absorb surplus labour from the traditional agrarian sector. In fact, this further deepened the dependency between the two sectors, and the predictions of the fading away or merging of the unorganized sector were falsified.

Keith Hart coined the term 'Informal Sector' in early seventies, "referring to a number of income and employment generating activities in the 'unenumerated' sector of urban settlements, thereby covering self-employed individuals and the urban proletariat" (Hart, 1973, pp. 61-89). The concept was formalized by the ILO at its Employment Strategy Mission in Kenya, leading to policy research in this area. Overemphasis on formal sector activities led to a neglect of the mass of informal sector workers, resulting in an increasing concern with 'Decent Work'. The failure of percolation theories further worsened the condition of informal labour, as their 'worker' status remained out of the definitional coverage of 'employed labour'. This in turn accelerated the marginal, temporary, and residual nature of informal work despite proliferation of this segment and its activities. Also, the poorest amongst these like women, migrants, and home-based workers became more vulnerable and exploitable despite their rising numbers.

The various definitions of the urban informal sector became more elusive and difficult to pinpoint, as different people used it in different contexts. The ILO's earlier definition in 1970's of the informal sector referred to the working poor involved in the production of goods and services, whose activities were not recognized, recorded, protected or regulated by public authorities.

Two decades later, the ILO introduced a definitional change, as the focus shifted from workers to employers of the informal sector enterprises. There was a further enhancement in this definition to cover the informal sector beyond the traditional confines of the type of workplace, to the use of fixed capital assets, duration of the operation of the enterprise to detailed activities generated by the informal sector. The nineties demonstrated a widening of the earlier definitions to include OAME's and also 'Enterprises of informal employers'.

Most of the studies by individual researchers have somewhat similar conclusions that focus on emerging trends and issues in the labour market. There is an increase in the amount of employment, income, and activities in the informal sector; thus causing 'informalization of the formal sector'. This is evident in falling shares of the organized vis-à-vis the unorganized segment. The words 'informal' and 'unorganized' are used as synonyms, as are 'formal' and 'organized' used interchangeably. The growing informal sector is characterized by a large amount of women workers due to easy entry and exit, and no skill or education bar thus, cutting across the gender, class, colour, and race bars. All this results in 'feminization of the informal sector' itself. The nature of work is temporary, casual, and insecure, reiterating the flexibilization of labour markets. Reforms led to growth in tradables, but not in employment that culminated into a 'jobless growth'. Women's entry into the market arena has caused several conflicts on their home front, as the divide between paid and unpaid work increases. Simultaneously, multi-tasking further masks their invisibility and leads to under-counting and lower estimation of this segment of workers. A paradoxical fragmentation occurs, as females compete with men, and vice-versa. The former arises due to loss of male earnings, compelling women to undertake income augmentation that is popular among the poorer sections. Men try to enter the female-dominated informal sector, due to loss of jobs in the formal segment. The competition becomes stiffer, as women themselves stand divided. Globalization and export-led growth readily provide jobs to young and unmarried girls as they are docile, non-unionized, and exploitable. Employers do not prefer married women on account of frequent leave, maternity benefits, crèches, and other related services associated with them. Women who are poor are doubly dis-advantaged due to gender, and class differentiation.

Globalization reduces all guarantees of employment, and cut-back in subsidies also challenge women's adjustment. Thus, meager incomes have to match increasing expenditures worsened by inflation and falling public distribution support; all causing poverty, indebtedness, migration; along with deteriorating mental and physical health. The number of Female Headed Households, divorces, and loss of male members are common repercussions. Expenditure and living standards are hit, forcing people to either live with poverty, or work harder to maintain pre-reform standards. Women and female children bear the brunt of restructuring on account of rising school dropout ratios, as the burden of the girl child also increases. Strangely, women do not control their own earnings, thereby continuing to remain asset less, as well as without resources. A major part of the above findings are also reflected in our field work of Charkop.

Summary of Macro Level Studies on the Informal Sector

This section briefly summarizes the findings of major macro studies that point to the growing importance of the informal sector which were mentioned briefly in the earlier part. Leading institutional studies show that this segment is growing rapidly, accounting for a higher share of women to the tune of over 90 per cent. Despite the dominant trend of 'feminization of work and the informal sector', its contribution goes unaccounted, and under-reported in official national accounts. This sector has increased in size, and operations that cover services and industries, apart from traditional agrarian ones. Thus, the initial predictions of its transitory nature are highly debatable, especially in post-nineties. In fact, the formal sector is shrinking, while the informal section shows a reversal.

Restructuring labour markets, urbanization, population explosion, and rising migration have posed challenges that the formal sector is unable to address. The unorganized segment is becoming pivotal in terms of livelihoods, incomes, and production. Majority of its employees are women, thereby further raising their wage and non-wage burden, thus escalating the debate between paid and unpaid labour. The quantitative dimensions of work in a globalizing world may have risen, but the quality and security of employment is questionable. Many researchers through their case studies have captured the emerging trend of informalization as a result of reforms in both the organized and unorganized segments of the labour market. This was primarily caused by the inherent casual and low-yielding nature of informal work, on one hand; coupled with lack of estimation in national income accounting, on the other. All this resulted in widening of the gender gap and exclusion of female workers from the organized stream in terms of employment opportunities and upward mobility. Women in the unorganized sector were worst hit due to gender-based segmentation of the labour market, and their 'marginal' status (See Breman, 2005, pp. 2500-2506; Census of India, 1991, pp. 527-43; Dewan, 1999, p. 427; Planning Commission, 2000, p. 225).

Globalization has accelerated the imbalance between paid and unpaid work, and as documented by time use surveys across the globe; women continue to carry a disproportionately greater burden of non-market activities representing the care economy, exceeding that of men (Economic Survey, 2001-02, pp.240-250). Thus, almost universally, women's contribution to the economy, society, and the household went unrecognized, as most of their activities were not in the sphere of the market, and remained non-monetized. Also, most of female work being interspersed with other household chores makes it difficult to measure their economic work and differentiate it from the extra-economic tasks. This was further complicated in developing economies like India, as women were traditionally involved in non-market, subsistence, economic activities; that were not recognized as work, despite representing basic survival strategies, especially of poor households (See Bardhan, 1985, pp. 2261-69; Dewan, 1999, pp. 425-427; Government of India, 1988). Emerging trends of 'feminization of work and poverty' were confirmed, as globally the ratio of women to men in economic activity more than doubled over the two-decade period of 1970-90. Also, women increasingly shouldered the bulk of 70 per cent of unpaid work, thereby leading to 'feminization of poverty'. Export-led globalization increased the invisibility and vulnerability of mainly women in the third world due to EPZ's, and BPO proliferation (See Brigitte, 1985, pp. 279-80; and Date-Bah, 1997, pp. 2-5).

Chaganti, (2004, pp. 2220-2224); Dubey, (1996, p. 56); and Panitch, L. and Colin Leys, (2001, pp. 280-295) point out an emerging contrasting trend of a new class of 'mommy managers' or 'home-makers', who have given up their professional careers to settle down as caregivers, and thus, focused on extra-economic roles at the cost of economic ones. This has created an imbalance of gender-biased development, as women with capabilities became victims of gender stereotyping, and their illiterate and poor counterparts also suffered due to additional burdens they faced as income-augmenters. Thus, the current occupational class structure has created two groups of women in relation to domestic work and the care economy, those who have no time to do it, and those who have no alternative, but to do it.

Also, another segment of women workers emerging are 'Home workers' or 'flexi workers' that further increase their invisibility and vulnerability, along with over-representation in all kinds of irregular work (Mukherjee, 2004, pp. 282-84; Ratna Kumari, 2001, p. 3603). Three noticeable outcomes of the on-going reforms and deregulation are visible in the form of informalization, feminization, along with widening gender differentials, and re-emergence of home-based work as an important part of industrial production (See Kelkar, 2005, pp. 4690-4693). All the above trends have been documented and tabulated by our field work analysis in an exhaustive manner.

We now focus on the conclusions of results of prominent macro level data analysis at the national, state, district, and ward level data sources generated by various Economic and Population Censuses, Annual Survey of Industries, and National Sample Survey in India. The National Sample Survey (NSS) provided valuable State-level information, especially pertaining to the informal sector, along with special data generated for our study in the chosen areas of economic activity. The Directorate of Economics and Statistics was very helpful for Mumbai level data, which was enriched by the Brihan Mumbai Corporation's ward level information. As noted in the chapter on secondary data, its incorporation is essential to make any research complete and holistic, which may seem an easy due to an apparent 'ready reckoner' nature.

Unfortunately, we experienced a series of snags and gaps in the collection, tabulation, and availability to general public due to administrative delays, funding issues related to publishing, worsened by frequent transfers of research officers, government files and documents. Despite these teething problems, secondary data has enriched our analysis, and helped to draw few contrasts and comparisons with our primary data. More importantly, it becomes imperative to link macro and micro level analysis to draw conclusions on recent trends in the labour market.

The world of work is being drastically affected by reforms world over, especially in India, which has almost universally led to the 'informalization and feminization of livelihoods'. The informal sector accounts for about 95 per cent of employment in India, as the share of the formal sector has been continuously and rapidly shrinking. The Population Census data was analyzed at the levels of Maharashtra State, Urban Maharashtra, and Greater Bombay (Mumbai) for the decades of 1991 and 2001. In terms of total workers, at the All-India level, males represented over three-fourths of main workers that increased in the categories of cultivators; and livestock, forestry, fishing, plantations, orchards, and allied activities, and other services to about 80 per cent. The presence of females' further reduced to approximately 10 per cent in trade and commerce, and other than household industry. The Maharashtra State figures portrayed an improvement in women worker ratios of about one-third in case of main workers, which were seen to particularly rise in the category of cultivators to about 40 per cent, with one-thirds contribution to household industry. At the Greater Mumbai level, the share of women main workers was lower at 14 per cent, along with one-fifth contribution in case of all other chosen sectors. Similarly, a further downturn was observed in all categories at the R/S Ward level, as the percentage of female workers ranged between 10 and 20 per cent. The falling ratios continued even at the Kandivali and Charkop level, with the exception of the 'other services' category, where female shares rose to one-third.

The 2001 Census figures showed a rise in women workers in the category of cultivators to one-thirds, and an almost equalization with males in case of household industry at the national level.

Similar results were reiterated at the State, and Urban State, and Mumbai levels. No disaggregated data was available at the Ward, and Kandivali and Charkop levels due to administrative delays. Besides, no comparisons could be made in terms of occupational codes, as the 1991 Census had clubbed together various activities like livestock, forestry, fishing, other than household industry, trade, and commerce, and other services. On the other hand, the 2001 Census had introduced 2 new categories of household workers, and other workers; which cannot be compared with the earlier decade due to lack of reference category. In percentage terms, the analysis looked quite different, as 1991 figures showed that the metropolis accounted for over one-thirds of Urban Maharashtra's main workers, with hardly any male majority. The mega city also accounted for one-thirds of Urban State's secondary sector workers, maximum of who were males. The 1991 data had clubbed a number of activities from the primary, secondary, and tertiary sectors in the category of 'other than household activity'; that showed 40 per cent representation at the Mumbai level, with no female domination. The R/S Ward level accounted for 4 per cent of main workers, majority of who were men. Cultivators accounted for a similar proportion as Mumbai's main workers, the only difference being that these were equitably distributed between the two genders. The ward represented about 6 per cent of Greater Mumbai's household industry that also mirrored maximum males. We were unable to look at the respective shares of 'other than household industry', and trade and commerce, as these were clubbed together at the Greater Mumbai level. Kandivali and Charkop represent half of the ward's main workers, with a female share of 60 per cent, thus showed a reversal. Surprisingly, cultivation constituted a major occupation accounting for 60 per cent of activity, which represented two-thirds male presence. This conclusion was reversed in our field survey of Charkop Village, as females were the major cultivators. Two-thirds of ward level workers were involved in the category of 'livestock, forestry, fishing, hunting, and plantations, orchards, and allied activities', of which women accounted for an 80 per cent majority; which was similar to our field data. One-third of household and half of non-household industry involving a female dominance were observed in the Kandivali and Charkop figures as a share of the ward figures that coincided with our findings.

The area also accounted for two-thirds of trade and commerce workers, with a male majority that mirrored in our field survey. Similar results were seen in case of other service workers, along with their female prominence.

The 2001 Census figures showed a relative drop from one-third to one-forth in case of Mumbai's share of main workers as a percentage of Urban Maharashtra, maximum being males. The proportion of cultivators had more than doubled in the metropolis in comparison with the earlier census. Similar results were observed in segments of household industry and 'other workers' depicting male concentration. On the whole, the decadal variations denote an increase in non-formal employment, as well as primary sector due to lack of secondary sector jobs in the post-reform period. Most of these were dominated by men because of shrinking avenues in the organized segment, along with escalation of female participants on account of income-augmentation. This trend of 'informalization, casualization, and feminization of work' become almost universal, and was also mirrored in our field survey.

The Economic Census data for the State of Maharashtra for 1990 and 1998 according to major industry groupings reiterated the findings of the Population Censuses seen earlier. The number of persons working usually had decreased marginally, along with similar results in the category of manufacturing and repair services. Small increases were also observed in the segment of 'community, social, and personal services' in actual and percentage terms. Agriculture showed a small percentage decline, despite a rise in the actual number of workers employed. Thus, the secondary sector and formal job shares fell in the post-reform period with a rise in the tertiary and primary sector employment. Unfortunately, no gender-disaggregated data was available, and neither was any information released on the current decade to enable suitable comparisons with other secondary sources.

The National Sample Survey (NSS) data was of great importance to our study, as it dealt with most of the occupational activities carried out by the field respondents, and also because the officials were very helpful in generating special data for us. Various rounds conducted by the NSS provided valuable information on employment trends in different sectors at the national and state levels. We used the data generated by the 50th and 55th rounds for five chosen areas of livelihood at the

Maharashtra, Urban Maharashtra, and Mumbai levels. A summary of NSS results at the 50th and 55th round relevant to our fieldwork activities showed mixed trends in employment. In accordance with the two rounds, an overall decline followed by constancy was noticed in the area of 'retail sale of meat, fish, and poultry'; with a marginal uptrend for females. Besides, no exclusive information on fish is available, as it is clubbed with meat and poultry; thereby probably reducing its separate contribution. However, women's employment was even higher than total, thus confirming female-domination of this industry.

Turning to 'manufacture of rubber, plastic, petroleum, and coal products; processing of nuclear fuels', an improvement was observed over the two rounds; particularly for females that was double of overall figures in Mumbai. Thus, the importance of new avenues of livelihood is depicted. Ofcourse, employment in only plastic products were studied at the field level, which is not segregated at the national level. Another major work segment was domestic service due to its rising popularity at the Urban Maharashtra, and Mumbai levels at both the rounds on account of easy entry, and low skill requirement. This was seconded by our field experiences, as it was commonly found amongst female migrants. Another category of growing vegetables or 'kitchen gardens' depicted low priority accorded to this activity at almost all the levels of various NSS rounds. This could probably be explained by the scarcity of landed property for cultivation, especially noticed in case of migrants. Lastly, for the category of 'retail trade of fresh fruits and vegetables', only 5-digit level data was available as there was no previous information on this category. Barely, a per cent sold vegetables and fruits, of which half were women. However, we came across a trend reversal in Mumbai's data due to growing importance of these items in the daily diet; thereby employing more people, especially females. Our field study considered only fresh vegetable retailing, as fruits being seasonal were not sold on a regular basis.

Despite valuable contributions made by NSS data to enrich our analysis, there were various flaws in this source due to generality as it was collected at macro levels, and sample sizes were restricted to only a few blocks. Apart from that NSS's own definitional concepts of 'usual', 'daily', and 'weekly' status employment were highly ambiguous and not scientific in nature;

thereby making comparison with other secondary sources difficult. The invisibility of women's work got further masked due to inappropriate questionnaires, fielded by inexperienced teams of male-dominated enumerators using highly misleading probes that often tricked women about their own worker status. This data covers only the formal segment, thus leaving out a major source of livelihood that is becoming more important than the organized sector. The separate bloc approach to collect data on marginal labourers among women was faulty, and could lead to under-reporting of work. The definition of 'work' itself was highly ambiguous, and could not be compared with other secondary sources of the Census primarily due to agency differences in enumeration of women's work. There was no consensus on the treatment of activities related to non-market output of the primary sector other than cultivation; as the NSS considered it as 'work', while the Census did not. Also, NSS data missed some of the activities defined in the United Nations system of National Accounts, and its adoption of 'time criterion' excluded some of women's activities. This could defy our time-use patterns, which attempted to bring out multi-tasking that females generally undertook, as it is difficult to compartmentalize various economic activities that are normally carried out with extra-economic ones. Thus, female contribution to total production of the informal sector is not properly assessed, as women workers are underestimated by both NSS and Census data (SEWA Academy, 1996).

On account of various definitional snags regarding the 'worker' status, particularly of women in the informal sector, we decided to analyze Work Participation Rates (WPR's) to help estimate the economically active population lying in the age group of 15-59 years, which depicts the dependency load, along with information on the gender component of labour force. This economic indicator may not be fully accurate in India, due to the existence of child and old age labour; as we also brought out in our fieldwork, especially with respect to old age labour in case of non-migrants. The NSS data on WPR's brought out low participation rates among females, especially in the urban areas, which were nearly half of their rural counterparts. WPR's of rural males were slightly higher at 63 per cent in comparison with 60 per cent for urban males. The dependency load in India was not so high, as about 3 to 6 per cent of children are employed in urban, as well as rural areas, respectively. Also, a majority of the aged, largely in rural areas continues to work.

The Government of India data at the national level showed similar results as NSS, confirming higher participation rates among males, particularly in rural areas. Also, females in the countryside depicted greater participation than urban women, primarily on account of the nature of agrarian occupations. The post-reform period demonstrated a sluggish behaviour of WPR's for all workers, except urban females. The trend of 'feminization of work' was reiterated in our urban field study. An in-depth age-group analysis of WPR's mirrored almost the same trends, wherein the pre-reform WPR's for urban women were the lowest, and rose in the post-reform period on account of their post-restructuring income-augmentation role. At the State level, WPR's for main and all male labourers fell, largely due to unemployment and informalization that mainly affected men. Female main workers rates were 20 per cent lesser than for total women labourers, which clearly demonstrates the acceleration in their marginal status. We also observed this development during field surveys, especially in case of migrant occupations of labourers, as well as home-based workers. Almost identical behaviour of WPR's is echoed in the Brihan Mumbai experience.

Also, a review of the Own-Account Manufacturing Enterprises (OAME's) and Non-Directory Manufacturing Establishments (NDME's) was attempted on account of their valuable contribution to industrial employment and entrepreneurship, especially in the post-nineties due to falling shares of formal sector employment. OAME's represent family-operated businesses/ household enterprises run without any hired worker, whereas, NDME's are non-household industries that employed less than 6 workers. We took into account secondary data on NDME's only, as our field study showed the emergence of these in Charkop, especially in case of plastic products. To a certain extent, NSS-generated special data made comparative analysis easier. The ASI's data on the organized sector enterprises, including information on the plastic industry; that was classified as 'Rubber, Plastic, Petro Products' showed a doubling of employment growth, despite a general slowdown in the overall industrial sector jobs. Similar results were also observed at the ward level, which were confirmed by fieldwork findings of Charkop.

The NSS generated special data on OAME's in the plastic division at different levels that depicted a male predominance of over 90 per cent at the state level, despite accounting for less than a per cent of total male labour in Maharashtra. The Urban State level also showed a furthering of this trend, contrary to the general low contribution of this sector to employment. The figures were so negligible at the Mumbai level, that the NSS considered them to be nil. The NDME experience for this industry was reverse only at the general and Urban Maharashtra level accounting for about 2 per cent of male employment options, and 3 per cent in case of female workers. However, field surveys of Charkop depict a different picture as NDME's have gained prominence on the employment front, whereas OAME's were rare, and sited in the sole case of a laundry set up by a Koli for his widow sister. Besides, contrary to macro data that showed majority of male workers, field analysis depicted more of women due to the home-based nature of this activity. However, new male entrants, particularly migrants were also noticed on account of loss of formal sector jobs.

FIELD SURVEY RESULTS

The field survey results have been considered separately for the two groupings of resident local and migrant population.

Analysis of Resident Local Population

The analysis of local residents used detailed questionnaires, both structured, as well as unstructured, supplemented by personal interviews, and several life histories. Apart from the income-expenditure analysis, the major focus is on livelihoods that are concerned with employment changes from formal to informal, various kinds of informal activities of women, effect of declining male jobs on women's employment, thereby impacting expenditure patterns.

The socio-economic profile dealt with different aspects like sex ratio, age-group analysis, relationship with the 'cultural' head of household, and literacy levels of the sample. Our survey is divided between resident locals, comprising two-thirds of households, while the remaining one-third constitutes migrants. The religious and caste analysis are not carried out for Kolis as they represent the upper caste of 'Soan Kolis', majority of who later changed to the reserved category of 'Mahadev Kolis' for seeking employment in government services. All the fisher folk are Hindu, with no other religion being followed. The analysis of 120 Koli households brings out an almost equal gender distribution. The headship of households is determined by economic or income parameters, and not the cultural factors. Patriarchal trends are reinforced by the headship of a majority of households resting in males as portrayed by two-thirds of Male Headed Households. Female Headed Households seem to be circumstantial in nature, as they arose out of death, debility, or loss of employment of male members. The age group distribution shows highest concentration in 40 plus category, thereby largely representing a middle-aged population. The proportion of one-sixth each, of child and old age composition brings out an apparently lower dependency load. Lesser number of females is seen in the marriageable and child bearing group of 16-40 years on account of high maternal mortality and morbidity. Female survival rates are seen to worsen in later years due to the double burden of production and reproduction, as women increasingly take to multi-tasking due to economic pressures and emerging labour market paradoxes. However, a reversal of the male bias is seen in Female Headed Households, as women constitute a $3/5^{th}$ majority with a concentration in the productive age group of 16-40 years. Few females are seen to survive over 60 years due to increasing stresses of multi-tasking. A similar trend of falling longevity is also seen among men largely due to alcoholism.

Literacy data depicts a skewed graph at higher levels, particularly in case of females, as demonstrated by a doubling of illiteracy of Female Headed Households in comparison with Male Headed. Thus, an emerging trend of 'feminization of illiteracy' arises largely due to poverty and women's pre-occupation with the care economy that gets typified by the social construct of gender.

The economic analysis focuses on occupational distribution of population, emerging trends in livelihoods of men, and specially women in the post-reform period. Local residents are involved in the traditional activities of fishing and cropping, along with new sources of livelihood found in plastic enterprises and rickshaw driving for men. Even within the activity of fishing, we come across a change from creek fishing to fish retail, that is mainly bought from nearby suburbs due to a host of factors like environmental degradation and formation of the amusement park of Essel World that impacts marine life, land reclamation by government and non-government agencies, especially of the industrial estate and the dumping of waste into the creek is worsened by pollution caused by urban housing. The retail market of Charkop is monopolized by women, as a few men who sell fish are seen in adjacent suburbs. The local market represents a resident local women's domination due to entry restrictions imposed for outsiders. Reforms have impacted the residents of Charkop as they are increasingly pushed back into primary sector activities of fishing and kitchen gardens, especially in case of women, largely due to a cut back in employment generated in the organized segment. Declining formal sector jobs, along with government's de-reservation policy, in accordance with which Kolis are no longer recognized as 'Scheduled Tribes', thus compelling people to join the informal sector. Women are largely involved in this section due to loss of male incomes on account of closure of enterprises, casualization of formal sector jobs, and emerging employment opportunities in the informal sector. Thus, income augmentation is seen in a number of new jobs like the plastic industry, as it facilitates their multi-tasking and fine-tuning between productive and reproductive activities. However, they are not generally involved in domestic service, which is prominent amongst migrant women.

As observed in field analysis, we have introduced an interesting feature of 'cultural' head versus 'economic' head of household, as the latter focuses on headship on the basis of income, and not patriarchy. Our study being non-sociological in nature, we emphasize the 'economic' headship. In accordance with this classification, almost one-thirds of the resident local households are 'Female-Headed' in economic terms; as women constitute sole or major earners of family income. Thus, we do not consider the additional 24 households that could probably be taken as Female-Headed, but continue to be termed as, 'Male-Headed' in the cultural sense. Female Headed Households show the occupational predominance of fish retailing, followed by casual labour, majority of who were men, and also vegetable sellers or kitchen gardens monopolized by women. Few Koli men are observed to start new enterprises of plastic, poultry farming, laundry services, and auto rickshaw driving, all of which migrants have no access to. Unfortunately, a negligible portion of women are seen to be entrepreneurs due to basic lack of resources, skill, and time. Few female entrepreneurs like the sole example of a laundry lady, along with a majority involved in illicit trade of alcohol seen during field visits are largely helped by their male counterparts in terms of finance and infrastructure. Female entrepreneurs are totally missing amongst migrant women due to poverty and lack of resources. Thus, there is a reaffirmation of the emerging intertwined trends of 'feminization of livelihoods, incomes, poverty, debt, and illiteracy'.

An analysis of conditions of work show that almost 85 per cent of women earn daily wages, primarily on account of the nature of their occupations that are largely piece-based. This makes their earnings highly unpredictable and uncertain, on one hand, and do not provide any benefits or job security, on the other due to the prominence of self-employment or home-based work. Most of these women are target earners, and income-augmenters as their market work is seen to rise on account of falling family incomes due to loss of male jobs. Thus, female employment becomes a function of male unemployment caused by labour market reforms.

A pivotal aspect of the field study is an analysis of the intensity of women's work measured through detailed time use surveys. These provide an insight into women's contribution to both, economic and extra-economic activities, an area that is largely under-represented, under-valued, and ignored in economic theory and practice. Time-use surveys bring out the fluidity, flexibility, and interspersion, as females are generally known to combine two to three activities together as mirrored in our time schedules. Uniformly, all of them are found to be early risers, largely due to their extra-economic activities and contribution to the care economy, coupled with occupational requirements in a few cases of reaching the city in the early hours to buy fish at low cost from wholesale markets of Ferry Wharf and neighbouring suburb of Malad. Also, women wake up early for morning ablutions due to poor sanitation facilities, and paucity of drinking water. Domestic chores of cooking, cleaning, washing of clothes, dropping children to school, caring for the old and sick are an endless list of activities that preoccupy them, as hardly any male help is received in these areas. The care activities of spending time with children and the aged, largely pushed into the evening time-slots are generally found to be multi-tasked with cooking. Women in Female Headed

Households being primary earners are pre-occupied with economic activities, thereby leaving hardly any time for extra-economic ones.

The nature of women's work covering time span of work, and job change is analyzed. They are largely seen to be working in the age group of 14-45 and almost half of them are employed for over a decade with hardly any new entrants in the recent past. This brings out an interesting facet of women's lives, wherein they get pre-occupied with extra-economic roles in the early part of their lives, and find time for economic activities in later years. Data on job change shows a general trend of constancy in almost 90 per cent of the resident local women. 10 per cent who switched their jobs are generally found in the 14-45 years category. Male Headed Households largely demonstrate that job changes are undertaken by females working for over two years, but less than a decade. A reversal of this trend is seen in Female Headed Households, as a majority of the ones associated with this trend are older women, whose reproductive burden is relatively lesser. Detailed analysis of occupational changes highlights few cases of working women exclusively going back to the care economy. Majority of Koli women have not changed their jobs and the one-tenth who have are governed by income-augmenting concerns due to decline or loss of male earnings. Women in Male Headed Households portray a greater flexibility with respect to occupational changes, as they are subsidiary earners, in contrast with their economic headship seen in Female Headed Households.

The income, expenditure, and asset data is studied exhaustively to get a better picture of the impact of reform on livelihoods and resultant survival strategies devised by women. The income analysis covered the average monthly income, and earning months in a year. Income is divided into six slots beginning at less than Rs. 500, and ending at over Rs. 4000. The lowest slot covers only a single person constituted by a woman, thereby confirming that poverty has a woman's face. Income distribution gets skewed at higher levels of earning as the gender divide worsens due to the number of male earners increasing from 60 per cent to 90 per cent as income slabs rise from Rs. 2000 to over Rs. 4000. Male Headed Households show a predominantly lower middle class population, especially comprising women workers earning between Rs. 500 and Rs. 2000. After this grouping, male earnings exceed those of females with the largest gender disparity seen at the highest income level over Rs. 4000, where one-fifth of total male earners and a sole woman are found. Female Headed Households depict the reverse, as female earnings exceed male incomes at all levels due to their status as head of household. Thus, the income analysis confirms the emerging trend of 'feminization of poverty' that worsens on account of gender-based earning differentials.

A further insight into the earning months in a year demonstrates that barely 5 per cent of people work for less than six months in a year with males comprising the majority. This primarily arises out of the seasonal nature of male-dominant occupations like fishing, coupled with the temporary nature of jobs in the post-reform period. Female Headed Households portay a negligible proportion of people working for less than six months, all of whom are males. Women workers being target earners in Male Headed Households or sole earners in Female Headed Households are highly flexible, as fisherwomen are found to sell vegetables and flowers during monsoons or the festive season. This brings out the multi-tasking of women's labour, along with their secondary worker status.

The expenditure analysis of households demonstrates less than one-fifth of people allocate below Rs. 1000 with 60 per cent of middle class people expending up to Rs. 4000 per month. Barely 10 per cent of people spend over Rs. 5000 per month. Contrastingly, Female-Headed Households show a majority expend not beyond Rs. 3000 due to low earnings.

A detailed break-up of various expenditure groups gives us a better picture of standards of living and priorities of people. Over 90 per cent of Koli households spend up to 75 per cent on food with the sole exception of a widow who is unable to manage even 25 per cent for the same. Clothing, shelter, and transport allocations are uniformly low for all households primarily due to simple lifestyles depicted in the attire, along with bare minimum expenses on housing as they are owned by Kolis. Transport spending is also low on account of proximity to work places.

Health and education are low priority areas due to ignorance and prevalence of home-based remedies in case of the former, coupled with free primary education in case of the latter. Female Headed Households are seen to allocate little to education, thereby confirming the trend of 'feminization of illiteracy'. Allocations on drinking are universally large to the extent of Rs. 100 to Rs. 150 justified by the monotonous and strenuous nature of occupations, and are male-specific. People claim to spend less than Rs. 50 on rituals, but when asked about 'other' outlays they confessed to spend anything up to Rs. 250 on marriages, births, festivals, and the like.

An insight into the ownership of assets demonstrates that almost all households possess the basic items of reasonable living like gas, stove, vessels, and fridge in the kitchen, along with cots/beds and wardrobes in the bedrooms, coupled with telephones, television sets, music systems, sofas, chairs, and the like in the living rooms. Few rich people have two-wheelers, three wheelers, as well as four wheelers. Some households own vast expanses of land in Charkop, as well as in Vajreshwari that is cultivated seasonally. Kolis are also involved in the construction of buildings and industrial galas. Women are seen to hold assets in the form of gold ornaments on account of their intrinsic safety and liquidity. They have shared personal experiences of mortgaging or selling their ornaments in times of family crisis, thereby perpetually keeping them impoverished and asset-less. Contrastingly, few men have started investing in shares, debentures, and fixed deposits of companies, but majorities continue to refrain from these areas due to inherent risks.

The most pertinent question of the impact of globalization on resident locals has differing responses from various households surveyed. However, almost all admit to experience a decline in their living status. A few confess to use unscrupulous means like charging heavy rents or selling kerosene, water, and electricity to the migrants. Some Kolis are seen to trade in illicit liquor that mainly involved their wives, as police authorities least suspect women. This clearly brings out the vulnerability of females as most of them took the cover of vegetable selling as they carried hooch to avoid suspicion. The 'New Economic Policy' has practically affected all aspects of livelihoods, ranging from occupations and incomes to expenditures and asset holdings. This is especially true in case of Koli men in government service and organized employment, as the 'Exit Policy' has forced many to accept 'Voluntary Retirement Schemes'. Thus, a majority is pushed from the formal to informal sector, thereby reducing incomes, benefits, and certainty of employment. Besides, new entrants are denied jobs due to industrial restructuring in the post-reform period, and also on account of de-reservation of their status as a 'Scheduled Tribe' pushing them into the informal segment. All these transitional changes on account of reforms have their bearings on incomes, expenditures, and asset holdings. Falling male incomes force women to take to income augmenting activities that are largely home-based in nature. This results in an increase in women's burden, as they switch between productive and reproductive work. Despite their additional economic roles, most of them receive no help from their counterparts in extra-economic activities, thereby adversely impacting their health. Also, the burden, especially of girls increases as they are found to help their working mothers in household chores. This results in increasing absenteeism and dropout rates in schools in many cases. Women also cut expenditures by buying cheaper foodstuffs, mixing vegetable stalks in daal, adding maida to expensive wheat dough for chapattis, and reducing their own consumption. Periodically, they mortgage or sell their gold ornaments during family crisis and indebtedness. All this increases the assetlessness and poverty of women. Women in Female Headed Households are worst affected, being sole earners and are trapped in the vicious circle of illiteracy, poverty, and low skills.

During fieldwork, we came across a unique trend of unionization, peculiar only to fisherwomen. About 30 of them have formed the 'Jari Mari Mahila Mandal', which is registered in 2002 with all women as office-bearers (Jari Mari Mahila Mandal, Reg.M.A.H./2001/Charkop Koliwada). They employ men for administrative purposes and routine jobs like meeting with government officials, ward personnel, and the like. The prime reason for starting this union is driven by survival, as the local market place of Charkop will be eventually taken over by government authorities because it encroaches on the public road. The government has decided to give alternative vending places to these women in the newly formed local mandai, which is already leased out to private operators for administrative purposes. Fisherwomen are resistant to be relocated, as the spaces provided in the BMC mandai are too small and cannot accommodate all of them. Besides, none of them are in a position to pay the exorbitant rents and municipal taxes levied on these premises. Thus, women's work, earnings, and survival are at stake in a reforming market-driven economy, thereby accelerating the trend towards 'feminization of poverty and illiteracy', along with a general trend of 'informalization of work', and 'feminization of the informal sector'.

Analysis of Migrants

An analysis of migrants becomes essential for any study to be complete and holistic, as the changing nature of women's employment, especially with respect to this segment is largely impacted by globalization. Another important reason for covering resident non-locals is on account of their valuable contribution to employment and income, primarily in the city's informal sector. The coverage of all 60 migrant households comprising 225 persons shows interesting results, as they form one-thirds of Charkop's population and add to its economy. Most of these people have come from regions outside Mumbai, thus making such transfers largely intra-state in nature. Migration is primarily a result of 'push' factors, as natural calamities in the state of Maharashtra, especially droughts leading to an exodus of people into the city, supplemented by 'pull' factors of economic opportunities provided by the mega city. Some amount of inter-suburban transfers are also seen from the neighbouring suburbs of Malad and Goregaon on account of slum demolitions and forceful evictions in the last few years.

Surveys of the 60 migrant households show that barely one-tenth of these were women-headed, of which over half are categorized Male-Headed in the 'Cultural' sense. This is in contrast with one-thirds of resident local households that are Female-Headed. Thus, the trend partially brings out the economic contribution of Koli women, but should not be taken to represent passivity of migrant females as economic agents, because not all women from the countryside have migrated into Charkop. Similarly, the sex ratio may seem marginally adverse, as there are about 60 per cent males even in case of Female Headed Households. Majority of non-local households represent nuclear families on account of the pattern of migration mapped earlier. Also, women in Female Headed Households have come alone, and almost all of them are married. A striking difference between these and Male Headed Households is the presence of an immediate nuclear family constituted of an additional member or two, which is missing in case of the former due to economic reasons. Contrastingly, non-migrant households are seen to generally have large extended families with a few exceptions of nuclear ones, as Charkop is their place of origin and settlement.

Almost three-fourths of the Male Headed Households have a Hindu majority with about 50 per cent of Female Headed Households also following Hinduism, along with Buddhism as the second most popular religion. This kind of religious diversity is totally missing in case of Koli households, as they all practice Hinduism. The caste structure denotes that over ten per cent represents the 'Other Backward Classes' (OBC's) category, while a majority belong to the Kshatriya or open category. On the other hand, the non-migrant population has changed their previous upper caste status of 'Soan' Koli to a Scheduled Tribe status of 'Mahadev' Koli to secure jobs in the reservation list pertaining to the State of Maharashtra.

One-third of migrant population belongs to the child-age group with a nearly non-existent old age population of over 60 years portrays a low dependency ratio, as two-thirds of people are economically active. This stands in sharp contrast with the non-migrants having a large dependency load, as the aged and economically inactive stay with them.

The literacy data shows that every second migrant was illiterate, the figures being double for females. Despite this, paradoxically 20 per cent of these women have acquired primary education, as it is free, particularly for girls up to Class 12. The dropout ratio is seen to increase after this level and is typically higher in case of females, thereby increasing the gender asymmetry. The literacy graph gets more skewed at higher levels, as barely 0.25 per cent is fortunate to have higher education, majority comprised of males. One-tenth of Female Headed Households are illiterate, particularly with a concentration among female members. The non-migrant data also shows similar trends, the difference being in higher levels of literacy in comparison with the migrants. Thus, the trend of 'feminization of illiteracy' is almost universal for both the groupings.

The occupational distribution shows that half of the migrants work as casual labourers with a male majority of nine-tenths. The second largest source of livelihood is seen in the assembling of plastic products, which is largely female-dominated due to its home-based nature. Men have taken to new occupations of driving rickshaws, taken on hire from the Kolis. Other male-dominated occupations comprise of contract labour on farms and construction sites, along with entrepreneurship of small–time businesses of spoon polishing and dye-making. Women are seen to assemble plastic products and undertake domestic service to augment family incomes. An in-depth analysis of the occupational profile of Female Headed Households shows that one-thirds of the women resort to domestic work and gets plastic products home. One-fifth of them sell vegetables, while a similar proportion works as labourers on farms and construction sites. The remaining women combine the above-mentioned jobs to augment family incomes. Migrant women have no fixed jobs and kept on switching to make ends meet. Apart from basic migratory behaviour, their husband's unemployment compels them to become target earners. Male Headed Households reinforce the occupational concentration as most of the men are labourers, with no single case of male vegetable seller or domestic due to gender stereo-typing and female prominence, as also seen in non-migrant households.

A peculiar trend is that the numbers of women workers are higher in comparison with men, despite which their earnings are lower due to the nature of jobs. Also, a large part of migrant women's work is home-based in nature, and almost double of their non-migrant female counterparts, thereby bringing out the increased burden of poverty amongst them. Non-local resident women do not retail fish, as it remains the exclusive domain of non-migrant women, and instead sell vegetables bought from nearby wholesale markets of the adjacent suburbs of Malad and Borivali, unlike the Koli women who grow and largely retail vegetables from their own kitchen gardens. Similarly, almost 15 per cent of migrant women did domestic service due to survival, contrasted by barely 0.25 per cent of their non-migrant counterparts. This clearly brings out the fact that the poorest, least skilled, and migrants among women workers themselves are the most vulnerable, as they lack assets and productive resources, thereby getting deeper into the poverty trap.

Low literacy almost universally pushes men in both the groupings into low-skilled labouring jobs. Migrant men are seen to increasingly hire rickshaws owned by non-migrants to earn additional income. All these emerging trends in the post-reform period make the labour market highly uncertain and promise almost no guarantee of employment. Thus, exit seems to be simpler than entry into both, the formal and informal sector for migrant men that leads to a rise in female income-augmenting activities. Non-local resident men resort to risky and uncertain avenues of survival like night-time rickshaw driving to earn double fares, or selling illicit liquor for the Kolis. Entrepreneurship is largely missing in case of migrants, particularly females due to poverty, and lack of resources.

An exhaustive analysis of the employment status of women covers different aspects like conditions of work, history of job change and intensity of work. The time-span analysis shows that three-fourths of migrant women are working since the past 6 years, with a majority in the 19-35 age groups that is largely governed by natural calamities. Contrastingly, women in Female Headed Households are found to have come to the city over a decade ago along with their husbands, and have subsequently become heads due to loss of main male earners. Rest of them has been working since the last 3 years to as secondary workers or breadwinners in single-parent households. Thus, most of them are target earners, unlike their non-migrant female counterparts.

The job change analysis of Male Headed Households shows that one-third have changed their jobs, and are primarily found in the productive age group of 14-45. A major job change is seen in the recent past of 2-4 years on account of newly set-up plastic industries. A reversal of this trend is observed in case of Female Headed Households, as two-thirds have changed their jobs mainly due to income augmentation, and inflationary pressures.

A study of activity change portrays that nearly half practically every second woman has switched from domestic service to plastic products due to the occupational stigma associated with the former, coupled with the convenience and home-based nature of the latter. However, their incomes have become more uncertain on account of its intrinsic piece-based remuneration that is worsened by foreign competition particularly from cheap Chinese goods facilitated by liberalization. A change from growing vegetables on hired plots, or factory employment to plastic products is noticed in case of 20 per cent of female workers. This largely arises due to seasonality of the former, along with low and uncertain income in case of the latter associated with reform and industrial restructuring. It leads to closure of units, increasing male unemployment in the formal sector, and resultant entry into informal activities, thus adversely impacting women. Non-migrant households mirror a mixed trend, as most of the Koli women have retained their traditional occupations, along with income-augmenting activities of kitchen gardens, plastic products assembling, and private tuitions with the exception of domestic service.

The income, expenditure, and asset analysis brings out interesting observations in case of migrant households. The income data looks at earning months in a year, average monthly income, and intensity of work. Males of one-tenth of these households work for less than 6 months a year due to seasonal migration for harvesting purposes, coupled with the emerging labour market scenario that largely offers temporary and casual jobs. Contrastingly, women are found to work throughout the year due to relatively less frequent village trips that are further restricted by children's education. The situation gets pronounced in Male Headed Households, wherein two-thirds of men and one-thirds of women work for less than six months, whereas a majority of 90 per cent women are employed throughout the year. Not a single person in Female Headed Households is found to work for less than 6 months, as one-thirds of men and two-thirds of women work for almost the entire year for survival. Migrant conclusions stand in contrast with the non-migrant ones, as about 90 per cent of the population is occupied throughout the year. Local residents working for a lesser time is either due to loss of employment or break in service due to personal illness, or voluntary retirement given almost compulsorily.

Data on average monthly income depicts that 75 per cent of migrant population earn between Rs. 500-3000, thereby representing a predominantly low-income grouping. Hardly anyone draws below Rs. 500 or more than Rs. 4000, thus showing negligible inequalities. Male Headed Households brings out 20 per cent low-income people earning below Rs. 500, all represented by women. Negligible proportions of earners at the higher end of the spectrum exceeding Rs. 4000 are found, all being men. Gender asymmetries in income are confirmed by this highly biased distribution. Inequalities are directly related with income levels.

Contrastingly, Female Headed Households do not have anyone earning less than Rs. 500 at the lower end of the spectrum, as well as a negligible proportion above Rs. 3000. Most of them are middle-income categories of about Rs. 2000, and exceed male incomes at almost all levels. We came across a sole exception of the highest income earner being a woman, which is easily explained in these households. A comparative analysis of the Kolis brings out a negligible proportion of low-earners, with about a quarter of high-earners above the income slot of Rs. 4000. However, 90 per cent at the top levels are comprised of men, who are all self-employed. More women earners are found in the income range of up to Rs. 2000, with a reversal of the situation at higher levels, thereby demonstrating gender discrimination in income.

The intensity of work analysis for migrant women portrays a dismal picture, as they are seen to go through greater hardships for survival purposes, due to lack of basic infrastructure like water, sanitation, and electricity. Almost all of them are multi-tasking and continuously working to fine-tune their economic and extra-economic activities. They waste more time on daily purchases on account of insufficient wages, and paucity of storage and refrigeration. Hardly any of them find time for children, due to pre-occupation with survival. They look over-burdened, as their landladies' extracted free work from them. Female Headed Households demonstrate a worsening of women's work schedules because of extended hours, thereby falling sick on account of general neglect of health and nutrition.

The expenditure patterns of migrant households denote high spending leading to low or practically no savings. Hardly anyone is found to expend less than Rs. 1000, and so also above Rs. 5000. Over three-fourths are forced to allocate up to Rs. 5000 due to the high cost of living in the metropolis. The major outlay is on food that comprises about 75 per cent of total outlay. Clothing outlays are very low, as a majority allocated almost negligible amounts, with the exception of 30 per cent in case of a few. Shelter is another expenditure head, as three-fourths of the households spend about 15 per cent due to the intrinsic high cost of living in the metropolis. Ownership is a distant dream, as they usually live on either high deposits and low rents, or alternatively, no deposits and high rents. Despite huge allocations, housing conditions remain sub-human. Contrastingly, the non-migrants being original inhabitants spend almost nothing on housing. The other two basic necessities of food and clothing portray an almost similar trend in case of both the groupings.

Three-fourths of the migrants spend one-tenth of income on medical treatment due to common ailments like malaria, diarrhea, and anemia, particularly associated with malnutrition and lack of hygiene. Education comprises a low priority expense, as a majority incurs less than 5 per cent on this outlay due to free schooling at the municipal school in Charkop up to class seven, coupled with complementary notebooks and uniforms donated by the affluent Kolis, and the newly formed Rotary Club of Kandivali West in 2003. A similar trend with respect to health and education is also mirrored in the case of Kolis, largely due to the fact that primary education and public health are provided free in the state of Maharashtra. Despite this, health remains a generally neglected area, on account of ignorance, and practice of home-based remedies.

A majority of migrants like their non-migrant counterparts claim to spend almost nil on drinking, rituals, and 'other' outlays, but our field surveys clearly falsify these, especially with respect to drinking being a social taboo. Paradoxically, it is justified by non-migrants on grounds of occupational hazards and monotony. Despite denial, migrants are seen to spend large amounts on 'other' outlays in the form of gifts and allowances to their relatives in the countryside. Almost universally, a typical gender-specific pattern arises, wherein Male Headed Households are seen to allocate more to drinking; while Female Headed Households to rituals and 'other' outlays. Similarly, basic necessities, along with health, and education are low on the agenda of Female Headed Households, barring a few exceptional cases in comparison to Male Headed Households due to economic reasons of income, and nature of earnings. Transport too figures low on the expenditure list, due to short geographical distances between their residences and work places, or covering of long distances by foot to cut expenses. Besides, the need to travel does not arise on account of home-based work.

Thus, on the whole, Male Headed Households portray better income and standards of living with respect to Female Headed Households, denoting a feminization of poverty. Similarly, migrant households are seen to be less privileged and go through greater hardships, in contrast with non-migrant households, thereby demonstrating the vulnerability of the weaker sections. This picture gets magnified when we consider the asset holding of migrants, especially Female Headed Households, as they hardly have any possessions due to meager incomes and migrant status of living, and also stand in total contrast with the resident locals, as they inherit landed property and assets, thereby providing a better economic base.

The impact of reforms is quite adverse in case of migrant households, as their employment and incomes are jeopardized in an uncertain labour market. Migrant men are seen to face more competition from their own women, and largely from the Koli men, especially in the categories of labourers and home-based segments. Thus, migrants continue to face erratic employability worsened by low skills, illiteracy, and lack of resources, coupled with high costs of living in the city. Very few, especially the ones who have stayed for over a decade, consider them lucky, as private builders have given them a lakh or two as compensation for evacuation. A few of these migrants have taken the sum and are going back to their villages, which could partially reverse migration.

RECOMMENDATIONS

The growing importance of the informal segment of production, along with feminization has promoted the government to propose somewhat delayed policy recommendations at the macro level. We have attempted to suggest probable field level measures that could be incorporated and implemented for improving the status and livelihoods of the residents of Charkop.

Policy Suggestions at the Macro Level

We need to review concrete suggestions to make the informal sector's contribution to work and livelihoods more inclusive, rather than exclusionary in nature. This can be achieved by revisiting the very definition of this sector, which will help to precisely define its coverage and contribution that would enable the formulation of supportive policy framework. A major area of concern is the problem of measurement, especially with respect to women's work at home that is perceived as housework, despite its addition to the family's real income. In today's era of globalization, the dividing line between the formal and informal sector is blurred, particularly in case of home workers that are steadily rising. The estimates of unorganized sector employment are calculated as a residual, after subtracting employment in the organized sector from the total employment. The informal sector is defined negatively denoting a non-formal one, along with absence of characteristics belonging to formal activities like security and regularity of work, wage earnings, union protection, and the like (Eapen, 2001, p. 2390). Thus, this negativity associated with the definitional aspect needs to be addressed in order to proceed with the framing of condusive policies for this segment.

Policies at the macro level need to be re-looked at to make them women and informal-sector friendly, as both these form important components of the new development process. Traditionally, as well as presently, women continue to face marginalization and discrimination at work and home. As highlighted earlier, time use surveys have shown that women spent 53 hours, while men spent only 17 hours per week on an average in housework. Females also put in double the amount of time compared to males in taking care of children, the aged, and the sick. The Human Development Report states that, 'All the group parameters that influence inequality between individuals' remains potentially relevant for estimating equity-sensitive indicators. The focus on gender inequality is only a beginning in this respect, but it is an important stating point, since a widespread gender bias severely affects the social, economic, and political situation of many countries', thus reiterating the need to measure gender inequality via an appropriate gender disparity tool (Human Development Report, 1995, p. 72).

The measure of gender disparity suggested by the HDR, 1995 should be adopted by all nations, as it uses simple composite indices-that is, the absolute differences in average time spent by males and females in different categories of activities like housework, extended housework, and activities performed outside the house taken together and combined to arrive at a composite index of gender disparity.

National income accounts need to be revamped and broadened to include workers who are invisible and vulnerable in the labour market like outworkers, informal employment in the formal sector, and domestic workers, mostly constituted by women. Thus, it reinforces the link between gender, informality, and poverty which requires to be taken into account by policy makers in order to make economic policies women-friendly and gender neutral.

Multilateral institutions have emphasized different labour strategies in various decades ranging from the 'trickle-down/ growth-oriented' of the sixties to the 'basic needs of development' of the seventies to 'poverty alleviation' of the eighties to 'guardians of informal sector' in the later decade. Unfortunately, all these being indirect methods have proved to be less effective in their impact. One of the major programmes focuses on social protection, but the important nuances in this very definition lack synchronization amongst international organizations (Lund, F. and Jillian Nicholson, 2003, preface-p. 9). This is evident from the view of the World Bank that defines social protection as consisting of public interventions, 'to assist individuals, households, and communities in better managing income risks (Holzmann, R. and Jorgensen, S. 2001). However, the ILO believes social protection to be basic rights defined as, 'entitlement to benefits that society provides to individuals and households-to protect against low or declining living standards arising out of a number of basic risks and needs'. Thus, it advocates social insurance funded by agencies like governments, employers, and organized labour (Von Ginneken, 2000). Contrastingly, WIEGO's approach to social protection focuses on informal workers and suggests that the emphasis should be on specific needs of the informal workers. Thus, a multi-institutional approach using divergent interest groups of the government, private sector, as well as organizations of formal and informal workers, individuals, and the NGO's should be appropriately devised.

Stiglitz (2002, pp. 1-9) contends that, "Apart from merely reviewing labour markets and suggesting reform measures, it's important to look at the root cause of this change process, namely globalization. Despite its contribution to incomes, growth, trade, and tradables across the world; it is becoming controversial and spreading discontent, especially in the Third world. Thus, the notion of 'one size fits all' and 'globalization as a panacea for all economic ills' must be revisited". The social equity and distribution aspect of reforms must not be sacrificed for economic growth that increases the disparity between the haves and have-nots and thus, gender-neutral and women-friendly labour policies be followed for a gender-just development pattern. These growth trajectories could be unique to every nation, and need not be tailored in Washington at the behest of world donors, as domestic solutions must be sought for local problems in order to promote sustainable development. Thus, developing countries could experiment with 'glocalization' strategies.

Unfortunately, in countries like India, despite the increasing presence of women in the expanding informal sector to the tune of 95 per cent they continue to be marginalized and excluded. Female workers are the most vulnerable of the working people, according to the ILO director, Herman Van Laan. He felt that the unreached and excluded groups in India found primarily in the informal or unorganized sector faced several challenges, and thus, suitable strategies should be evolved to bring these workers to the mainstream. The secretary of the All India Trade Union Congress (AITUC), Amarjit Kaur pointed that neither the Remuneration Act governing equal pay, nor the Maternity Benefit Act was applicable to women working in the informal sector and thus, laws be modified to benefit these women (AITUC Seminar on Unorganized Sector, 2005).

A multi-pronged solution should also provide a resource base to women since they are generally poor, assetless, and resourceless. The Indian inheritance laws are not entirely women-friendly, as seen from the archaic Hindu inheritance law that discriminates against them. A son enjoys the birth right of inheritance of his father's property, while a daughter has no rights except to the father's share of ancestral property if he dies in testate. The recently introduced Equal Rights Bill in the Rajya Sabha in December 2004 allows girls equal entitlement to ancestral property as a member of the undivided family-a provision earlier available only to males. Unfortunately only the four states of Maharashtra, Karnataka, Andhra Pradesh, and Tamil Nadu have passed it, but activists feel that these are largely on paper and there needs to be a change in the mindset of society. Many girls avoid claiming stake to property to avoid tensions and misgivings with their brothers. Kerala is the only state that has abolished the concept of joint family property which is beneficial to females.

The government in October 2005 mooted to pass a bill on the Informal Sector Workers, which should be made an Act, and urgently implemented to protect the majority of our workforce, as it is represents the most vulnerable section of our labour that is growing rapidly. The National Commission for Enterprises in the Unorganized Sector's (NCEUS) first report on social security for unorganized workers has been submitted to the government on May 16, 2006 with the prime objective of providing a national minimum social security to the estimated 30 crore unorganized workers with independent earnings (See Kannan, K. *et al.*, 2006; pp. 3477-3480). The NCEUS is highly ambitious and aims to provide health insurance, life insurance, old age security, and pension with the contributions of the Central government at around Rs. 20,583 crores, along with the State governments at Rs. 4.819 crores, or Re. 1 per day per year by workers, employers, and governments. A distinction between workers below the poverty line (BPL) and above the poverty line (APL) are also made for pension of around Rs. 200 per month for the former, coupled with provident fund in case of the latter (NCEUS, 2006). However, this all-India level effort to legislatively help and institutionalize social security in a phased manner over the next 5 years faces severe criticism. The sequencing of this reform is questionable as its proposed future report on the working conditions and livelihoods of informal workers should have logically preceded the national social security scheme. Also, the implementation of this scheme needs a supportive institutional framework that can be built via structural changes. Most importantly, the definition of informal workers mooted as those working in all unincorporated private enterprises engaged in production and sale of goods and services, operated on a proprietary or partnership basis and employing less than 10 persons needs to be re-looked at (Jose, 2006; pp. 3480-3483). If this target group's calculation is faulty, the success of implementation is questionable. Other experts criticize the categorization of targeted groups on the basis of BPL and APL due to problems of genuine exclusion and needless inclusion. This could lead to a further segmentation amongst workers due to inherent heterogeneity and unwillingness to contribute, especially amongst female-headed households, landless labourers, and other marginalized segments that prefer employment and income security to social security (Rao, V.M. *et al.*, 2006; pp. 3488-3490). Some economists also disagree with the segmentation of workers and social security that the implementation of this proposed bill will create. It would be better to include the informal sector into the mainstream organized segment, instead of exclusion (Duggal, 2006; pp.3495-3497). International experiences in social welfare of Germany, America, Singapore, and others show that it is a long process requiring administrative and implementation skills of various levels of governance; thereby questioning the mass target population, as well as time period of meager 5 years proposed by the NCEUS (O' Keefe, P. and Robert Palacios, 2006; pp. 3483-3487).

Field Level Recommendations

Most of the aspects in terms of nature of employment, working and living conditions, and apathy of government policy found in our discussion in the above section are common to the field level experiences. Most of the workers in Charkop Village, especially the migrants were found to work in the informal segment due to dearth of formal sector jobs, aggravated by lack of skills and training. Thus, they had temporary jobs with frequent breaks, and no benefits of organized sector employment. Thus, majority could not be members of trade unions, and lack collective bargaining because of lack of 'worker' status. Their socio-economic conditions have deteriorated due to hardships in the city, accentuated by the labour reforms and industrial restructuring in the post-reform period. Migrants have meager and uncertain incomes with no job security, thereby forcing many of their women to take to income-augmenting activities. Thus, they face the double burden of work at home and work, thus creating clashes between the economic and extra-economic roles. This has also taken a toll of women's physical and mental health, especially the girl child in some cases. Female workers encounter worst employment conditions in comparison with their male counterparts due to lack of skills, education, and resources that were worsened by restricted mobility on account of socially constructed gender roles.

Migrants are found to be doubly disadvantaged, as their meager incomes are not sufficient to combat rising prices and costs of living. Besides, they have to pay for every basic necessity like water, electricity, sanitation, and shelter in the metropolis. We find women waste time in the early hours of the day for their morning ablutions (by sitting in open spaces) to save money and the waiting period associated with queues at the two public toilets. Worst are the water queues, which are longer at cheaper locations. The strife and stresses of city life increases their sense of alienation resulting in frequent visits to their villages for occasions like marriages, deaths, festivals, harvesting, and the like. All this vitiates the circle of poverty and unemployment, as they lose their jobs in the city, and also incur expenditures and debts. The plight and drudgery of domestic work of women rises with income-augmenting activities as they multi-tasked to maintain the fine balance between falling family incomes and rising expenditures. Often, the coping strategies vary from sacrifice of self or the girl child in terms of food, clothing, or education to working extra hours for supporting the family. Non-local resident women also face subjugation and exploitation at the hands of their Koli landlords, and often work free for them. Migrant men have hardly any occupational choice and mostly undertake menial and lowly paid jobs. Their position is declining due to reforms and industrial restructuring as the labour market conditions are worsening in terms of the nature of employment, earnings, and benefits. Despite hardships, the migrants are found to be optimistic and work longer hours. Most of their children are going to schools and taking private tuitions as their parents consider education to be the only way out of poverty and debt. However, girls are not allowed to study beyond Standard VII due to poverty, as education in private schools was expensive. Thus, drop out rates have been higher amongst girls, particularly in case of working mothers who solicit domestic help from their daughters.

A few migrants have been thinking of going back to their native places as living in the city is becoming more difficult and expensive. Besides, most of them have landed property and farming to fall back upon. Also, the ones who have stayed in the city for over two decades are receiving compensation ranging from Rupees one to two lakhs from private builders and thus, have been contemplating to return to their villages.

The government must evolve development strategies that devise labour and employment reforms simultaneous with industrial restructuring. Also, weaker sections of society like migrants or women must be given special attention in order to include the marginalized segments of society. Labour flexibility is being propagated to make the entry and exit meaningful for the private sector and multinationals. However, proper matching of new types of skills required must be undertaken for new entrants, along with retraining and rehabilitation of retrenched workers. The soft cushion of welfare must be given to smoothen the transition from a 'Command' to a 'Demand' economy. Basic amenities of physical and social infrastructure must be offered to everyone affected adversely by reform and equity-blind market policies. More importantly, economic opportunities should be legitimately given in order to recognize the 'worker' status of informal labour. Thus, benefits and security of livelihoods enjoyed by their formal segment counterparts be extended to this area of growing importance.

The situation of the non-migrants may seem a little better than the migrants as they are the original inhabitants and settlers, thus enjoying the security of landed property and traditional occupations of fishing, farming, or government jobs. Unfortunately, personal interviews and life histories of elders and prominent locals tell a different story. The Kolis are fast losing their traditional occupations like fishing due to urbanization and development of amusement / water parks like Esselworld, thereby adversely affecting the ecology and marine life, worsened by the entry of migrants-especially North Indians into the sale of fish in adjacent wholesale markets. The Kolis once supplied fish to the adjacent wholesale market in Malad, have been buying on a retail basis from this market to re-sell in the Charkop due to depletion of fish in the creek. Apart from the earlier causes of industrial pollutants and effluents from units in the governments industrial estate, development of residential and commercial premises on 'agricultural' land and resultant household and commercial dumping of waste into the creek, several other developments like amusement parks and the proposed tourism at Gorai in the adjacent suburb of Borivali and the emerging private builders lobbies have changed the landscape and destroyed the livelihoods of the original settlers. Also, the entry of multinationals and foreign trawlers has led to over-fishing and depletion of stocks, apart from the ecological damage and loss of livelihoods of the Kolis. Organized protests organized by the National Fishworkers Forum helped in the withdrawal and cancellation of several foreign operators licences. However, the resultant deep fishing has caused irreparable damage to the spawning process. Unfortunately, in the post-reform period, the fisher folk are seen to resort to over fishing due to difficult living and working conditions, thereby preferring present survival over future concerns. Older fishermen are emotionally attached to the traditional occupation and have no education or requisite skills for alternate jobs, thus hindering their occupational mobility. Few of the younger ones seem to be better off, as they have using the landed property for starting their own enterprises, as observed in few cases during our fieldwork. Unfortunately, they lack the entrepreneurship and specialization, thereby restricting their sales to local markets that are generally low priced. The prominent plastic enterprises are increasingly finding it difficult to survive as cheap Chinese goods have been flooding local markets. Thus, globalization is deteriorating their condition, and does not usually generate expected high incomes due to the emerging export industries. In fact, most of the locals are losing their secured government jobs in the ports and aircraft industries. Many have availed of these opportunities by changing from the upper caste of 'Soan Koli' to the lower one of 'Mahadev Koli', as the latter are regarded as a Scheduled Tribe and given jobs. The de-reservation of this tribal status is prohibiting entry of younger Kolis into the formal sector, and leading to unemployment amongst the older ones due to the 'Voluntary Retirement Schemes' on account of industrial and labour reform caused by changing policies from command to demand oriented ones.

Two other prominent occupations have become extinct-namely, toddy tapping and farming, as the government confiscated surplus property during the seventies to set up its own industrial estate. Urbanization and the sale of land to private builders have also contributed to this extinction. The huge paddy fields of the past have been reduced to kitchen gardens today, where women are seen to grow vegetables and flowers to augment falling family incomes. Toddy tapping is degenerating to selling hooch illegally, especially by women, thereby increasing their vulnerability. The number of women-headed households in the 'economic' sense is rising, as ironically the 'cultural headship' remains with the males. Thus, females are found to always bear the greatest cost of change and reform, be it in case of migrants or locals. Yet, the dual responsibility of the home and market continues to go un-noticed, un-accounted, and un-estimated. This is worsened by the socially constructed gender roles, which increase the multi-tasking and drudgery of women. It calls for a re-look of the very definition of 'head of household' that should be changed from culturally determined to the economic based, thereby making income the deciding factor.

The individual experiences of the resident local population shows variations in some aspects, primarily arising out of their location advantage, resource and asset position vis-à-vis their migrant counterparts. But, almost universally females bear a greater burden of reform due to their lack of basic resources, assets, skills, training, and education, thereby widening the gender divide. Inequalities of all kinds, ranging from income, wealth, assets to opportunities between men and women increase in post-reform period. Chandrasekhar C and Jayati Ghosh, (2002, p. 172), rightly state that, "Globalization tends towards centralized decision-making governed by a few, pulling the weaker and poorer nations and sections of society into its vortex". This trend is echoed by the marginal segments of women and migrants. Migrants, almost universally are documented to face sharper discrimination and insecurities that probably result in the vicious trap of poverty and unemployment. They face continuous evictions from different powerful lobbies and particularly, women are known to bear the greatest burden of restructuring and relocation. Thus, females are vulnerable to a confluence of multiple marginal identities in a patriarchal society, as migrants, informal workers, members of minority communities, and householders (Menon-Sen, 2006, pp. 1969-1974).

The apathy of the government in terms of de-reservation, coupled with industrial restructuring has hit labour markets. The human aspect of reforms has been ignored, thereby questioning the very purpose of such changes. The absence of social security and a welfare state in India could jeopardize the continuity and sustainability of the 'New Economic Policy' in terms of its social impacts that are gender blind. Thus, marginalized segments like women, fisher folk and informal producers must be given protection and recognition in order to avoid extinction in the process of internationalization.

The social construct of gender needs to change to an economic one, and role reversals must be encouraged. Also, political structures and labour markets must be made more women-friendly by granting powers, reservations, and positions to women in policy framing and implementation to make empowerment and enlightenment meaningful. Basic support systems of crèches and day care centers, along with sharing of domestic responsibilities within the household would help to reduce obstacles to women's market activities. Reports like Shramshakti (1988, pp.249-250), establish that all women are workers because they are producers and reproducers; thus their work as homemakers must be recognized as social/economic production. The vulnerabilities of women informal sector workers extend to health, family problems, and menace of dowry that need to be tackled. The existing socio-political and economic organizations are weak, powerless, practically non-existent, or defunct, and perpetuate hierarchical gender relations. Women workers need to be addressed on a priority basis, as they face gender discrimination in the labour market with ever-widening wage disparities between male and female earnings. Unorganized sector women workers are the worst hit, which calls for gender sensitive policies to enhance women's productivity and work participation. Mere tokenism or part measures are no real solutions, as specific informal sector policies covering all workers, focusing on the marginal segments like women and migrants are required.

In conclusion, the post-nineties development experiences of major world economies reiterate the need for a balance between the governments and markets. Globalization needs to be democratized so that the voices of the developing countries, especially the poorest among poor, and the most vulnerable workers, namely women workers can be heard (Stiglitz, 2003, pp. 25-30, 343-345). Also, one need not accept the emerging trend of a single unified pattern of the market economy that exists in the developed world, to be totally applicable to the developing world, especially for India. Besides, the informal sector cannot be subject to a uniform policy tailored for the formal segment due to its vastness and heterogeneity. Thus, flexible measures encompassing the needs of women workers differentiated by characteristics like age, education, occupation, and employment status should be considered. This will enable to form a rational view of the two segments of formal and informal as a continuum of production processes and labour markets that are peculiar to reforming economies (Deshpande, S. and Lalit Deshpande, 1998, An Abstract). Nevertheless, reforms, informalization of work, and prominence of women workers in the urban informal sector are becoming almost universal trends cross cutting all barriers of nations, races, religions, castes, classes, and sectors of the economy; especially in developing countries like India. This development represents a necessary concomitant of reform that characterizes India's change from a command economy to a demand one, and probably also inherits few problems associated with this transition. These difficulties can be overcome by appropriate policy changes that are gender-just and inclusive in nature. These could take care of marginalized segments of society like women, informal workers, slum dwellers, religious minorities, and the like. Government efforts need to be supported by non-governmental support that creates social awareness and collective public action like the cases of the National Fishworkers Forum that helped to oppose foreign trawlers due to their detrimental effects on local livelihoods that account for 92 per cent of below the poverty line families (nff@vsnl.com). Also, the Nivara Hakk Suraksha Samiti is actively involved in the crusade fro slum dwellers for relocation and rehabilitation, as evictions create worst slums that have made Mumbai the nation's 'slum capital'. However, 40 million slum dwellers constitute 23 per cent of urban population of India that accounts for a majority of informal workers. Thus, slums have become synonymous with urban habitat and need rehabilitation and reform due to their invaluable contribution to the unorganized production, employment, and income streams.

CONCLUSIONS

The detailed gender analysis of the impact of domestic reform and globalization at the macro and micro levels proves our hypothesis correct. The field study of Charkop Village brings out the impact of transition at the national level on the micro level. The Fund-Bank doctrine of LPG is seen to affect all major sectors, especially labour and employment. The ramifications of systemic and functional changes since the advent of liberalization in the eighties, followed by the reforms of nineties are manifold. These deep-rooted changes have impacted people's livelihoods, particularly of women in a major way. It has created several paradoxes and anomalies in the development process, wherein macro-economic growth parameters have been given priority over the grassroots impact of percolation, and moreover, lack of percolation due to the 'jobless nature of growth' in reality. Industrial restructuring has led to severe dis-equilibrium in the labour markets, as there is an observed shift from the formal to the informal segment. Also, the formal sector itself is experiencing an informalization, as employment is increasingly becoming temporary, casual, insecure, and ad hoc in nature. Despite a large degree of informalization and the continuous growth of the unorganized section, workers lack the benefits enjoyed by their counterparts in the organized sector due to policy lags and virtual absence of trade-unionism on account of an unclear 'worker' status. Marginalization is seen to be worse among weaker segments constituting women, migrants, religious minorities, and the like. Women are documented to bear a major burden of transition in the economy due to an acceleration of their 'productive' and 'reproductive' shares. Labour market reforms on account of a shift from a 'Command' to 'Demand' economy has led to unemployment, especially of males that has put the onus of income-augmentation on females. Shrinking family incomes and rising expenditures have put additional burdens of women that have led to the evolution of various survival strategies. This has accelerated the gender divide, thus increasing the gap between their 'paid' and 'unpaid' work as portrayed by the time use patterns. Women continue to work longer hours earning low or no wages. This causes a deterioration of female health, rising absenteeism and drop-out rates of school-going girls that result in the vicious circle of 'feminization of the informal sector, poverty, debt, illiteracy, and livelihoods'. All these emerging trends must be addressed with the help of an appropriate macro policy framework, along with socio-cultural changes in 'gender-prescribed roles' in a patriarchal system for a gender-just development.

SHORTCOMINGS OF THE STUDY

Our fieldwork analysis has tried to capture the micro-economic impact of macro-policies of globalization, along with industrial restructuring and labour market reform in the post 'New Economic Policy' regime. The grassroots level experiences are important, as they largely mirror the macro-economic trends, but our analysis of fieldwork was largely delayed due to data gaps at the secondary data level. Nevertheless, this source of information was essential to incorporate national developments. Apathy of government officials, especially at the ward levels to part with information, frequent transfer of files and personnel from government offices, along with time over-runs in publishing of official data, especially the NSS on account of paucity of funds and pending government sanction, further slowed our comparative analysis. Thus, ready availability of reliable and timely data; with standard and uniform classification, unbiased questionnaires, sufficiently large and representative sample sizes, and surveys carried out by experienced surveyors, along with gender-disaggregated data on employment, especially in case of informal workers, and mainly women workers are vital to enrich the vast secondary database. Future research could use statistical tools beyond tables and time-use surveys resorted by this thesis, to improve upon the accuracy and measurement of results. There also arises an urgent need to develop synergies between the vast macro-level, and highly personalized local level of micro analysis by way of a meso-analysis that could be taken up by others. Thus, measurement of informal work, especially in terms of gender-disaggragated data for female workers must be undertaken, as is the case with formal employment, and not treated as a residual activity. Women's status as 'marginal' workers should be revamped, and their 'non-market' or 'household' contribution, along with the 'care economy' also should be accounted for at market value. Also, informal work within the formal sector be accounted for, and be granted the same status as formal employees enjoy. Besides, the universally growing 'home-based' category be given worker status, Thus, gender mainstreaming and gender budgeting are powerful tools that new studies can look at to innovate with 'bottom heavy' models of development in contrast with the popular 'top heavy' models. Recognition of the failure of 'trickle-down approach', thereby stressing the 'basic needs facilities'/target group approach is imperative for alternative development strategies to emerge. Devastating effects of globalization are seen in developing countries, especially the poor in these countries, as markets promote growth, but not equity. Thus re-invention of Governments and markets is needed (Stiglitz, 2002, pp.ix-xiv) to find solutions for re-fashioning globalization to meet the local needs of individual nations (Friedman, 2005, pp.324-25). This could probably resolve the age-old dispute between economic growth and social concerns by developing suitable models of development that incorporate social security into the market model. The strategy needs to be gender just to eliminate gender-blind market policies (Rao et al, 1996, pp. 133-36).

The World Development Report (1996, p.66) contends that, 'A nation's transition will be judged by whether its citizens live better than they did before'. It thereby becomes imperative to focus on equity concerns, as it is important to view the gains, pains, and problems created by transition; especially for the human factor of labour, along with other physical, and natural resources.

Human development must emphasize the role of women workers that is enlarging in a shrinking world facilitated by globalization, as the trend of 'Global Feminization' and 'Fexible Workforce' is universal (Razavi, 2000, pp. 259-60). Future studies should focus on the disaggregation of economic and extra-economic statistics by gender to study the magnitude of relative disparities between male and female segments of population. Gender just studies must use progressive tools like the 'time use surveys' used by our field work analysis to recognize the extra-economic activities of women, as these contribute to real incomes of households. In the absence of female labour, these would have to be economically accounted and paid at market wage rates. Women's production and reproduction are equally important as they augment family incomes and exclusively create supplies of labour on a continuous basis. Thus, these 'invisible' and 'under-accounted' activities need to form a part of national income calculations, along with a 'realization of decent work' especially for marginalized segment of workers comprising women and informal workers.

SELECT BIBLIOGRAPHY

AITUC, March 8, 2005, *Seminar on Unorganized Sector*, New Delhi.

Annual Survey of Industries; 1990-91, 1993-94, 1997-98, 1998-99, 2000-01, *'Summary Results for the Factory Sector'*, Ministry of Statistics and Programme Implementation, Delhi.

——(2000), *Special Data Generated*, pp. 00179; 38-142.

Atkinson, J. (1986), *'New Forms of Work Organization'*, Report 121, Institute of Manpower Studies, Brighton, U.K.

Awasthi, I. *et al.*, (1994), *'Employment Promotion in India'*, Institute of Applied Manpower Research Study, New Age International (P) Ltd, New Delhi.

Bagchi, A. (1999), 'Globalization, Liberalization, and Vulnerability: India and the Third World', *Economic and Political Weekly*, Volume 36, No. 52; pp. 3219-3230.

Bardhan, K. (1985), 'Women's Work, Welfare, and Status: Forces of Tradition and Change in India', *Economic and Political Weekly*, Volume 20, No. 50; pp. 2207-2220.

Becker, G. (1981), *'A Treatise on the Family'*, Harvard University Press, U.S.A.

Bhalotra, S. (1998), 'The Puzzle of Jobless Growth in Indian Manufacturing', *Oxford Bulletin of Economics and Statistics*, Volume 60, No. 1; pp. 5-32.

Bose, A. (1973), *'India's Urbanization, 1901-2001'*, Tata McGraw Hill Publishing Company Limited, New Delhi.

Breman, J. (1996), *'Footloose Labour: Working in India's Informal Economy'*, Cambridge University Press, Delhi.

——(2000), *'Down and Out: Labouring under Global Capitalism'*, Oxford University Press, Delhi.

——(2005), 'Work and Life in the Informal Economy', *Economic and Political Weekly*, June 18, Volume 15, No. 25; pp. 2500-2506.

Brigitte, B. (1985), 'Women in the Third World Cities: Paths to a Better Future', United States Agency for International Development, in Panitch, L. and Colin Leys, *'Working Class Realities: Socialist Register'*, Merlin Press, London.

Brihan Mumbai Corporation, (2002-2003, 2003-04, and 2004-2005), *'Know Your Ward'*.

Bullock, S. (2000), *'Women and Work'*, Women and World Development Series, Zed Books, U.K.

Census of India (1991), *'India Provisional Population Totals'*, Series 14, Part-B, Controller of Publications, Government of India, Delhi.

——(2001), *'India Provisional Population Totals'*, Series 1, Paper 1, Controller of Publications, Government of India, Delhi.

——(2001), *'India Provisional Totals'*, Paper 3, Series 28, Statement 1 and 2, Controller of Publications, Government of India, Delhi.

Central Statistical Organization (1998), *'Men and Women in India'*, Government of India, Delhi.

——(2004), *'Proceedings of the National Seminar on Gender Statistics and Data Gaps'*, Government of India, Delhi.

Chaganti, S. (2004), 'Creation of a Third World in the First-Economics of Labour Migration', *Economic and Political Weekly*, May 29, Volume 34, No. 32; pp. 2220-2224.

Chakrabarty, C. and Jayachandran, C. (2001), 'Software Sector: Trends and Constraints', *Economic and Political Weekly*, August 25, Volume 36, No. 34; pp. 3255-3261.

Chandrasekhar, C. and Jayati Ghosh (2002), *'The Market that Failed-A Decade of Neo-Liberal Reforms in India'*, LeftWord Books, New Delhi.

Chhachhi, A. *et al.* (eds) (1996), *'Confronting State, Capital, and Patriarchy: Women's Organizations in the Process of Industialization'*, Macmillan Press Limited, Britain.

Chossudovsky, M. (1997), *'The Globalization of Poverty'*, The Other India Press, Goa.

Cornia, G. *et al.*, (1987), 'Impact of Crisis', Volume 1, *United Nations Development Programme*, India (mimeo).

Date-Bah, E. (ed) (1997), *'Promoting Gender Equality at Work'*, Zed Books, U.K.

D'Cunha, J. (1987), 'Domestic Workers: Isolated and Powerless', *National Survey of Domestic Workers Report*, Akshara, Mumbai.

Despande, S. and Lalit Despande (1998), *'Reforms and Labour Market in India'*, at a Symposium on 'Reforming India's Social Sectors: Strategies and Prospects', April 16-17, Indian Merchants Chamber, Mumbai.

Deshpande, L. *et al.*, (2004), 'Liberalisation and Labour: Labour Flexibility in Indian Manufacturing', *Institute of Human Development*, New Delhi.

Dev, M. and Jos Muoji (2002), 'Social Sector Expenditures in the 1990's: Analysis of Central and State Budgets', Economic and Political Weekly, April 12, Volume 37, No.9; pp. 853-866.

Dewan, R. (1997), *'Runways across Villages: Critique of the Proposed New International Airport for the City of Mumbai'*, Himalaya Publishing House, Mumbai.

——(1999), 'Gender Implications of the New Economic Policy: A Conceptual Overview', *Women's Studies International Forum*, Volume 22, No. 4, Elsevier Science Limited, U.S.A.; pp. 425-429.

——(2000), *'The Warp and the Web: Organized Production and Unorganized Workers in the Informal Food Processing Industry'*, International Labour Organization, Working Paper 156, Geneva.

——(2000), *A Ceentury of Work and Workers in Bombay (Mumbai)-Gendered Occupational and Demographic Patterns of the Process of Urbanization in Mumbai in the Regional Scenario of Maharashtra State'*, Research Issue 12, Planning and Development Unit, Department of Economics, Mumbai (mimeo)

——'Unorganized Workers in Bombay Metropolis: A Study', *Maniben Kara Institute*, S.N.D.T. University, Mumbai.

District Primary Census Abstract, Government of India, Delhi.

Dube, L. and Rajni Palriwala, (eds) (1990), *'Structures and Strategies: Women, Work, amd Family'*, New Delhi.

Dubey, M. (1996), *'An Unequal Treaty: World Trading Order after GATS'*, New Age International, Delhi.

Duggal, R. (2006), 'Need to Universalize Social Security', *Economic and Political Weekly*, August 12-18, Issue 16, No. 32; pp. 3495-3497.

Dunlop, J. and Victoria Velkoff (1999), *'Women and the Economy'*, United States Department of Commerce, Economics, and Statistics Administration, Bureau of Census.

Dwyer, D. and Judith Bruce, (eds) (1988), *'A Home Divided: Women and Income in the Thirld World'*, Stanford, CA, U.S.A.

Dyson, T. *et al.* (2003), *'21st Century India-Population, Economy, Human Development, and the Environment'*, Oxford University Press, London.

Eapen, M. (2001), *'Rural Industrialization in Kerala: Some Emerging Tendencies'*, Manohar Books, New Delhi.

——(2001), 'Women in Informal Sector in Kerala–Need for Re-examination', *Economic and Political Weekly*, June 30, Issue 36, No.26; pp. 2390-2393.

Economic Census of Greater Mumbai (1991), Directorate of Economics and Statistics, Government of Maharashtra, Mumbai.

Economic Survey of Maharashtra (1998-99 and 2001-02), Directorate of Economics and Statistics, Department of Planning and Policy Implementation, Government of Maharashtra, Mumbai.

Gandhi, N. and Nandita Shah (1992), *'The Issues at Stake-Theory and Practice in the Contemporary Women's Movement in India'*, Kali for Women, New Delhi.

——(2002), *'Contingent Workers-Women in Two Industries in Mumbai'*, Akshara Publication, Mumbai.

Ghose, A. (1994), 'Employment in Organized Manufacturing in India', *Indian Journal of Labour Economics,* Volume 37, No. 2.

——(1999), 'Current Issues of Employment Policy in India', *Economic and Political Weekly,* September 4, Volume 34, No. 36; pp. 2592-2608.

Glover, J. (1995), *'Women, Culture, and Development'*, Clarenden Press, Oxford.

Goldar, B. (2000), *'Trade Liberalization and Manufacturing Employment: The Case of India'*, International Labour Organization, Employment Paper 34, Geneva; pp. 1191-1193.

Greenhalgh, S. (1991), *'Women in the informal enterprise: Empowerment or Exploitation'?* World Bank, Washington D.C.

Gugler, J. (ed) (1976), *'The Urban Transformation of the Developing World'*, Oxford University Press, London.

Harris-White (2002), *'Globalization and Insecurity: Political, Economic, and Physical Challenges'*, Palgrave, London.

——(2003), 'Inequality at work in the informal economy: Key Issues and Illustrations', *International Labour Review,* Volume 142, No. 4, pp. 459-463.

Haq, Mahbub-Ul (2003), *http://www.undp.org.in,* pp. 1-6.

Hart, K. (1973), 'Informal Income Opportunities and the Structure of Urban Employment in Ghana', *Journal of Modern African Studies,* Vol. 2, No.1; pp. 61-89 as quoted in The Institute of Applied Manpower Research, (2002), *'Reform and Employment'*, New Delhi.

Holzmann, R. and Jorgensen, S. (2001), *'Social Protection Sector Strategy: From Safety Net to Springboard'*, World Bank, Washington D.C.

http://hdrc.undp.org.in/APRI

http://hdrc.undp.org.in/GngrInitv.

Human Development Report (1995), United Nations Development Programme, Oxford University Press, Delhi.

Indian Council of Social Science Research (1997), *'Non-Conventional Indicators-Gender Disparities under Structural Reform': A Monograph;* p. 7.

Institute of Social Advisory Service (1985), *'The Informal Sector: Concepts, Issues, and Policies'*, The Netherlands.

International Labour Organization (1989), International Labour Office, *'Key Indicators of the Labour Market'*, World Labour Report, Geneva.

——(1992-97), *'Eight Plan-Workshop on Strategic Approach to Job Creation in the Urban Informal Sector in India'*, Geneva.

——(1999), *'Key Indicators of the Labour Market'*, World Labour Report, Geneva.

——(1999), *'Decent Work'*, Report of Director-General at the 87th Session of International Labour Conference, Geneva.

——(2002), *'Women and Men in the Informal Economy: A Statistical Picture'*, Geneva.

——(2004), *'Report on Global Employment Trends for Women'*, Geneva, p. 24.

Institute of Applied Manpower Research (2002), *'Reform and Employment'*, Concept Publishing Company, New Delhi.

Jhabvala, R. *et al.*, (eds), (2003), *"Informal Economy Centrestage – New Structures of Employment"*, Sage Publications, New Delhi.

Jose, A. (2004), 'Dignity at Work–Strategies for Labour in Developing Countries', *Economic and Political Weekly*, October 2, Volume 39, No. 40; pp. 4447-4450.

——(2006), 'Is Legislation the Only Solution?', *Economic and Political Weekly*, August 12-18, Issue 16, No.32; pp. 3480-3483.

Kalpagam, U. (1994), *'Labour and Gender: Survival in Urban India'*, Sage Publications, Delhi.

Kannan, K. P. (2006), 'Social Security for Unorganized Sector'-A Major National Initiative, *Economic and Political Weekly*, August 12-18, Issue 16, No. 32; pp. 3477-3480.

Kapadia, K. (ed) (2002), *'The Violence of Gender Biased Development'*, Kali for Women, New Delhi.

Kelkar, G. (2005), 'Development Effectiveness through Gender Mainstreaming: Gender Equality and Poverty Reduction in South Asia', *Economic and Political Weekly*, October 29, Volume 40, Nos. 44 and 45; pp. 4690-4693.

Kumar, N. (2001), 'Indian Software Industry Development: International and National Perspectives', *Economic and Political Weekly*, March 4, Issue 35, No. 10; pp. 4278-4290.

Kundu, A. (1999), *'Urban Informal Sector in India: Macro Trends and Policy Perspectives'*, International Labour Organisation, Discussion Paper No. 25, Geneva.

——(1999), *'Key Indicators of the Labour Market'*, World Labour Report, International Labour Organization, Geneva; pp. 817-819.

Kundu, A. and Lalitha Kundu (1998), 'Informal Sector in Urban India: Sectoral Trends and Interdependencies', *Indian Journal of Labour Economics*, July-September, Volume 41, No. 3; pp. 6-9.

Lebra, J. *et al.*, (eds) (1984), *'Women and Work–Continuity and Change'*, Promilla and Co. Publishers, U.K.

Lever, W. (1991), 'Deindustrialisation and the reality of the post-industrial city', *Urban Studies*, No. 28; pp. 983-999.

Lewis, A. (1954), 'Economic Development with Unlimited Supplies of Labour', *Manchester School of Economics and Social Studies*, Volume 22, No. 2; pp. 139-191.

Lund, F. and Jillian Nicholson, (eds) (2003), *'Chains of Production–Ladders of Protection: Social Protection for Workers in the Informal Economy'*, School of Development Studies, South Africa, preface- p. 9.

Mahbub ul Haq (2003), *'Report on Human Development in South Asia'*, http://www.undp.org.in.

Mahmud, S. and Wahiduddin Mahmud (1989), *'Structural Adjustment and Women–The Case of Bangladesh'*, Bangladesh Institute of Development Studies; pp. 31-33.

Majumdar, D. (1975), *'The Theory of Urban Under Employment in Less Developed Countries'*, World Bank, Staff Working Paper No. 198; pp. 3017-3051.

——(2004), 'Reforms and Employment Elasticity in Organised Manufacturing', *Economic and Political Weekly*, July 3, Volume 39, No. 27; pp. 3045-3051.

McGowan, J. *et al.*, (eds) (1987), *'Poor Women and the Economic Crisis: The Invisible Adjustment'*, Americas and the Caribbean Regional Office, Regional Programme of Women in Development, UNICEF, Santiago.

Menon-Sen, K.________ (1995-96), Indian Labour Market and the Trade Union Movement Today, *Women's Link*, Labour File, Volume 1 & 2, Nos. 3 & 4, p. 21.

——(2006), 'Better to Have Died Than to Live Like This', *Economic and Political Weekly*, May 20-26, Volume 16, No. 20; pp. 1969-1974.

Mies, M. *et al.*, (eds) (1986), *'Patriarchy and Accumulation on a World Scale: Women in the International Division of Labour'*, Zed Books, London.

Mitra, A. (1998), 'Industry, Informal Sector Employment, and Poverty', *Indian Jounal of Labour Economics*, Volume 41, No. 3; pp. 3-6.

——(1998), 'Employment in Informal Sector', *Indian Journal of Labour Economics,* Volume 41, No. 3; pp. 3-6.

Morgan, R. (ed) (1984), *'Sisterhood is Global',* Harmondsworth, Penguin, U.S.A.

Moser, C. (1980), 'Informal Sector or Petty Commodity Production–Dualism or Dependence in Urban Development', *World Development,* Volume 6, Nos. 8-10.

Mukherjee, D. (2004), 'Informal Manufacturing Sector in India: Pre-and-Post Reform Growth Dynamics', *Indian Jounal of Labour Economics,* Volume 47, No.2; pp. 293-304.

Mukherjee, M. (2004), 'Women and Work in the Shadow of Globalization', *Indian Journal of Gender Studies,* Volume 11, No.3; pp. 282-295.

Nagraj, R. (2003), 'Industrial Policy and Performance since 1980: Which Way Now', *Indira Gandhi Institute of Development Research,* Reprint Report, No. 542.

National Commission for Enterprises in the Unorganized Sector (2006), Government of India.

National Sample Survey Organisation (1993-94), Round on Employment-Unemployment Survey, 50th Round, Government of India, New Delhi.

——(1999-2000), 'Employment and Unemployment in India', 55th Round, Government of India, New Delhi.

Nayyar, D. (2003), *'Governing Globalization: Issues and Institutions',* Oxford University Press, New Delhi.

——(2003), *'Gender, Technology, and Development',* Volume 7, No. 1, Asian Institute of Technology, Thailand; pp. 2377-2380.

Neft, E. and Ann Levine (1997), *'Where Women Stand',* Random House, New York.

nff@ vsnl.com

Noronha, E. (1996), 'Liberalization and Industrial Relations', *Economic and Political Weekly,* February 24, Volume 31, No. 8; pp. 298-299.

Oberoi, A. *et al.,* (2000), *'Strategic Approach to Job Creation in the Urban Informal Sector in India',* Background Paper for National Workshop, 17th-19th February, Haryana.

O'Keefe, P. and Robert Palaios (2006), 'Evaluating NCEUS Social Security Proposals in Light of International Experience', *Economic and Political Weekly,* August 12-18, Issue 16, No. 32; pp. 3483-3487.

Organisation for Economic Co-operation and Development (1994), 'Women and Structural Change–New Perspectives', Paris.

Panda, M. (1999), 'Growth with Equity: Policy Lessons from the Experience in India', Report No. 366, *Indira Gandhi Development Institute Report*, pp. 9-11.

Panitch, L. and Colin Leys, (eds) (2001), *'Working Classes Global Realities: Socialist Register'*, Merlin Press, London.

Papola, T. (1980), 'Informal Sector: Concept and Policy', *Economic and Political Weekly*, May 3, Volume 15, No.18; pp. 817-824.

——(1992), 'Labour Institutions and Economic Development: The Case of Indian Industrialisation', *Indian Institute of Labour Studies*, Research Series, No. 97, International Labour Organization, Geneva.

——(1994), *'Indian Labour Market'*, International Labour Organization, Geneva.

Parthasarthy, G. (1982), and Visaria, Nalin. (1985), *'Rural Poverty and Female Heads of Household–Need for Qualitative Analysis'*, Paper presented at Technical Seminar on, 'Women, Work, and Employment', Delhi.

Patel, S. and Alice Thorner, (eds) (1996), *'Bombay: Metaphor for Modern India'*, Oxford University Press, Delhi.

Patel, V. (2002), *'Women's Challenges of the New Millennium'*, Gyan Publishing House, Delhi.

Phongpaichit, P. (1982), *'From Peasant Girls to Bangkok Masseuses'*, International Labour Organisation, Geneva.

Pillai, K. R. Lakshmi Devi (1985), *'Women Beedi Workers in a Kerala Village'*, Asian Regional Conference on Women and the Household, January 27-31, New Delhi.

Planning Commission (2002), *'Task Force on Employment Opportunities'*, Government of India, Delhi.

Ramanujam, M. *et al.* (1998), *'Employment Promotion in the Urban Informal Sector'*, New Age International (Pvt.) Limited Publishers, New Delhi.

Ramaswamy, K. (1984), *'Power and Justice'*, Oxford University Press, Delhi.

——(1999), 'The Search for Flexibility in Indian Manufacturing–New Evidence on Outsourcing Activities', *Economic and Political Weekly*, February 6, Volume 29, No. 41; pp. 363-368.

Rao, N. *et al.*, (eds) (1996), *'Sites of Change'*, Tulika, New Delhi (Proceedings of the Workshop sponsored by Friedrich Ebert Shiftung and UNDP, New Delhi).

Rao, V. *et al.* (2006), 'Putting the Cart before a Non-Existent Horse', *Economic and Political Weekly*, August 12-18, Issue 16, No.32; pp.3488-3491.

Ratna Kumari, B. (1997), 'Work and Gender: A European Perspective', *Economic and Political Weekly*, September 17, Volume 36, No. 38; pp. 3603-3605.

Ray, B. (2000), *'Globalization and Women in India: A Women's Studies Perspective'*, file:/ / CI/Bharati Ray.htm.

Razavi, S. (2000), *'Gendered Poverty and Well being'*, Blackwell Publishers Ltd, U.K.

Reddy, N. (2005), 'Challenges of Decent Work in Globalizing World', *Indian Journal of Labour Economics*, Volume 48, No. 1; pp. 3-9.

Roy, S. *et al.* (1996), 'New Economic Policy and Old Trade Unions', *Economic and Political Weekly*, March 8, Volume 31, No. 11; pp. 33-35.

Safa, H. *et al.*, (1990), *'In the Shadows of the Sun: Caribbean Development Alternatives and US Policy'*, West View Press, U.S.A.

Sanyal, B. (1991), 'Organizing the Self–Employed: The Politics of the Urban Informal Sector, *Indian Labour Review*, Volume 130, No. 1; pp. 39-56.

——(1991), *'Measuring Women's Unpaid Work'*, United Nations International Research and Training Institute for the Advancement of Women's News; pp. 9-42.

Sarvekshana (2002), Volume 35, No.2 and 3, Government of India; pp. 1-3.

Savara, M. *et al.* (1986), *Organisations and Informal Sector Women: Social Control or Empowerment'*, Indian Association of Women's Studies, Chandigarh.

Sen, A. (1992), *'Inequality Re-examined'*, Clarender Press, Oxford.

Self-Employed Women's Association Academy (1996), 'The contribution of the Unorganised Sector to the Indian Economy' (mimeo).

Sharma, A. (2006), 'Flexibility, Employment, and Labour Market Reform in India', *Economic and Political Weekly*, May 27-June 2, Issue 16, No. 21; pp. 2078-2086.

Shramshakti (1988), 'Towards Equality: Report of the Committee on the Status of Women in India', Government of India, New Delhi.

Sparr, P. (ed) (1994), *'Mortgaging Women's Lives: Feminist Critiques of Structural Adjustment'*, Zed Books, London.

Srivastava, N. (1997), 'Striving for a Toe-holds-Women in the Organized Sector', *Indian Journal of Labour Economics*, Volume 40, No. 3; pp. 527-543.

Standing, G. (1999), 'Global Feminism through Flexible Labour: A Theme Revisited', *World Development*, Volume 27, No. 3; pp. 583-602.

Statistical Outline of India (1991), Government of India.

Stiglitz, J. (2002), *'Globalization and its Discontents'*, Penguin Books, England.

——(2003), *'The Roaring Nineties–Seeds of Destruction'*, Penguin Books, England.

S. Uma Devi (2002), 'The World of Women's Work', Economic and Political Weekly, April 20, Volume 37, No. 10; pp. 4421-4427.

Sundaram, K. (2001), 'Employment and Poverty in 1990's: Further Results from National Sample Survey's 55th Round, Employment-Unemployment Survey's 55th Round, Employment-Unemployment Survey', *Economic and Political Weekly,* August 11, Volume 36, No. 32; pp. 3039-3051.

Talwar, S. (2005), 'Economic Reforms and Female Employment: Issues and Challenges', *Man and Development,* Volume 27, No. 1; pp. 4-6.

Tripathy, S. and Soudamini Das (1991), *'Informal Women Labour in India',* Discovery Publishing House, New Delhi.

Tsikata, D. (2003), 'Globalization-the Cause of Poor Women's Woes', *Third World Network;* pp. 1-3.

Tsjeard, B. *et al.* (2005), 'Gender, Conflict, and Development', *The World Bank,* Washington, D.C.

United Nations (1987), 'Measuring Women's Unpaid Work', Inter-regional Seminar for Women and the Economic Crisis, (1987), Geneva.

——(1999), 'Women Looking Beyond 2000', Bureau of Statistics, Geneva.

UNDP India Web Books (1995), *Human Development Report,* Oxford University Press, New York; pp. 1-8.

——(2003), *http://www.undp.org.in/web book;* pp. 2-9.

UNICEF (1985), 'Indian Informal Sector', Santiago.

——(1988), 'Poor Women and the Economic Crisis: The Invisible Adjustment', Americas and the Caribbean Regional Office; Women in Development; pp. 66-67.

Unni, J. (2001), 'Gender and Informality in Labour Market in South Asia', *Economic and Political Weekly,* June 30, Volume 39, No. 40; pp. 4447-4450.

Veltweyer, H. (ed) (2004), *'Globalization and Antiglobalization: Dynamics of Change in the New World Order',* Ashgate Publishing Limited, England.

Visvanathan, N. *et al.* (eds), (1997), *'The Women, Gender and Development Reader',* Zed Books, London.

Von Ginneken, W. (2000), *'The Extension of Social Protection: ILO's aims in years to come',* Dept. of International Development, London.

Webster, L. and Peta Fidler (1996), 'The Informal Sector and Micro Finance Institutions in West Africa', *World Bank Regional and Sectoral Studies,*Washington D.C.

World Bank (1989), World Survey, Washington D.C.

——(1991), 'Gender and Poverty in India', Washington D.C.

——(1995), World Development Report, 'Workers in an Integrating World', Washington D.C.

——(1996), World Development Report, 'From Plan to Market', Washington D.C.

——(2004), 'New Study on Women at Work: Equality Remains Elusive', World of Work, Washington D.C.

APPENDIX-I: QUESTIONNAIRE

HOUSEHOLD QUESTIONNAIRE

Questionnaire Number

(I) HOUSEHOLD IDENTIFICATION:

1) Name of the Respondent:
Sex: 1. Male. 2. Female.

2) Name of the Head of Household:
Sex: 1. Male. 2. Female.

3) Age of Head of Household: (in years)

4) Address:

5) Religion:
1. Hindu.
2. Muslim
3. Christian.
4. Sikh.
5. Buddhist/Neo-Buddhist.
6. Others.

6) Caste:
1. O.B.C.
2. S.C.
3. S.T.
4. N.T./D.N.T.
5. General.

7) Name of the Caste:

8) Languages Spoken:
1. Marathi.
2. Hindi.
3. Telugu.

4. Kannada.
5. Gujarati.
6. Konkani.
7. Bengali.
8. Oriya.
9. Urdu.
10. Others (specify)

9) Does your family belong to this place?
   1. Yes.
   2. No.

10) If no, which is your original place?
   1. Within Mumbai.
   2. Outside Mumbai District.
   3. Outside State.

11) When did you move here? (years)

12) Why did you move here?
   1. Marriage.
   2. Employment.
   3. Loss of employment in resident area.
   4. Displacement.
   5. Others (specify)

(II) LIVING CONDITIONS:

13) House Structure:
   1. Kutcha.
   2. Semi-pucca.
   3. Pucca.

14) Ownership Status:
   1. Owned.
   2. Rented.
   3. Public Space.
   4. Employers.
   5. Others (specify)

15) Availability of Toilet Facilities:
   1. Community Toilet.
   2. Individual Toilet.
   3. Open.

16) Source of Drinking Water:
   1. Individual Tap/Well/Hand Pump.
   2. Public Tap/Well/Hand Pump.
   3. Water Bodies such as River/Stream/Ponds.
   4. Others (Please specify)

17) Electricity: Yes / No
If Yes Number of Hours.

III) SOCIO-ECONOMIC PROFILE OF HOUSEHOLDS MEMBERS

18) Please furnish following information on all your family members (Begin with the Head of Household).

(1) RHH	(2) Sex	(3) Age (yrs)	(4) Migrated (1) In (2) Out	(5) Literacy Level	(6) Skill Status	(7) Occupation	(8) AMI (Rs)	(9) Earning months

Codes:

I Relationship with the Head of the Household (RHH).

1. Self.
2. Wife.
3. Husband.
4. Brother / Brother-in-Law.
5. Sister / Sister-in-Law.
6. Son / Son-in-Law.
7. Daughter/Daughter-in-Law.
8. Mother / Mother-in-Law.
9. Father / Father-in-Law.
10. Others (specify)

II Gender: 1. Male
2. Female

III Age: Actuals in years.

IV Migrated: 1. In this place.
2. Out of this place.

V Literacy Level:

1. Illiterate.
2. Literate.
3. 1-5 (Primary Levels) Standard.
4. 5-8 (Middle) Standard.
5. 9-10 (High) Standard.
6. 11-12 (H.S.C.) Standard.
7. Degree & above.
8. Technical (ITI, Polytechnic etc.

9. Others (specify)

VI Skill Status:

1. Unskilled.
2. Semi-skilled.
3. Skilled-on-the job.
4. Skilled-Formally Trained.

VII Occupation:

1. Fishing (Creek).
2. Retail / Selling Fish.
3. Crop-grower (Owner)
4. Selling / Cleaning of Vegetables (crops)
5. Labourer.
6. Owner of enterprise (Plastic Products).
7. Working in factories.
8. Getting work home.
9. Domestic Service

VIIIAMI (Average Monthy Income in Rupees).

IX Earning months p.a. (actual number of months in a year)

IV) HOUSEHOLD ECONOMIC PROFILE: (Female Employment)

19) A) What is the position of female employment w.r.t.

Sr. No.	*Women's Time Span of Women's Work*	*Job Change, If yes, Why?*	*Duration of Job Change*	*Activity changed from*	*Activity changed to*
1.					
2.					
3.					
4.					
5.					

Codes: Types of Female Employment (Activity):-

1. Fishing
2. Kitchen gardens growing Vegetables, Flowers & Fruits?
3. Domestic Service.
4. Factory Employment.
5. Assembling Plastic Products
6. Others (specify)

B) Intensity of work (Time Use Pattern)

Sr. No.		TIME SCHEDULE:			
		4.00 a.m. to 6.00 a.m.	6.00 a.m. to 8.00 a.m.	8.00 a.m. to 10.00 a.m.	10.00 a.m. to 12.00 p.m.
1.					
2.					
3.					
4.					

TIME SCHEDULE:					
12.00 p.m. to 2.00 p.m.	2.00 p.m. to 4.00 p.m.	4.00 p.m. to 6.00 p.m.	6.00 p.m. to 8.00 p.m.	8.00 p.m. to 10.00 p.m.	10.00 p.m. to 12.00 p.m.

Activity codes for time schedule:

1. Morning abulations.
2. Carrying water for drinking.
3. Carrying water for washing utensils.
4. Carrying water for washing clothes.
5. Carrying water for cooking.
6. Getting household items like atta, vegetables, fish etc.
7. Dropping & picking up children from school/tuition.
8. Spending time with children
9. Taking care of the aged/ill.
10. Studying.
11. Cooking.
12. Going to work/getting work home.
13. Resting time.

C) Conditions of Work:

1) Total income/wage:
   a) piece-rate.
   b) time-rate (daily/monthly)
   c) kind benefits (like old clothes, furniture, food, T.V. etc.)

2) Toilet facilities
3) Medical, creche & other facilities.
4) Leave
5) Increments & bonus.

D) Child Labour:

1) Increase.
2) Decrease.
3) Its impact on the female children

E) Female as 'Economic' Head of Household:

1) Yes
2) No
3) If yes, its impact on women's health?

F) (i) Expenditure Patterns (Rs. per month / % share):

Number of items	*Items*	*Rs.*	*% in Total*
1.	Food		
2.	Clothing		
3.	Shelter		
4.	Health		
5.	Education		
6.	Rituals		
7.	Transport		
8.	Loans		
9.	Drinking		
10.	Others		
	Total		

ii) Effect of Price Fluctuations on Expenditure Pattern:

1. Price rise & its effect on consumption quantity & quality.
2. Price fall & its effect on consumption quantity & quality.

V) Ownership of Assets:

20) Do you possess any or all of the following assets (Tick):

A	*Household Assets*	*Year of Purchase*	*Value (Rs.)*	*Financing Mechanisn: (i)/(ii)/(iii)*
1)	Cot / Bed			
2)	Cupboard			
3)	Chair/Stool			
4)	Table/Vessel Rack			
5)	Stove/Gas			
6)	Cycle			
7)	Radio			
8)	T.V.			
9)	Fridge			
10)	Sewing Machine			
11)	Others (Specify)			

21) What is your source of agricultural income?

i) Vegetables.
ii) Fruits.
iii) Flowers.
iv) Toddy.
v) Others (Specify)

22) Have you heard of the Government's 'New Economic Policy'?

What is it? How has it affected you (Listed below are some of the components):

1. (a) Retrograde. (b) Bettered living conditions.
2. Wage fall/rise.
3. Urbanisation.
4. Government's Industrial Policy (vis-à-vis setting up of the industrial estate by the Government).
5. Government's Slum Policy.
6. Price fluctuations of essentials: & their availability. (i) Increase (ii) Decrease (iii) Constant
7. Government's privatization programmes, labour retrenchment & temporary/contract services.
8. 'Globalisation'.
9. Other developments (Specify)

INDEX